THE GOVERNMENTAL
HABIT REDUX

THE GOVERNMENTAL HABIT REDUX

ECONOMIC CONTROLS FROM COLONIAL TIMES TO THE PRESENT

JONATHAN R. T. HUGHES

PRINCETON UNIVERSITY PRESS

PRINCETON, NEW JERSEY

Library of Congress Cataloging-in-Publication Data

Hughes, Jonathan R. T.

The governmental habit redux : economic controls from colonial
times to the present / Jonathan R. T. Hughes.—2nd ed.

p. cm.

Rev. ed. of: The governmental habit. c1977.

Includes bibliographical references and index.

ISBN 0-691-04272-1

1. United States—Economic policy. I. Hughes, Jonathan R. T.
Governmental habit. II. Title.

HC103.H76 1991 338.973—dc20 90-20145

To M.G.

FOR PATIENCE

Creation of the "legal environment" for economic endeavor is the most fundamental function of government and one which cannot be avoided or abdicated. It may range from a pure "hands-off" policy to one of total state control. The cardinal sin in this area is neither intervention or nonintervention, but ambiguity. The "rules of the game" should be clear, unequivocal, and enforceable.

—Rondo Cameron, 1976

CONTENTS

PREFACE

TO THE FIRST EDITION

WHEN I STARTED WORK on this book in the late 1960s the prospect before us was a great expansion of government influence in the private lives of Americans. That would have been inevitable, even without the Vietnam War, since the expansion of the welfare state (the "Great Society" in that particular avatar) is by definition the expansion of government power. When Martin Kessler (now editorial director and associate publisher of Basic Books) and I discussed my plans for the book, I argued that a decade of 1965 style federal government would cause the question of its rightful place in the American economic system to overshadow all else.

Such has now come to pass. I thought it inevitable and, perceiving the singular characteristics of government economic participation in this country, I wanted to study its development.

As it turned out the research carried me far back into history, farther than I imagined I would need to go. It also involved me in the study of topics I had no reason to suppose would confront me. As a result I have several institutional debts: to the Ford Foundation, to All Souls College, Oxford, and to Northwestern University. I wish to express my gratitude to them here.

As this book developed I presented parts of my results in lectures to mainly academic audiences and was both delighted and appalled by how little even professionally interested people know about the overall nature of American government response to economic problems, the form of that response, and its historical development. The major institutions and policies are familiar enough in the light of current problems. But what seems not to be known, and needs to be, is the fact that there is a totality of social control beyond the decisions of the market in this country, and that totality has a certain shape. It can be comprehended in aggregate. That is what this book is about. If we ever are competently to reform our social-control "technology" (and surely someday we must), we need to know what it is.

J.R.T.H.

PREFACE

TO THE SECOND EDITION

I N ITS INITIAL VERSION, this book was published slightly before
its time. In 1977 most academic economists of my ken were still
of the liberal Democratic political persuasion. When this book became current some of my old colleagues thought I had taken leave of
my senses. How could I have so misunderstood the signs and por-
tents? Everyone knew that government regulation of the private sector was a good thing, needed to protect the public from market failures and the general rascality of business executives. Fiscal policy,
the triumphant macroeconomic legacy of the Keynesian Revolution,
was meant to stabilize the economy and prevent inflation, depression, and unemployment. The federal government played a stabilizing role. That was the standard textbook gospel. Redistribution of
wealth and income through taxation and expenditure was a Robin
Hood venture: taking from the rich to aid the deserving poor by government transfers.

My answer to my distinguished colleagues was simply: That is not
how it is. Read the book. We have a history, and it really isn't what
you seem to think. The world did not begin in 1933, and neither did
our American habit of superimposing the decisions of regulators
upon those derived from free-market contracting. We have politi-
cized the economy in favor of special interests since colonial times: it
is the All American way. If market-clearing contracting by private
bargaining be considered a superior method of achieving economic
efficiency (by economists, at least), then what we have always done
and still do, massively, makes sense as history, politics, and sociology, but not as economics. This message, in 1977, was unwelcome to
those who saw every year's new regulatory increments as automatic
progress.

Some other scholars (as I soon discovered) were on to the same
story that had disturbed me, although not from a historical viewpoint. In 1977 such work was not in the mainstream of economic wisdom, nor was this book. However, in only four years Ronald Reagan
and the neoconservatives were settling into Washington, D.C., on
the promise to "get the government off the people's backs." A tooth-
less threat, as it turned out.

The Governmental Habit became well known in its own right despite
its offbeat message. It was then the only book that traced American

government intervention in the private economy from its remote origins to modern times. In its first version the narrative ended in a tone of deep pessimism. I could see the inflation and the huge federal deficits coming, and said so. I could not foresee, nor could anyone else, how the American economy would adjust to such forces operating year after year. Apart from wartime emergencies we had never been a country plagued by inflation. With our vast resources, huge labor force, and relatively open economy, we had not experienced banana republic style prices and fiscal regimes. Historically the federal government's expenditure ambitions had tended to be at least in the neighborhood of tax revenues. But in the middle 1970s, drastic changes were coming down the tracks: the steep upward movement of prices, the sharp increase in unemployment levels, the precious-metals boom and collapse in 1979–80, and the appearance of unimaginable federal budget deficits in the Reagan years. The low levels of productivity that began in the mid-1970s continued into the 1980s. We experienced the flight of domestic manufacturing capital to foreign shores while, at the same time, huge foreign investment poured into this country as the balance of payments opened giant current-account deficits. The agricultural crisis that began with Carter's grain export embargo to the USSR continued through the 1980s. Unimaginable financial debacles followed "deregulation" of the banking system. In October 1987 there was a huge stock market meltdown, and another in 1989.

None of that could have been foreseen in 1977. We survived it all only to face the sudden implosion of Soviet-style communism in 1989–90, leaving American macroeconomic policy hanging in midair, with a gigantic defense economy and, initially, no apparent plan to dismantle it and return to the kind of peacetime economy last seen on these shores in 1946–48. During World War II companies had made plans for reconversion to a peacetime economy. The Cold War, which had lasted ten times as long, ended suddenly with the U.S. defense establishment still planning new weapons systems, a $300-billion annual federal expenditure built into the economy on a permanent basis.

The end of the Cold War, if that indeed is what we have in 1990, gives Americans a chance to do some major *perestroika*, or restructuring, of their own. And these developments make the message of *The Governmental Habit* more germane than ever. The problems of 1977 are all still there, even bigger and more complex than they were. I do not mean to be tiresome about this, but now, as in the 1970s, we need to understand our vast structure of government regulation—nonmarket economic controls—and to make it less destructive of productivity and wealth-creating activity. Where did it all originally come from, and what is (or *was*) its purpose? Can the means at hand, the organizations, rules, control techniques, really achieve the ends legislators envisaged when this tangle of administrations, offices, managements, authorities, and bureaus was established? That needs to be known. The origins and evolution of American nonmarket controls are what this book is about.

In this new edition I have made appropriate cuts and additions to compensate for the change in perspective after the wild ride of the past fifteen years, and to include, however briefly, a survey of new thinking about the problems of government intervention and control of economic life. I have kept the treatment spare, a tactic that was thought to have been a virtue of the first edition. This is a huge subject, of course, and I have indicated in the notes to each chapter my major sources for those who wish to pursue these topics at greater depth. Nearly four hundred years of an American tradition are treated within these covers, so an element of brevity was the only practical way to write the book, and, realistically, to expect anyone to read it.

My intellectual indebtedness on the subject matter of this book is far too extensive by now to elaborate here. I do want to thank especially my colleague, Joel Mokyr, for his thoughtful criticisms. I also want to publicly thank my college teacher, Professor Evan Murray of Utah State University, who might not agree with some of what is written below, but who first introduced these topics to me. His insightful teachings more than forty years ago stayed in my mind as the decades advanced, one after another. I spoke with him of these matters again in 1990, when he was in his eighty-ninth year. Studying this book to create a new edition, I often could hear the echo of his voice in my pages.

Modern inflation has reduced the quality of many things, and the words *great teacher* have been, alas, diminished in meaning and value by excessive issue. But there really can be great teachers. I know.

J.R.T.H.
Evanston, Illinois
April 1990

THE GOVERNMENTAL
HABIT REDUX

Chapter 1

INTRODUCTION

THIS BOOK is a study of social controls over economic activity, the way we use the powers of government to change the allocation of resources from patterns that a completely free-market economy might produce. The main thesis is that our methods of social control make sense as history, as law, and as sociology, even though they often appear to make no sense at all as economics, narrowly defined. Would an economically efficient system of social control be equally compatible with our history, our legal tradition, and in the end, our whole way of life? This is a critical question, and probably one this country will have to face at the end of the twentieth century.

USES OF THE PAST

Whether it be called big government, the growth of government, bureaucracy, or whatever, intervention in economic processes to alter outcomes the free market has produced, or would produce if left alone by the governmental power, is my basic subject matter. We achieve this interference by direct regulation, rule-making, taxation, expenditures, subsidies, and licensing. We have a long history of distrust of the free-market bargain and the resulting interference with its functioning. The reader of this book will find deep-seated and ancient roots in our behavior patterns, largely unique to us, and repeated, not just for decades, but for close to four centuries. We need history to comprehend even the most basic features of the American economy: how we own property, and how we control its social consequences. No amount of theorizing alone can produce, say, the essential features of fee simple. To ignore the history of American non-market control while studying merely its current structure and operation is just willful ignorance. It is like trying to imagine a tree—roots, trunk, branches, limbs, twigs, leaf structure, and all—by studying only crosscuts. The thing has a shape, and a purpose in the world. No matter how elaborately festooned with the hieroglyphs of modern social science, lack of the historical dimension turns the study of big government into mere pretense. I am not opposed to theory and to theorizing, but theory is supposed to be about something, and that something, in this case, is our path-dependent evolution of nonmarket social control. After all, if the facts are incorrect, it makes little difference what the explanations of them are.

To comprehend how big government in the United States grew from its very modest beginnings, three basic sets of information need to be understood at the outset.

1. The nature of the original models used and developed.

2. The endowment of the federal government with powers originally exercised only by state and local governments.

3. The desire, expressed politically over time, to have a central government with wide powers.

The governmental apparatus set out by the constitutional convention of 1787 in Philadelphia was not the kind of all-embracing federal establishment we now enjoy. It took more than two centuries of economic growth and change in a popular democracy, together with legislative and judicial responses and initiatives to achieve our present happy situation. It is obvious that this is a most complicated subject. Indeed, intensive study of our methods of mixing government with private economic activity is like viewing the firmament with successively more powerful telescopic lenses: the greater the magnification, the more dense and complex is the universe of phenomena seen.

Is there a single person alive today who professes a comprehensive knowledge of our economic control mass and intervention devices at even the federal level alone?[1] Federal nonmarket controls—laws, regulations, subsidies, and taxes—by themselves are now complex phenomena reminiscent of a forest ecology. To study them at all, we need hypotheses, simplifying assumptions to guide our questions. We need to analyze the nature of our own questions. Our hypotheses must be informed by the relevant known facts, but an infinity of facts does not speak for itself. We must have sure intellectual organization of our questions about the undifferentiated mass of data. The study of the relevant history provides the bases for such an organization and for believable explanations.

It is said that you cannot know where you are going without knowing what road you are on. I would rephrase that aphorism by arguing that, in our modern nonmarket control universe, you cannot tell where you *are* without knowing where you have *been*. After all, the ultimate destination of American institutional evolution, in any of its parts, is unknown. We do not know in any depth what a given institution is achieving unless we know who is supposed to be served and who is being harmed by it. Such knowledge requires that we know why the institution came into existence in the first place. In modern computer parlance, our institutional development is *path-dependent*. What originally was placed into the system matters: unless it is excised, its influence continues as institutions evolve from the origins. Institutional innovations can change the direction of movement. But because of the law and a written constitution, we also experience a certain amount of determinism.

Most studies of modern nonmarket controls consider that the relevant history extends back to the New Deal. A few go back further, into the late nineteenth century. But in fact the powerful and *continuous* habit of nonmarket control in our economy reaches back for centuries. The colonial origins were our institutional gene pool for these government controls. What originally was encoded largely remains until now. It is shown in this volume how those beginnings still influence us in varying degrees; for example, in our land tenure (the way we own real estate) where modern practice is little changed from the rights and obligations of land ownership in this country in, say, 1650. Why, if I refuse to pay my property taxes, does my tenure, my ownership, become subject to reentry by the state?[2] The answer is: no modern law, but a practice going back to the original land tenure planted here by British governments—the same one in every single colony established, from the 1607 Virginia colonization to Georgia in 1732. We seem to have found it more convenient over the centuries to continue this system than to change it. We have never voted for it, we just have it. A modern conveyor of real estate is still "seised with the fee," even though neither he nor his lawyer is likely to know beyond boiler-plate repetition what those words actually mean.

The same holds true of our modern system of business licensing, of detailed regulatory controls, and of the powers to intervene in the interests of safety, health, and welfare—the police powers. They were all implanted, in full force, in colonial America, and have evolved directly from those ancient seedlings. Direct transfer of such practices, or laws, was a technology transfer. It was a most efficient way to move a social system from one location to another. I can offer a spectacular example of this. When the miners of Idaho Territory in January 1864, in order to govern themselves, passed the common law of England by voice vote, they borrowed and implanted an instant solution to their problem (having no law at all), and solutions for generations to come.[3] What Idaho implanted was simple: it was most probably mainly Blackstone's *Commentaries* to live by. What a pity Third World and former Communist states cannot so simplify their own transitions to democracy in our time. If the USSR could adopt eighteenth century English common law, it would save itself a lot of grief.

Of course we (including Idaho) have changed a great deal since Blackstone. Indeed, the modern federal control Leviathan recalls the words of Cassius: "What meat doth this our Caesar eat that he is grown so great?" How did the federal government come to exercise those powers that were in place before there was a federal government, and that were not transferred to the federal government by the states when the original constitutional settlement was reached? Thomas Jefferson did not believe that George Washington's government had the right to establish the Bank of the United States in 1791. Madison and Monroe did not believe the U.S. Constitution empowered their administrations to subsidize internal improvements in the states. The federal Constitution is a short document. According to Madison's account of the constitutional convention in Philadelphia in the summer of 1787 the delegates, each representing states with full sovereignty, gave away as little as possible, despite their need to create that more perfect union. Consequently, the federal powers given up by the states were explicitly limited. No code of law is included in the original federal document. There are limitations upon preexisting powers of the states, and some restrictions upon the new federal government; for example, it could not tax trade between the states. It was clearly understood that the states would continue to rule themselves, apart from the powers they had surrendered at the constitutional convention.

But then in American history came implied powers, Supreme Court decisions, concurrent powers, a civil war, subsidies, tariffs, controlled land sales, homesteads, a regulatory agency and a law against trusts and other business forms thought repugnant, more federal agencies, war, depression, war again, the welfare state, and the Cold War. In the fullness of time it all added up to big government. In a 1985 ruling, *Garcia v San Antonio*,[4] the conservative Supreme Court held that even state employees were subject to federal minimum wage rules. Some believe that the *Garcia* ruling actually wiped away the last vestiges of the Tenth Amendment's rights reserved to the states, and that federal control is now legally unlimited. It gives one pause. In this book I will show how even modest beginnings evolved into the mass of bureaus, boards, offices, and managements that fill the marble and granite buildings of modern-day Washington, D.C.

To what extent did the American people ever vote for the growth of government? Or did they merely succumb to it? Robert Higgs, in his 1986 book, *Crisis and Leviathan*,[5] documented the argument that the necessary reactions to modern crises had made a sequence of emergency expansions of government, whose expenditures and bureaucracies then lingered on into bureaucratic perpetuity (his "ratchet effect").[6] For complex reasons, Higgs continued, the population adjusted its ideology to accept such new expansive realities until it finally reached the supine condition of modern times when further extensions of federal powers are scarcely resisted at all. Again, one is reminded of ancient Rome, watching the Republic drift insensibly into the decadence of empire, as Gibbon might have put it.

The crises did have such results, as, indeed, I argued in the first edition of this book. But there was more to it. Already a fertile and ancient seedbed was waiting. In 1893, James Bryce, in *The American Commonwealth*,[7] argued that Americans even then were willfully canceling out their unique economic achievement, the late nineteenth century market-driven economy. Bryce noted this paradox: that the American people believed axiomatically in sturdy individualistic values, yet freely legislated against all those beliefs. (I will treat these problems in due course.) Bryce understood the great difference between government controls in America and in Europe at the end of the nineteenth century: in the United States, government policy tended to boil up from below; it was not a grant of privilege given from the top down.

Why did the late nineteenth and early twentieth century judicial apotheosis of free contract—*substantive due process*—vanish without trace in the 1930s? Was it really a change of ideology? I am not dealing here with a religious mystery: in the context of American economic history, these paradoxes have explanations.

New Perspectives

Modern writers have been attracted to the phenomena of growth of government, and it will be useful here to survey their findings at the beginning of this enquiry. Since the 1960s, in the New Frontier, Great Society, and Nixon administrations, when the largest peacetime additions to nonmarket controls since the New Deal were imposed, analysis of government growth has slowly moved into the mainstream. Scholars have sought to understand both the amazing size of the federal government and its tendency toward continuing expansion. A Nobel Prize in economic science has even been awarded for new wisdom about the nature of government and its growth.[8] So a field of enquiry which, if not moribund in the late 1960s, was at least in a condition of the near stasis of conventional explanation, became potent and scintillating.[9] Nearly all of the new scholarship, despite its varying identifications of the prime causal forces behind growth of government, has achieved a surprising degree of agreement on one point: *government will grow if it can*. These findings are reminiscent of Joseph Schumpeter's argument in his essay, "Imperialisms," that all nation-states tend to "objectless . . . unlimited forcible expansion" unless or until they are stopped by force.[10]

Time was when economists believed, and taught, that regulation was done in the interests of the general welfare, and that the relative size of government was a matter of discretion: in expansions, there were to be countercylical budget surpluses (relatively smaller expenditures) and deficits (relatively larger government expenditures) in times of recession. Not emphasized, but surely possible, balanced budgets (relatively neutral government expenditures) were justified somewhere in between. This beneficial mechanism of fiscal policy, derived for economists and developed from the writings of J. M. Keynes, was designed to promote economic growth (or stability), price stability, and full employment. Thus the Employment Act of 1946 was not merely hubris.[11]

The most general objection to nonmarket control of all kinds comes from the primal American belief that property and income belong, by variously derived rights, to those who own and earn them, and that the disposition thereof is a private matter. Any economy based on free contracting between owners of property (including labor) maximizes both individual freedom and efficient aggregate output. That old-fashioned view has been dominated in this country for decades by a vote-rich political economy that postulates that negative externalities and market failures from private contracting reduce the general welfare, and that regulation to correct these imperfections improves society at large; the public interest is served by such healing and correcting amendments to market decisions. Because the real-life outcome of those healing and amending corrections is modern big government, scholars have sought to discover how that could have resulted from the purest of motives.

By the 1970s interested scholars had detected reasons other than pure public interest to explain the proliferation of regulation and regulatory agencies.[12] Also, the growth of government expenditures in excess of gross national product growth was found to be rooted in the self-interests of organized coalitions of those receiving federal largess. By the 1970s the goal of stabilizing countercyclical expenditure (its greatest moment, Walter Heller's fine tuning along the New Frontier, having passed) had been swamped by the relentless increase in expenditures, deficits every year, no matter what. With that the era of modern fiscal policy began, to be enhanced later by the Reagan-era genius stroke: tax cuts and simultaneous expenditure increases as the country added World War II-style armed forces—including aging battleships hauled out of mothballs—to the endless proliferation of hi-tech Cold War expenditures.

A few facts will demonstrate the fiscal puzzles of the modern era. Total government—federal, state, and local—purchases of goods and services as a portion of GNP were about 10 to 11 percent in the mid 1920s, 14 percent in 1940, 18.6 percent in 1960, and are now about 45 percent. Only at the height of World War II (46 percent in 1944) was such a figure achieved. After 1960 the federal share surpassed those of state and local governments combined. In 1929 private investment, the planned future of the wealth-creating sector, was five times the size of federal expenditure. Today private domestic investment is less than one half the size of annual federal outlays. By the 1980s, 15 percent of the civilian labor force (more than one out of every six) were government workers, compared to 10 percent in 1950 and 6.5 percent in 1930. In 1841 there were 11 federal workers per 10,000 of population, 52 in 1920, and 125 by the mid-1980s.[13] Regulation blankets the country, from water to steel. In 1979, on the eve of the Reagan Revolution there were 2,897,000 federal civilian employees. By 1985, one term later, there were more than 3,000,000.

It is only a modest exaggeration to say that the modern American economy is what government says it should be. After five decades of high income taxes, an economy adjusted by businesses primarily to minimize tax obligations, with tax savings higher than normal profit rates, must be radically different from the one that might have existed at lower tax rates. Since the income tax has only marginally been used explicitly over the years to create economic structure (e.g., various investment credits), the economy we have surely is not the one anyone, people or government, would want, given free choice in the matter.

In gross, the fiscal changes have become, by the standards of only a few years ago, hair-raising. The general price level no longer falls in recessions; its rate of increase merely slows down. In the late 1970s the accelerating rate of increase in prices produced experts reminiscing on the TV talk shows about the 1923 German inflation. The economist Herbert Stein, who had consistently feared inflationary policies in the past, admitted in 1980 that he had not known the half of it: "in our naivete we meant by endless inflation an endless rise in the price level, not an endless increase in the rate of increase in the price level."[14] The rate of increase in consumer prices, 5.9 percent in 1976, was up to 13.5 percent in 1980, and 10.4 percent in 1981. Then the

Federal Reserve System imposed a regime of tighter money, a recession ensued, unemployment rose, and by 1983 the rate of increase in consumer prices had been compressed to 3.2 percent. The Fed was hailed for ending the inflation. Rates of price increases that would have terrified the Eisenhower conservatives of the 1950s were acceptable to the Reagan neoconservatives of the 1980s. Times had changed.

In the new fiscal regime, expenditures increase every year without regard to phases of the business cycle. Deficits occur because of taxation shortfalls, not explicitly to buoy up a sagging economy although that was the consequence of the 1983–85 deficits.[15] The central bank's policies still are sensitive to business conditions, but the money supply rises every year, and now (1990), with such a huge influx of foreign investment, is only questionably within the Fed's discretionary control. The conventional wisdom regarding debt and deficits as bankrupting the country, seemed to be seriously devoid of content. The national (gross) debt outstanding grew to unimaginable absolute levels: in 1975, $544.1 billion; in 1981 it passed a trillion dollars ($1003.9 billion), by 1986 it had passed two trillion dollars ($2132.9 billion); and by 1990, three trillion dollars. All of the federal debt accumulated in the country's first two centuries—to 1975—was multiplied by a factor of more than five during the next fifteen years, and was still rising. The country was not seeking a receiver, although some claimed that surging foreign investment in the United States was a form of near-bankruptcy—"selling the assets," but hardly at knock-down prices. In 1989 foreign ownership of U.S. assets came to about $1.5 trillion, and as the terror mongers on the evening newscasts emphasized in funereal voices, the United States had become the world's largest debtor on foreign account. It was so in the nineteenth century too, when we realized real rates of economic growth the world had never seen before—or since.[16]

These are the kinds of modern phenomena that have lighted the imaginations of a new generation of students of government. With some snipping here, and stretching there, the major findings of this work take the form of ten general propositions.

  1. Regulation creates economic rent. This is really a truism. Regulation is interference with normal market outcomes. Someone loses, someone gains. The gains are economic rents—returns in excess of competitive returns. Resources flow to the highest returns and therefore to the rents. The economy adjusts accordingly. It becomes a different economy because of the rents—the regulation.

2. The rents made available by regulation encourage free-riding by stretching the rules or ignoring them. If most people are held in check by regulation, it will pay, potentially, for individuals to violate the regulations, getting a free ride at the expense of the rest.

3. Free-riding might be seen as immoral by the general public, but in terms of economic values alone, free-riding is rational behavior to the free rider.[17] Should he toss his cigar butt out of the car window, or take it home and include it in his household trash? The free rider tosses; the simplest and cheapest solution for him.

4. Rent-seeking activity is socially wasteful.[18] Resources are withdrawn from productive, that is, wealth-creating, activities to pursue rents. Those who fail to gain the rents take a total loss, and the winners are merely participating in wealth redistribution.

5. It pays special-interest coalitions to manipulate the power of the state to create rents.[19] Thus rent-seeking activity will tend to be organized. Individuals usually will have little chance to control the political mechanism, but groups, representing both voting power and organized money, have the ability to gain rule-making or legislation favorable to themselves. This is the case especially because the benefits are concentrated (available only to the rent seekers) and the costs are disbursed to the public at large. By forming rent-seeking coalitions, a few can benefit at the expense of everyone else.

6. Dominant groups will tend to use the state to redistribute wealth to themselves. Although this is not surprising, stated thus boldly, it explains what has been a surprising outcome of nonmarket control in this country: most of the wealth redistribution is from the rich and the poor to the middle classes. This corresponds to "Director's Law," which states that the chance to redistribute will always be acted upon if the chance arises.[20]

7. Economic growth encourages growth of government, supported by the middle classes. This flows from the previous proposition, and explains to a large extent why big government (large ratios of government expenditures relative to gross domestic product) is the luxury of the richest countries. The ratio is much smaller, half or less, among the poorer countries.[21]

8. While market power tends to be oligarchical (rich people have more dollar votes than do poor people), the political system is egalitarian—one person, one vote. Those who lose out in the competitive market may gain, or win, through organized manipulation of the political system: through lobbying, and in the worst cases, payoffs to legislators and regulatory personnel.

9. The shares through redistribution of organized special interests will exceed their proportion of the population.[22]

10. It pays those inside the government regulatory establishment to

push for expansion of regulation. The more regulation, the greater the career opportunities for experienced hands in the regulatory game.[23]

Note that these propositions are essentially ahistorical. What happened before the time they came into play is not germane. But in
American history there was a *process*, in law and constitutions,
through which nonmarket control evolved. Society's acceptance of,
or demands for, controls has been conditioned by experience. In a
country of law not all control methods are options for the government.[24] The origins and evolution of the controls therefore matter.
There was no time in American history free of nonmarket controls
over economic life, especially at the more basic level—how the country's land was occupied, owned, and exploited. There have been
times of more, and times of less, regulation. Moreover, the federal
government, which began its existence in 1789, was a minor player
compared to states and municipal authorities until the late nineteenth century. The federal government has become the giant controller in a process whose study I now undertake.

A Synopsis of Change

The nature of this subject may be capsulized, by way of introduction,
in a brief examination of two watershed events in 1877 and 1887. In
these may be seen the characteristics of our problems in social control
and the way we have tried to solve them until now. Legislatures,
laws, and agencies are motivated and constrained by history.

In the spring of 1877 the U.S. Supreme Court, still officially sitting
in its 1876 autumn term, handed down the fateful decisions known
collectively as the Granger cases.[25] Most of these cases involved legislation by Midwestern states to control railroads. However, the basic
case, *Munn v. Illinois*, concerned the refusal of a Chicago warehouse
firm, Munn and Scott, to apply for a state license and to have its
services and charges controlled. The Court said that Munn and Scott
must comply if they wanted to continue in that line of business.
Thus, they were compelled to operate their private business affairs
according to the collective wisdom of the Illinois legislature. If private
businesses were important enough to be "affected with a public interest," as the court ruled, then they were subject to whatever concepts of social control the statesmen of that state body might hold at
the time.

Munn was not *obiter dictum*; it was an application, said the Chief
Justice, Morrison Waite, of fundamental rules of Anglo-American

law. Such powers to control, he wrote, were part and parcel of our system of government: when the people of the "United Colonies" separated from England, they had "changed the form, but not the substance" of their government. Such powers to control private business had existed in England "from time immemorial," in the colonies before independence, and in the states ever since. Businesses affected with a public interest were not to be free of government control.[26]

However much the decision rocked the American legal profession (and it did), in that age of triumphant laissez-faire economics, *Munn v. Illinois* was not the beginning of something new; it really measured the limit of something very old. Waite was right. The power to control business was vested in the state governments; it had indeed been exercised by the colonial governments and in England for centuries before that. What *Munn* measured the limit of, and ended, was an era in American history when businessmen (apart from those in banking, railroad building, and foreign trade) commonly had experienced the control powers of only state and local governments. *Munn v. Illinois* marked the high tide of those powers, driven at last to the legal apex, the Supreme Court of the United States, and successfully defended there. Until then, it could be argued in retrospect, business organizations had been of such size and propensities that American society and American businessmen had been largely content with the consequences. But some American business organizations were growing larger than any before known, overstepping local jurisdictions and existing in part beyond the grasp of any local or state governments. The largest of these emerging giants were the railroads.

Accordingly, a decade after *Munn*, a new page was turned in American history. The railroads, writhing under *Munn*, were in court with Illinois again in 1886 in *Wabash, St. Louis & Pacific Railway v. Illinois*. The railroads were charging higher rates, per given weight, for short hauls than for long ones—the "tapering principle"—and this was forbidden by Illinois law. The Supreme Court, recognizing both economic reality and constitutional principle, forbade the state of Illinois to interfere with commerce between the states: "It cannot be too strongly insisted upon that the right of continuous transportation from one end of the country to the other is essential in modern times."[27] The commerce clause of the Constitution would be "feeble and almost useless" if states along transportation routes were allowed to regulate carriers and obstruct that commerce, the court ruled. Accordingly, the law of Illinois was overturned.

This was the dawn of the new age of federal control. The railroads had jumped from the frying pan into the fire—from state to federal control. There began in 1887, with the Act to Regulate Commerce establishing an Interstate Commerce Commission, the periodically growing and ultimately ubiquitous imposition at the federal level of those ancient control powers Waite outlined in *Munn*. From 1887 onward American business would never again be free from federal regulation; before 1887 such regulation had been extremely rare, and indeed unknown to most. As it happened, unsuccessful efforts had been made previously in both the Senate and the House to set up federal controls over the railroads, so the *Wabash* decision came upon ground already well prepared. Hence the 1877–87 decade was a fundamental watershed in American economic history: the end of one era and the beginning of another. The Sherman Antitrust Act came three years later, in 1890, setting out an institutional sumptuary law for business enterprise. Many old habits and methods of doing business were now declared to be illegal.

But there was continuity; that is fundamental. The principles of law were not changed. There had been a change in order of magnitude, and federal commissioners were to perform tasks formerly undertaken by state commissioners, township selectmen, justices of the peace, vestrymen, and other minor officials of colonial and English governments in a sequence stretching back into the mists of the Middle Ages. The new dimension of control, the federal dimension, grew and flourished until now, in its myriad forms, federal regulation of private economic life is an accepted fact of life in this country.

In the pervasive economic troubles of the 1990s we face general economic problems with a bag of tools for government interference with economic processes that were fashioned piecemeal, over a long period of time, to cope only with specific problems. The mechanisms of control are not coordinated where they are effective; their effects spill over into areas of economic life that are not subjected to the same controls, and the consequences are generally disruptive. Consider some examples. If government policies produce overcrowded airports and empty passenger trains, demand for automobile and gasoline increases; people still travel. Yet other government policies (e.g., mileage requirements placed on automobile manufacturers) and agencies have as their object the conservation of petroleum products. The Federal Reserve System fights inflation (periodically leveling the home-building industry in the process) while tariff policies, federal spending, agricultural subsidies, and labor and management policies sanctioned by federal agencies are all designed to *raise* prices.

To the exasperated citizen the resulting disarray looks like willful sabotage, or at least gross incompetence. But the problem is that each control policy is targeted to a specific problem, without regard for its macroeconomic spillover effects. Economists may see as cartels and oligopolies what are really the natural products of larger social forces. Much of government regulation appears to produce cartel behavior; such behavior is subject to a body of theory.[28] So we are expected by some economists to see regulated industries merely as government-sponsored cartels, price-fixing and market-sharing rings designed to enhance profits of the regulated industries at the consumer's expense. When such cartels lose money—as did the railroads—they are additionally denounced as inefficient. Antitrust laws, applied for a century now, have not stopped the growth of massive industrial concentration and oligopolistic behavior. Hence it is argued by some that such results must have been the object of antitrust policy. The observed result identifies the motivation.

Such ideas are naive. Once the historical dimension is added we see our economic controls for what they are: living social artifacts. They do not constitute any kind of system. They are a nonsystem. They are not designed to be a system; a pile of disconnected mechanical parts is not a machine. Nor can our control bureaucracy be used for general economic planning, as some demand. Economic planning is not why the controls were created, and it is not what people who work in the attendant bureaucracy do. From the ICC and the Sherman Act down to the latest federal regulatory agency our federal controls were created to cope with, or to finesse, specific problems arising from everyday economic life at specific points in time.

The control bureaucracy tends to linger on long after the event that called the original controls into being has passed and been forgotten. It is charged, rightly, that such control bureaucracies, by continuing to exist even when they do not work, make efficient economic decisions impossible to achieve, since the signals of the marketplace cannot be followed by business.[29] So we get regulated economic malfunctioning, from agriculture to advertising. The following chapters will show that such is not only the inevitable outcome of our methods, but that *what we wanted was not efficiency but the market interference itself*. As economics such a conclusion is at best paradoxical. As history it is an insight into deeply rooted tendencies in American society. Despite Fourth of July and political campaign oratory and the self-serving pronouncements of business leaders, Americans distrust the free market and accept its decisions willingly only when it suits their needs. For example, when the market creates shortages of goods or services in response to the expressed desires of consumers, the consequences are resented and the call goes out immediately for the government to intervene. If a surplus results from producer actions—too much high-priced American steel produced or too many expensive American autos made—industry demands, and gets, quotas to halt the resulting flood of cheaper imports.

Two additional pieces of information will be of use at this point: (1) the scope of traditional nonmarket controls and (2) the typical historical circumstances in which they have been imposed by government.

First, consider the matter of scope. As will be seen in the chapters that follow, the tradition of law from England gave government even at the lowest levels extensive power to establish, disestablish, and regulate economic activity of all kinds. So far as colonial America was concerned, there never was an absence of such controls, a time of complete economic freedom. The common law came over with the colonists. The power to control, which seemed natural enough in the early economy of medieval villages and incorporated boroughs, covering everything from real property rights to labor obligations, became formal and structured as economic life grew more complex over the centuries. It was the genius, or the peculiarity, of the English and the Americans after them to avoid, for the most part, quantitative controls over physical output, except in rare cases or in such dire emergencies as war. What was controlled traditionally were four crucial points in the flow of economic transactions: (1) number of participants in a given activity, (2) conditions of participation, (3) prices charged by participants either for products or services, and (4) quality of the products or services. These four control points—number, entry, price, and quality—combine into sixteen basic combinations depending on which ones are controlled or free of control at any given time.[30] These sixteen combinations form a basic matrix of social control. The matrix can be more complex, of course, if there are mixtures, or corruption. Also the matrix could be smaller, since any one of the four control hints could be used to influence the others; for example, price could be so controlled as to regulate number. Entry conditions (licenses, apprenticeship rules) also could influence number, as could quality controls. But the tendency over the centuries, since each control method has a separate origin,[31] has been to regulate (or not regulate) economic life at each of the four control points, or at all points, none, or a combination of them. This social control matrix is the subtle and complex economy of controls we have experienced historically, and with a few exceptions (for example, output control over crude-oil extraction, or production by permit only, as in the case of peanut farming) still do.[32]

Since these combinations have existed so long in peaceful conjunction with Anglo-American ideas about property rights, their long-lived existence must be considered by the historian as somehow natural, given the reality of our laws and customs. A moment's thought should indicate that this is not a trivial point, since the mainstream view of American economists for so long, a view that still is espoused by a vociferous minority, is that only zero government regulation is fully compatible theoretically with free enterprise; government control is *interference*, and the normative load on that word is negative. Ideologically we are caught in a paradox, since what has been historically true, and socially congenial, was theoretically obnoxious. Experience with decontrol efforts at the end of the 1970s and in the 1980s left ideologues on all sides adrift. Decontrol seemed to produce improvements in some areas, such as communications and air travel, and catastrophe in others, as in commercial banking and huge failures in the savings and loan industry.

Second, a useful discussion can be made in advance concerning the circumstances wherein the nonmarket controls have typically been called into service in this history. As I already have noted, not only are our controls congenial to our social system, but the controls are believed to be desirable for their own sakes. Hence there has been little popular clamor to be rid of them. Abolition of such government interference had made good political fodder at election time for years but was scarcely mentioned by either presidential candidate in 1988. It has obviously become treacherous ground for politicians. Historically, Americans have proved to be more comfortable even with malfunctioning controls (like the ICC) than with decisions of the marketplace that influential groups find repugnant to their interests. There is nothing mysterious, cynical, or corrupt about this. The country's form of government not only lends itself to favoritist legislation, but *depends* upon it. A history of American government limited to those laws that sprang pure from the brains of the nation's politicians with no special interests as their objects would be a very short history indeed.

The first economic law passed by the nation's new Congress on July 4, 1789, was a protective tariff, designed to relieve American manufacturers of those inconveniently low prices that the more efficient producers of Europe (mainly Britain) found profitable. Here one of our most cherished traditions, consumer subsidies of protected infant industries, was born. Repeatedly—as can be seen in banking controls, the Populist agitation against the railroads (resulting in the Granger Acts and the ICC), the outcry against the trusts (the Sherman Act of 1890), the unemployment levels of the Great Depression (the NRA, then the Wagner Act), the damage done by modern technology to the environment—whenever the decision of the market has produced suitably unhappy consequences, the control power has been called up.

From this viewpoint it does not matter what part of the political or economic spectrum the imposition of the controls favored. The point is that the controls were sufficiently desired and imposed. Sometimes massive political forces have been involved, sometimes the narrowest special interests have been served; for example, the Federal Trade Commission Improvements Act of 1980, marvelously misnamed, which prohibits the Federal Trade Commission from applying the antitrust acts to farm co-ops, or issuing regulations for the funeral industry. Sometimes the public, or general, welfare as conceived by politicians was the proximate excuse for imposition of controls; hence the Federal Reserve Act of 1913, or the Safe Drinking Water Act of 1973. Whenever the market decision produced (or sometimes even threatened to produce) results which in terms of real costs were considered to be excessive to an effective group, there was a demand for controls—in the case of the funeral directors, for control of the controllers. So the appearance of large-scale business firms as a result of the generalized business incorporation beginning in the late nineteenth century produced new private centers of economic power and resulted in antitrust legislation.[33] Big business was not yet as influential as the agrarian interest. In 1890, most of the population, by nearly a two-to-one ratio, was still rural. Farmers were afraid of the shift in economic power that the rise of giant business combines in the cities implied. Here was an intermingling of mass agitation and an interested political response to it, as in more recent times the rise of consumer environmental interest has been productive of more nonmarket control. It paid some political leaders to be trust-busters a century ago, as it does to be devoted environmentalists now.

The result of this historical phenomenon is our modern congeries of nonmarket controls at both local and federal levels. But we must begin in the distant American past, in the 150 years before the bicentennial year celebrated in 1976, in that time when we were English. From there to the present the lines are clear enough. This is one piece of history that could hardly be more relevant and immediate to our own circumstances at the end of the twentieth century. Understanding of the origins is the key to understanding the present.

A word about the book's organization. I am examining a single thesis over a long period of history, so my organizational scheme is both topical and chronological. From this viewpoint our country's entire history has been organized into five basic stages: (1) the colonial era; (2) the initial continental expansion; (3) the primary appearance of nonmarket controls at the federal government level; (4) the major effort in the first half of this century to exploit federal power in the interests of economic stabilization; and (5) the failure of this control apparatus by the 1990s to meet the demands made on it. Consider these stages for a moment.

The colonial era contained the origins of our present system because of the continuity of law, rooted in the way we own real property and control private exploitation of it. Logically the colonial period may be treated separately because independence brought great political changes which, paradoxically, serve to highlight the theme of basic institutional continuity.

From the American Revolution to the nineteenth century's final decade, the country's major enterprise was westward expansion. Although actions of the central government set the basic frame for this expansion, social control powers at this second stage stayed mainly, by design, at local levels. This period in our history produced the experience myth of the market-driven private enterprise economy as the necessary handmaiden of American political democracy.

Thirdly, in roughly the final quarter of the nineteenth century the forces of private economic growth outran the control powers of state and local governments and were countered by the erection of extensive federal controls over private business.

Following the third stage, we experienced a long period of experimentation with the new federal powers, energized by the economic needs of two world wars and the Great Depression of the 1930s. By the first decade after World War II the results, sometimes called the welfare state, had achieved a basic institutional structure that, although enlarged and supplemented periodically afterwards, has retained its basic form.

Finally, while many of the objects of these powers (especially social reform) have been considered broadly satisfactory, many have not. The problems of federal social control have been magnified by war—Cold, Korean, and Vietnam. The inflationary and disruptive consequences, the stagflation of the 1970s, the continued inflation of the 1980s, despite a recession and a huge stock market crash, have brought into focus the unhappy fact that the federal nonmarket control structure is a halfway house, without the virtues of either economic planning or free-market economy. This is the one of the greatest economic problems of our time, reform of which makes elimination of the federal deficit seem like child's play. A general income tax increase without a compensating spending increase, *ceteris paribus*, would eliminate the deficits. But what one-shot policy change would cause our nonmarket control establishment to make sense?

The following chapters are not so much a history as a perspective upon our history. I begin with colonial America and the role of government control in that enterprise.

Chapter 2

A MATTER OF PEDIGREE

> But in all the English colonies the tenure of the lands,
> which are all held by free socage, facilitates alienation,
> and the grantee of any extensive tract of land, generally
> finds it for his interest to alienate, as fast as he can, the
> greater part of it, reserving only a small quit rent.
> —*Adam Smith, 1776*

THE ESSENCE of American capitalism was transplanted from England in the mainland American colonies. Adam Smith understood that the way land was owned, the property rights in real estate that constitute the tenure, would affect all else. His observation was at once correct and profound. For in the ancient English land tenure of free and common socage lay the seed of American capitalism as it would be in future, a powerful right of private ownership of land and natural resources, which in time was generalized to other forms of private property. In socage tenure the owner had the full rights to exploit, as he pleased, both surface and subsurface resources. Rapid alienation meant selling, buying, and settling land as fast as men and women were willing to take up new territories. The way Americans owned and exploited land and its resources molded the way the national economy grew. Free socage ensured that land, once it was open to private purchase, would be settled at maximum speed. It also meant that, if society at large was to be protected from the adverse spillover effects of private economic activity, government power would ultimately have to be imposed and private right controlled.

Free and common socage was the only kind of land tenure allowed by the Crown to exist in the American colonies. Under this tenure owners of land could inherit, will, lease, or sell it in whatever amounts, but they were required to pay the fixed and certain incidents of it—essentially taxes—or their property right vanished, and the land reverted to the "donor" from whom the socman had purchased his property rights. Hence one would not own more land than was profitable enough to at least cover the incidents, that is, the taxes due. This is why Adam Smith said that an owner of an extensive tract of land in free socage found it in his interest to alienate it as fast as he could; there would be no great idle land holdings as in Latin America. There would be, instead, the family farm. The exception was in the South, where legal ownership of human beings in plantation agriculture and very large holdings were profitable. But even in the South taxes had to be paid.

This form of private property rights in real estate made land essentially a commodity. For American capitalism this was to be a piece of good fortune, as commercialization of land was basic to other economic relationships that would develop later. Such commercialization we would later come to regard as freedom: the ability of individuals to bargain with each other for rights of all sorts, in the exchange of chattel goods, or even, ultimately, the labor contract. But at the beginning such rights were scarcely visible, and it took generations for them to emerge from the original seedbed. The collective powers of society—government—dominated the freedom of individuals. But what the American historian Max Savelle once called the "seeds of liberty" were there.[1] And indeed, personal liberty in economic life would become so pervasive that in our own time controls less stringent than those known to colonial America would be widely considered to be unwarranted interference with personal freedom. The extent of private power to own land in free socage tenure was basic to the development of other freedoms. Later on, for example, the right to vote that came to a freeholder would be extended in the Northwest territories to all male residents above legal age, thus marking the beginning of the end of property and wealth qualifications for voters in the United States.[2] But such freedoms were never to be absolute; much of the rest of the colonial tradition lived on because of the nature of our legal system.

In colonial America English laws were put to work in the interests of a frontier society. For a long period they served well. We are, and were, a common-law country. Statutes passed by our governmental units are not law unless they are unchallenged (as in the case of the Securities and Exchange Act of 1934) or the courts say they are consistent with the constitutional structure. Since the common law of England was claimed by the states, and even by the Continental Congress in 1774, the major corpus of colonial nonmarket control over economic life passed through the Revolutionary hiatus and the state constitutions into the life of the new republic.[3] Thus the Tenth Amendment to the United States Constitution reserved rights "to the states and to the people" that had not been specified in the federal document. This was consistent with the accepted doctrine that all common law before the colonial settlements and all English statute law specific to the colonies from the time of settlement to 1775 formed the basis of American law.[4] Moreover, much of English law, such as the *Statute of Frauds* of 1677 or the substance of the infamous English laws of trade and navigation, was simply restated in American statutes after the Revolution.[5] So the whole body of English laws relating to economic activity is of concern. And, as previously shown, the basic law in a frontier society was that of land ownership.

THE LAND

Agriculture engaged more than 90 percent of the colonial population, and it provided the basic substance of domestic colonial life, as well as trade with the outside world. Agriculture, and most other forms of primary production, are industries of the land. How land can be acquired is therefore a critical issue, for the conditions of holding land partly determine its price. Advantageous conditions of tenure would inspire creative and intelligent husbandry; onerous conditions would not.

In Anglo-American society, property in land is not the land itself, but a collection of rights to the land. It is the nature of those rights that defines the property holder's tenure. The strongest American tenure is fee simple; other tenures include such things as leases, fixed-term tenancy, and sharecropping. It would surprise most American landowners today, as it often does those who cannot meet their property taxes, to learn that the state owns the land outright. The state is the allodial owner, from whom all other property rights are derived. Owners in fee simple have possession only of rights in real estate: this phenomenon is part of what historians call the English heritage. As Blackstone said in his *Commentaries*, no one can understand English land-owning without studying the "doctrine of feuds." So for a moment, since the property rights in land have changed relatively little in this country since 1776, feudalism must be considered.

In medieval England the only absolute (allodial) owner of land was the king. All subsidiary tenures were tenements held "of the king." Thus all persons with rights in land derived their titles from the king. As William Blackstone described the system in 1765: "The king therefore only hath *absolutum et directum dominum*: but all subjects' lands are in the nature of feodum, or fee; whether derived to them by descent from their ancestors, or purchased for a valuable consideration; for they cannot come to any man by either of those ways, unless accompanied with those feudal clogs which were laid upon the first feudatory when it was originally granted."[6]

Fee simple means "the simple feud", a relatively unencumbered estate of inheritance. Theoretically, land held in fee simple can remain in perpetuity in the possession of the fee-holder, the property owner. How Americans came to hold and grant land in this way from the king of England is not a simple story, but it is well worth consideration. To this day we live in its shadow.

In medieval times the king granted land under varying conditions, for varying terms of years.[7] In theory a person might alienate, by sale, lease, or other arrangement, rights equal to or less than his own. It was through such grants from the king, alienated in parts by the great feudal lords down the feudal chain to the lowliest agricultural serf, that the property basis of the English feudal order was established. Rights in real property—to enjoy its use, to destroy, to exclude others—were granted in return for various services, for allegiance (homage and fealty), and for assistance, real and monetary, in special circumstances. These formed the complex structure of the feudal system of mutual obligation between the grades of the social order.

The object of English feudalism was support for the king. The king's vassals received their rights in exchange for military and administrative services, religious duties, and the obligation to render extraordinary assistance. Payments were due upon receipt of property (entry fines, or reliefs) and at regular intervals (military service). Upon death of the tenant the property theoretically reverted (escheated) to the donor, to be granted again for a fresh round of payments and commitments. Individuals could acquire rights in each other's property (hereditaments real and incorporeal) that also could be aliened and inherited. The main form of inheritance in England, primogeniture, was simple in theory. The military aspect of English feudalism is usually considered to be the origin of primogeniture, the definition of heir as the eldest male descendant. It was he who could first bear arms and fulfill the conditions of military tenure. Rights in real property thus had several dimensions: (1) vertical obligations, running from the Crown down to the lowliest serf, (2) horizontal, between individuals, and (3) secular (between generations).

As medieval English society developed, the needs of continuity and order were met by laws controlling rights in land, and restraints were placed upon all parts of society, molding and limiting the course of future development. The greatest medieval laws were those of Edward I: the statutes *De Viris Religiosis* (the Statute of Mortmain) of 1279, *De Donis Conditionalibus* of 1285, and *Quia Emptores Terrarum* of 1290. The Statute of Mortmain restricted future grants of land to the Church (the tenure of frankalmoign) to the king alone, thereby limiting the future power of the organized religious community. The statute *De Donis* established the English system of entail, making possible permanent restriction of certain estates to single bloodlines. The combination of primogeniture and entail established the classic English rule of descent in the noble families. *Quia Emptores* restricted feudal alienation of land in fee simple. The donor (seller) in fee simple after *Quia Emptores* had to vacate his place to the donee (buyer). No further subdivision of feudal obligations and tenures (subinfeudation) was now possible; as the great English constitutional historian, F. W. Maitland, put it, after *Quia Emptores* "no new rungs can be put in the feudal ladder."[8] Land purchase in fee simple was now "clean"; rights might be reserved, such as the mineral rights or the perpetual rents mentioned by Adam Smith, but no new conditions could be created. This is the system we inherited, and so to this day Edward I protects the rights of buyers of real property in this country.

Now consider the American land tenure, free and common socage.[9] This property right could be acquired by purchase. The tenure could carry certain incidents, or costs, such as annual payments for reserved ground rent paid to the seller (which in colonial America became quitrents); but the payments, including entry and alienation fines and reliefs, had to be fixed and certain. No extraordinary feudal payments were due from the socager. Moreover, lands in free and common socage descended directly to the heir without escheatment, and there was no right of wardship. After Henry VIII's *Statute of Wills* of 1540, lands held in free and common socage could be devised by will. Land held in this tenure became essentially a commodity, alienable in pieces of any size under known and fixed conditions.

Free and common socage tenure is specified in all of the colony charters, from the beginning in Virginia (1606): "in free and common Soccage only, and not in capite"[10] to the last colony, Georgia (1732): "to be holden of us, in our County of Middlesex, in free and common socage, and not in capite."[11]

The statute *Quia Emptores* was lifted in Maryland, Pennsylvania, and Delaware because of the special nature of the land grants to Baltimore and to William Penn, but the land was held in socage, so that rapid sale and development lay naturally in the future in these three colonies. New York's Dutch heritage produced curiosities in land tenures that plagued agriculture in the Hudson Valley "manor counties" until the mid-nineteenth century.[12] These feudal burdens were consistent with common law and passed through the Revolutionary state constitution into modern American history. Following the "rent wars" of the 1840s the new state constitution of 1846 boldly stated that "all feudal tenures of every description, with all their incidents, are declared to be abolished, saving however, all rents and services certain which at any time heretofore have been lawfully created or reserved."[13]

The last phrase concerning "rents and services certain" contained the hitch; these are the words of socage tenure, so the extraordinary tenure conditions of these counties continued for decades, and feudalism of a sort lived on, although to an ever-reduced extent, until at last no such contracts survived. The great American jurist, Chancellor James Kent, tried valiantly to make sense of all this in his *Commentaries on American Law* in 1826: "The title to lands is essentially allodial [in the United States], and every tenant has an absolute and perfect title, yet, in technical language, his estate is called an estate in fee simple, and the tenure free and common socage."[14]

The "absolute and perfect title" became less than that as the incidents of socage became property taxes and right of reentry was reserved by post-Revolutionary governments. Hence, failure to pay taxes still allows the "donor" to step in and realize his prior right by selling the land for taxes alone. The donor is not now the Crown, or a feudal lord, but he still exists—he is the state government. How the king became the individual American states was the legerdemain of Thomas Jefferson, wearing his legal hat, described in the next chapter.

Thus the powerful social control over land ownership characteristic of this country has an ancient and surprising provenance. The development of a continent would require an orderly and solid basis for division and sale of land, a basis provided, it turned out, by our English heritage. Whether disposed of by townships as in New England, by headright grants as in the South, or by proprietary governments, the tenure was simple and trustworthy. Individual property rights were secured by fixed financial conditions; the land could be subdivided and sold without the possibility of additional and onerous conditions being imposed. Property went directly to heirs or could be devised to others by will.

However, the further complication arose as to who the heirs might be. Massachusetts claimed the minor English system of gavelkind, together with the system of allotting a double portion to the eldest son, in force throughout New England and in Pennsylvania.

An English common-law rule stated that "only God creates an heir." In most of England that heir was the eldest son. Failure to produce an heir caused the inheritance to go to the nearest eligible heir, and to descend again by primogeniture. If land was entailed, the heir was merely a life tenant. Except for entail, property could be devised by will, so primogeniture ruled absolutely only in cases of intestacy.

The original colonial patents were contracts between the donor (the Crown) and the colonists, and hence, the place where the grant of land was signed was always specified. Here the plot thickens, for the grant from which the Massachusetts claim to a legal existence was drawn was seated as of "Our Manor of East-Greenwich in our County of Kent."[15] Descent in Kent was not by primogeniture, but by gavelkind, which provided for equal proportions to all sons. The Puritans of New England believed that their charter gave them gavelkind. An entry in the *Plymouth Colony Records* in 1636 reads that it was "enacted by the Court That Inheritances shall descend according to the commendable Custom Tenure and hold of east greenwich."[16]

The New England saints, revolutionaries at heart, not only divided inheritances among all the children of both sexes, but by Biblical exegesis (perhaps as a genuflection to primogeniture) allowed a double portion to the eldest son, in a practice, called "Mosaic law." Pennsylvania followed this custom. New York followed the code of Justinian allowing for straight equal division. Elsewhere the common-law rule seemed to apply. Richard Morris, investigating this matter, found an extraordinary confusion throughout the colonial period regarding inheritance in New England. [17]

The Revolution and its aftermath finally settled this aspect of the property right in America: Virginia abolished primogeniture in 1776, Georgia in 1777, North Carolina in 1784, Maryland and New York in 1786, South Carolina in 1791, and Rhode Island in 1798. The double portion was abolished in Massachusetts in 1801 and in Pennsylvania in 1810. In the Northwest Ordinance of 1787 the present American custom of equal division among all descendants of equal degrees of consanguinity was finally established. Entailment became generally limited to a single generation, although for a while fee tails were barred altogether in many states.

Thus, from free and common socage and a century and a half of adaptation, our version of fee simple evolved with our own system of descent. The contribution of this property system to American development was immense; for contrast, one need only consider the Russian's failure to solve their land problem among individuals, or the land tenure problems in all countries settled by the Spanish. With the addition of Jefferson's survey system in the Northwest Ordinance of 1785, together with the arrangements for political organization contained in the 1787 ordinance, and inheritance, and privatization of common lands, the way was open to divide, own, sell, and invest in the continent and in islands in the Pacific. It was an institutional machine for peaceful settlement, the like of which the world had never seen.[18]

INDIAN LAND

Establishment of American tenures implied, of course, disestablishment of the American Indians. The common, or public lands, of American history had been the home of another people, too few to exclude the conquering Europeans. Beginning with the patent from Isabella and Ferdinand to Columbus, Europeans presumed that lands in America not belonging to Christian monarchs could be taken. The relevant legal doctrine was known as "right of conquest." So far as the English were concerned the American colonies were English and the king was the sole allodial landowner. All others held their property rights from him. Colonial lands included Indian lands. The Crown was able to deal with the Indian tribes and nations with some fairness, but the underlying situation was unstable: an expanding European population shared the continent with Indian tribes who had no "title."

An essay attributed to John Winthrop and circulated in England before the Puritans sailed for Massachusetts foreshadows the succeeding two and a half centuries:

> That which is common to all is proper to none. This savage people ruleth over many lands without title or property; for they inclose no ground, neither have they cattell to maintagne it, but remove their dwellings as they have occasion, or as they can prevail against their neighbors. And why may not Christians have liberty to go and dwell amongst them in their waste lands and woods. . . . God hathe given to the sons of man a twofold right to the earth; there is a naturall right and a civil right. The first right was naturall when man held the earth in common, every man sowing and feeding where he pleased: Then, as men and cattell increased, they appropriated some parcells of ground by enclosing and peculiar manurance, and this in tyme got them a civil right.[19]

The civil right derived from "enclosing and peculiar manurance" is precisely what the Indians would never get, for they did not enclose land. To be fair, Massachusetts did respect Indian corn grounds at first, but there was no basis for such long-term coexistence between Europeans and Indians competing for the same resources. Theodore Roosevelt, in *The Winning of the West*, justified the "ultimate arbitrator—the sword" by employing this argument: "To recognize the In-

dian ownership of the limitless prairies and forests of this continent—that is, to consider the dozen squalid savages who hunted at
long intervals over a territory of a thousand square miles as owning
it outright—necessarily implies a similar recognition of the claims of
every white hunter, squatter, horse-thief or wandering cattle-man."[20]

Thus at the beginning and at the end of the massive Indian dispos-
session, aboriginal property rights in land had only slight recognition. In colonial times individuals were forbidden to purchase land
directly from the Indians. Such primary acquisition was reserved for
the colonial governments, agents of the Crown, the sole source of
legitimate title for whites and Indians alike. The British kept a kind
of peace with the Indians, but Crown protection of the Indians was
a notorious source of conflict with the land-hungry colonists. After
the colonies gained independence, the Indians, Christian and pagan
alike, were driven out as rapidly as Americans arrived at the frontiers
of the steadily receding Indian territory. For that is what the frontier
was after all—the outer limit of ground left to the Indians, that line
of forts celebrated by the historian, Frederick Jackson Turner. When
the Indians were confined to reservations the frontier was gone. One
legal view was expressed in 1810 in *Fletcher v. Peck*, a case before the
U.S. Supreme Court involving contract rights, but also involving, col-
laterally, the Indians. John Marshall agreed that the Indians should
not be thought bereft of all right to occupy their lands, but held that
the ultimate ownership—*seisin in fee*, the words of medieval England—was in the state, the successor to England's king: "The majority of the court is of the opinion that the nature of the Indian title,
which is certainly to be respected by all courts, until it be legitimately
extinguished, is not such as to be absolutely repugnant to seisin in
fee on the part of the state."[21]

There followed the Cherokee removal beyond the Mississippi, the
expulsion of the Miamis, and in the next seven decades, the com-
pression of the Indian populations into their present compounds beyond the pale of the main European settlement of the continent. Perhaps it is true, as Chancellor Kent argued, that "the settlement of
that part of America now composing the United States has been at-
tended with as little violence and aggression on . . . the part of the
whites . . . as is compatible with the fact of the entry of a race of
civilized men into the territory of savages."[22]

But perhaps it is not true. Expulsion of the Indians from their lands
certainly seems inevitable. Title to property that would have been
respected by Anglo-American law, secure tenure, had to come from
a source beyond the reach or understanding of the Indians. After independence, republican government displaced the Crown as the

source of secure title. What was therefore a triumph for Americans—a system for the orderly measurement, division, disposal, and settlement of a continent—contained nothing but reservations, lands set aside, for the Indians. It can be argued that the mechanism of control, which left only the state as the legitimate source of title, saved the Indians from genocide. Their lands could not legitimately be taken by force, except government force, and that in the end was stayed. Had there been uncontrolled right of preemption, the Indian doubtlessly would have been annihilated. There is little in American history to suggest otherwise.

THE COLONIAL LABOR CONTRACT

Once we have established property rights in the land, and its settlement, we must ask ourselves under what rules the work of settlement is to be done. Land must have labor to be fruitful. Here again English nonmarket control dates to colonial times. In our own era the labor contract is surrounded by laws regarding age, sex, minimum wages, safety, social security, and, if there is a union, legally enforced work rules as well as wages. In a closed shop, number, entry, price, and quality (work rules and conditions) are all controlled in the legally imposed collective bargaining process. So there is nothing obvious or inevitable about the "free contract" as the correct way to engage labor, and it is not surprising that the colonial labor contract was subject to extensive controls.

The colonial legacy continues to cloud our history in many respects even today. The fact that so many workers in colonial America labored under conditions of structural unfreedom has had profound consequences on the course of our development. American society English at first, structured labor following English guidelines. Labor would not come willingly to the New World wilderness in sufficient numbers, so force was required to acquire white as well as black laborers. Classed among the lowest rungs of colonial society, American labor, until federal establishment came with the Wagner Act, also failed to find acceptance for its organized aspirations in modern society.

The place to begin is with white servitude. It is safe to say that most modern Americans who read history are utterly unaware of this subject.[23] Yet for nearly two centuries legally enforced servitude was a common condition of white labor. In 1750, for example, every tenth person in Maryland was an indentured white servant. One can only now speculate on how typical that figure was, for we have no overall data for the colonies. But from other evidence it is clear enough that the practice was a major one. The U.S. Constitution records how the population was reckoned for congressional representation: "Adding to the whole Number of free persons, including those bound to service for a Term of Years, and excluding Indians not taxed, three fifths of all other persons."[24] (Three-fifths of a person was the constitutional definition of a black African slave.)

In 1787 the white bondmen and bondwomen were only the representatives of an army of indentured white servants who had labored for their freedom in this country since the Jamestown and Plymouth settlements. How many came across the ocean in servitude? A. E. Smith, in the classic study of the subject, *Colonists in Bondage*, states that, apart from the Puritan migration to New England, between one half and two thirds of all white immigrants to colonial America came as "indentured servants, or redemptioners or convicts."[25]

Who were these people? The answer begins with the famous statute of 1562, in the fifth year of Elizabeth's reign, the "act containing divers orders for artificers, labourers, servants of husbandry and apprentices," known commonly as the *Statute of Artificers and Apprentices*.[26] This comprehensive act, a no-nonsense "incomes policy," formed the background labor law for the colonial period—and long afterward. The object of this law, together with a later addendum concerning vagrants and "sturdy beggars," was compulsory labor, in agriculture if necessary, for all who did not have a fixed place in the social order.[27] Exemptions were granted for persons of wealth (amounts specified) or independent incomes, gentlemen, scholars, mariners, fishermen, miners, and journeymen and apprentices in specified trades, all strictly defined, in market towns, cities, and corporate boroughs. All others were to "be compelled to be retained to serve in husbandry by the year, with any person that keepeth husbandry, and will require any such person to serve."

Conditions for bonded apprenticeships were laid down in the law, as well as provisions for wage fixing by government officials, penalties for wages paid in excess of the legal wages, penalties for refusal to work, and rewards for informers. Women under forty, children over twelve, and men under sixty were covered. The act settled the terms for indentures of all sorts, and its provisions appeared in colonial statutes and haunted American law courts far into the nineteenth century. The *spirit* of the statute was one of social status with rigid stratification of social classes and the complete elimination of "idleness." The man or woman who refused the wages offered could be convicted as a vagabond. The penalty for a third conviction was punishment for a felony, possibly death.

Individuals could contract themselves into service for fixed periods of years and be transported by those who owned their contracts to the New World. Those who chose this form of escape from the rigors of the Elizabethan law in the subsequent two centuries were the poor. They contracted for wages, working conditions, ship passage, housing, food, sometimes for a fixed annual wage, and sometimes even for a terminal reward at the end of the contract. The latter was not mandatory, but was sometimes provided in the form of tools, equipment, and even grants of land, as in early Virginia and in Pennsylvania. The Massachusetts laws of 1641 contained a resolution that "servants that have served deligentie and faithfully to the benefit of the maisters seaven yeares, shall not be sent away empty."[28]

Seven years is the term specified in the *Statute*, although the terms in America varied. As in England, an indentured servant could not leave his or her employment except with a master's consent (or in the case of his death). Indentures, like other property, could be transferred by sale. Servants, unlike Negro slaves, had access to the courts and could prosecute masters for violation of the contract.

Poverty alone was not a sufficient motivation to insure an adequate supply of indentured servants, so more forceful methods were commonly employed. In the case of orphans and foundlings the *Statute* provided guardians with an incentive to "bind" children in articles of indenture. Children were in particularly great demand; they could be worked until they reached twenty-one years of age, which, if they were young enough when they began working, could be longer than a seven-year term. In the early days the Virginia Company bought young children at five pounds per head in London; in 1627 alone between 1,400 and 1,500 children were bound and shipped to Virginia.[29]

Demand for such labor had several determinants. Most colonies granted headright lands of fifty acres for each servant, so a servant transported and supported was also a land acquisition for the master. Servants were particularly valued as cargo by shipmasters who brought New World produce to Britain and needed cargo for the return journey.

Convicts were a notorious but plentiful source of labor in the colonies. Such human shipments could include war prisoners and political offenders. We have evidence of their treatment in a surviving letter from the Massachusetts Puritan leader, John Cotton, to Oliver Cromwell dated May 25, 1651:

> The Scots, whom God delivered into your hands at Dunbarre, and whereof sundry were sent hither, we have been desirous (as we could) to

make their yoke easy. Such as were sick of scurvy or other diseases have not wanted physick and Chryurgy. They have not been sold for slaves to perpetual servitude, but for 6 or 7 or 8 years, as we do our owne: and he that bought the most of them (I heare) buildeth houses for them, for every 4 an house, layeth some acres of ground thereto, which he giveth them as their owne, requiering 3 dayes in the weeke to worke for him (by turnes) and 4 dayes for themselves, and promiseth, assone as they can repay him the money he layed out for them, he will set them at liberty.[30]

Less respectable prisoners came from the jails and law courts of England. In the seventeenth century more than 300 capital crimes were on the books in England. Convicted criminals could be "clergied," however, by "calling for the book" and looking at the Bible to prove ability to read, on the ancient theory that one who could read was in holy orders.[31] Pardons were granted such clergied prisoners, but the royal pardon was more likely to be given if the prisoner agreed to be transported. Although under common law exile or transportation could not be imposed, an act of 1718 provided for the transportation of clergied prisoners. The royal pardons on condition of voluntary transportation also continued.

After a "gaol delivery," or major assize, the judges made lists of prisoners they thought worthy of saving by royal pardon and forwarded these to the king. Transportation of "offenders in clergy" was for a servitude of seven years—"His Majesty's seven-year passengers"—and fourteen years for pardon of nonclergyable offenses. Merchants made regular rounds of the courts, bought prisoners from sheriffs, turnkeys, or the Recorder of London, then paid for their transportation, or sold the indentures to ship captains outright. These indentures were sold in America again to colonists for whom the indentured servants worked out their terms.

The trade was perfectly regular, but not perfectly acceptable. Colonists objected to the quality of these immigrants, and colonial assemblies made unsuccessful efforts to halt the trade. Even after the Revolution, in 1783, a cargo of eighty felons was successfully shipped. Finally in 1788 Congress passed a resolution against the trade and the English were forced to turn to Australia to rid Britain of this particular class of population. We do not know how many prisoners were shipped to America; estimates are that in the seventeenth century as many as 4,500 convicts arrived, and 30,000 more in the eighteenth century. And, convicts were not the only targets for enforced passage and servitude. In 1655 the Venetian ambassador reported that "the soldiers of the London garrison had visited various brothels and other places of entertainment and forceably laid hands on more than four hundred women of loose life, whom they compelled to sail for the Barbados Islands."[32]

The colonists also put their own people to servitude—not just criminals and the poor and destitute, but also the children of ordinary citizens. Apprenticeship was a form of indentured service and was used to acquire training, education, and entrance into trades, business, and the professions. The element of compulsion was real enough[33], with corporal punishments prescribed; both law and religion bade the servant to serve faithfully.

Labor was a necessity throughout the colonies. Jefferson wrote that, in Virginia, "vagabonds without visible property or vocation, are placed in workhouses, where they are well clothed, fed, lodged and made to labor."[34] In Massachusetts the laws of 1639, 1646, 1655, and 1657 empowered magistrates to "settle" the poor upon the community and to commit "idle persons" to houses of correction to earn bread, water, and "other mean food," each receiving ten lashes upon entry, and more whipping, and starvation if necessary, in order to maintain "meet order." Such laws were enforced well into the Federal period of American history, when overseers of the poor were empowered to put orphan children into bondage in order to relieve the taxpayers of their keep. In the 1830s the courts were still engaged in measuring American laws in such matters against the "statute of 5 Elizabeth." Edmund Morgan, in *The Puritan Family*, wrote that "most of the inhabitants of seventeenth-century New England either were or had been servants."[35] The system was characteristic of the whole colonial period, and bondmen and bondwomen were common features of Federal America until the courts ceased imprisonment for debt and extensive settlement made forceable return of apprentices increasingly expensive.

Redemptioners were a separate class of immigrants, thought to have originated with German migration to the colonies. They came in families, owing the shipmasters for their passage, and were allowed time after arrival to engage in work contracts to pay for passage. Placement of one or more children in indenture was a common method of settlement.[36]

In the Elizabethan *Statute* officials were charged with fixing wages and hours of work (e.g., 5 A.M. to 7 or 8 P.M. in the summer months). Accordingly, the colonial statutes abound with efforts by local officials to fix wages and working conditions. As in England, penalties were levied for overpayment of wages. Craftsmen in New England, as in the *Statute*, could be compelled to labor in the harvest. Township roads were built and maintained with direct labor taxes. Such compulsion was a common element in colonial life, and the entire community was involved in the maintenance of discipline and order. Even local offices such as the night watch were, or could be, compulsory. The colonial hue-and-cry ordinances for the pursuit of criminals followed the *Statute of Winchester* of 1285, which had also provided for the local arming and discipline of military forces. Such military service, a ubiquitous feature of colonial life, was far cheaper than maintenance of regular military forces. Long after such laws had disappeared in England, sumptuary laws in Massachusetts were imposed on a class basis, forbidding the wearing of luxurious garments among the poor: "the Selectmen of every Town, or the major part of them, are hereby enabled and required from time to time, to have regard, and take notice of apparel of any of the Inhabitants . . . and whosoever shall Judge to exceed their rankes & abilities in the costliness, or fashion of their apparel in any respect, especially in the wearing of Ribbons or great boots . . . lace, points . . . silk hoods or scarfes, the Selectmen aforesaid shall have power to assess such persons."[37]

The spirit of most legislation toward the laboring poor was one of discipline and control. At the same time, labor in colonial America, as in England, was considered and treated as socially inferior, an attitude that was inappropriate to a frontier community, but one that would long bedevil efforts in America to make a respectable place for wage labor in society. Where guilds existed in the colonial world, the labor element in crafts was conflated with management, production, and merchandising, reinforcing labor's lowly position. The class structure was functional but not all persons had civil rights. Even in the early Federal period property qualifications for voters and officeholders lingered. The restraints upon laborers were attempts to maintain ubiquitous controls, but still they were light compared to those imposed upon an even more regulated stratum, black slaves.

The one labor force component that found no place in the laws of England, common or statutory, was black slavery. Hence, the social position of the Negro slave had to be created in the New World. By 1780 there were more than 574,000 Negro slaves in the thirteen mainland colonies, a fifth of the entire population. By 1800 the slave population had nearly doubled, to just over a million. By then, most of the black population, as well as the white, was the result of natural increase, not recent immigration; but a larger proportion of blacks than of whites was native born. As Fogel and Engerman show in *Time on the Cross*, death rates equal to those of the West Indies would have left the United States in 1800 with 186,000 Negro slaves instead of a million.[38] The problem for Negro slaves in America was not just the material condition of their lives, but the nature of their labor contract.

No matter how well an African slave was treated he was at an utter disadvantage compared to the indentured servant. First, the slave had no legal document setting forth his wages. The slave's only contract was whatever social pressure there may have been, plus the self-interest of his master, to mete out reasonable treatment. Second, because a contract of indenture was property, its terms and conditions gave the indentured servant his status before the law; the slave had no such status. Third, the slave had no fixed end to his servitude, and in most cases, of course, it was for life. Fourth, death of the master did not free the slave, who could be devised by will, as could his family. The slave could even be entailed. Lastly, because children inherited the condition of the mother, slavery was passed on regardless of the status of the father. In contrast, there were no such disabilities for children born of parents in white servitude. Late in the seventeenth century the laws governing slaves were codified;[39] other disadvantages were added, including prohibitions against legal marriage, religious and secular education, any craft training, and any property ownership. Compared to the white indentured servant, the Negro slave was scarcely a human being, legally, by the end of the seventeenth century. Hence, however many individual cases of kindly masters and mistresses, of good basic treatment, of education, training, religious instruction, all done in contravention of the colonial black codes, the laws were harsh, and were meant to be.

There is no doubt that slave labor had great advantages over indentured servitude in the southern colonies. But, by 1780, the numbers of Negro slaves in the North shows that slavery was clearly an active practice there. Of the 575,000 Negro slaves in the thirteen colonies in 1780, the South contained the vast majority: 221,000 in Virginia, 97,000 in South Carolina, 91,000 in North Carolina, 81,000 in Maryland, and 20,800 in Georgia. But 21,000 lived in New York, 10,500 in New Jersey, 7,900 in Pennsylvania, 5,900 in Connecticut, and 4,800 in Massachusetts. In other words, slavery was ubiquitous in the colonies, but concentrated in the South.

Slavery held economic advantages for Southern agriculture even before the cotton culture developed in the late 1790s. Wherever gang labor could be used—in the production of rice, tobacco, indigo, forest products, or corn—"management" and capital equipment could be specialized, and scale economies became possible. The "wage" (food, clothing, shelter) could be controlled arbitrarily as there was no contract to be honored and hence no problem with the legal system. The imposition of discipline in a harsh regime, with education and training severely restricted, could have been costly. But here the community provided a social overhead: the slave codes were enforced by the entire community (including those who owned no slaves), so the individual planter, especially the large-scale slave owner, benefited disproportionately. Hence the slave codes were actually external economies to the slave owners.

Negro slaves, moreover, were as good for headright land grants as were indentured servants, so slavery cheapened the cost of land acquisition as well as labor costs. And since the slave's contract was for life, the transaction costs were reduced compared to those of white servitude. If the normal indenture was seven years and a slave lived for twenty-eight years, his transport cost (as part of the slave price) was only a fourth that of four seven-year servants. In addition, the slave's resale value was higher for most of his term than were the sums of the remaining terms of partly expired indentures. Thus, seen strictly as a capital investment, the slave was a more vendable asset. The termination cost of a slave contract was simply burial; there was no provision for supplies of tools, equipment, and food to a living servant. Also, since servants commonly had contractual provisions for training and education, and slaves did not, the amount of pure labor value that could be extracted from a slave was proportionately greater. Finally, the female slave was herself a prime capital asset, since her children, from either white or black fathers, were automatically slaves of the same master. This factor alone must have made slavery an enormously attractive labor system compared to white servitude.

For these reasons the demand for slaves, given the moral tone of the era, was high. Since in the late seventeenth century the perpetual bondage and social condition of the black slave was fixed in law, there remained only the supply from natural increase and the transatlantic slave trade to solidify the system in the mainland colonies. Natural increase, as Fogel and Engerman have shown, was by far the major source of black slaves. But the transatlantic trade, initially provided by foreigners (at first the Dutch), then by a royal monopoly, and finally by a thriving domestic shipping industry, supplied a sufficient additional supply of black immigrants. The puritanical New Englanders became the main entrepreneurs, and Providence, Rhode Island, the center and entrepôt of the trade, although domestic slavery in that colony was negligible. The Crown's interest was fixed early in the eighteenth century by Chief Justice Holt's dictum that "negroes are merchandise and within the Navigation acts."

It is one of the tragic ironies of American history that the English legal mind changed in this regard, too late for the Americans. The first slaves had landed in Virginia in 1619. The practice and legal system of slavery were developed by the Americans for a century and a half with the Crown, during the reign of the Royal Africa Company, who financed it and provided official sanction. The original conditions of the Georgia charter, calling for an end to slavery, had even been overthrown by the demands of the white settlers for black slaves. But, in the Somerset case in 1772, a slave taken from America to England to be shipped to the West Indies was freed on a writ of habeas corpus in the court of the King's Bench on the ground that "slavery did not and could not exist in England, under English law."[40] Since the colonial laws could not be repugnant to the laws of England, it was only a matter of time until colonial slaves would be freed, as was done in 1834 in the Caribbean by compensated emancipation. For the Americans, unfortunately, ultimate emancipation would be far more expensive to achieve.

In addition to controls over wages, entry into trades, apprenticeships, indentured servitude, and black slavery, the labor contract was also subject to nonmarket controls over business enterprise in general. I will turn to that subject next, but enough has already been said to indicate that the colonial world was no hotbed of laissez-faire for labor. It was a world well described by A. E. Smith not as a democratic arcadia, but a place where men with money thrived by making the poor work. A tradition was established: "It is a familiar story that mankind, when confronted in America with a vast and trackless wilderness . . . threw off its ancient shackles of cast and privilege and set forth upon the road to freedom. Among the social institutions found most useful in the course of this march were those of African slavery and white servitude."[41]

CONTROLS OF BUSINESS

Detailed regulation of business activity was extensive in the colonial world. Such control continued at the level of state and local government after the Revolution. It was raised to the level of central government in the National Bank Act (1863), the Act to Regulate Commerce (1887), and the Sherman Antitrust Act (1890). But in some areas of economic life—for example, the enforcement of prohibitions against the slave trade after 1808, control of foreign trade to reduce smuggling, and land acquisition and disposal—central government nonmarket control was never entirely absent. Controls over business activity at the state and municipal levels were primarily by license to limit entry, to raise tax revenues, to control morals, and to regulate the quality and prices of franchised public-service enterprises. But since the federal government originally was meant to have limited power, detailed control of business activity by central government was constrained for many decades. This fact helped to give the new republic an aura of economic freedom.

The ubiquitous presence of controls in colonial times must be viewed against the medieval background from which such practices, like those related to landholding, were derived. Feudal government was military and theological, with peasant agriculture centered upon the manorial society as its basic social unit. While it is true that a place was always made within the confines of European feudalism for trade and commerce, it was marginal (however convenient) to the feudal order. Hence cities were given special charters, rights, and privileges. Certain towns were specified as market towns; a separate body of law and system of justice existed for commerce and those engaged in it.

Commerce, a ubiquitous adjunct of medieval life, was also disruptive of it. The vast majority of people in this time were either peasants or part of the military-theocratic superstructure that rested upon peasant society. The growth of a separate commercial sector was destined to undermine the feudal order. Hence suspicion of commerce and careful control of it by the feudal state was a well-conceived policy, if the feudal order was to survive. The place of commerce is reflected in a 1353 law of Edward III allowing separate justice for business disputes. The Crown said that because "the merchants cannot often tarry in one place in hinderance of their business, we will and do grant, that speedy right be to them done from day to day and from hour to hour."[42] The affairs of merchants were those of migrants, outside the boundaries of manor courts, royal courts, or the rules of religious and monastic orders. As trade and commerce grew and embraced increasing sectors of English economic life, rules governing business activities multiplied. The separate justice developed into equity proceedings in the courts of Chancery, the laws of bailment grew, and if the sea was involved, the courts of Admiralty applied laws derived from the Hanseatic League, which in turn were based upon the ancient rules of the sea, the laws of Oleron and Wisby. Business developed within a corset of law that defined acceptable rules of behavior.

By the time of colonial settlement, English regulations governing private business could be placed into four broad categories: (1) general laws, (2) specific rules related to municipal authority, (3) laws governing businesses that fell into geographic interstices between ordinary jurisdictions, and (4) laws governing trade with foreign countries. Such nonmarket controls had as their objects regulation of one or more of the four basic control categories: number, entry, price, or quality. These rules, transplanted to the New World, formed part of the legal framework of American economic development. Subsequent American history was greatly influenced by these English and colonial usages.

Two medieval concepts, the prohibition of usury and the doctrine of a just price, were imbedded in the general colonial laws. The English, like other medieval (and modern) communities, prohibited moneylending at exorbitant rates of interest in accordance with the Biblical injunction against usury. Massachusetts legislated 8 percent as its maximum in 1641, saying of that rate that "neither shall this be a colour or countenance to allow any usurie amongst us contrarie to the law of God."[43] There is no evidence that usurious moneylending then, anymore than now, was inhibited by such laws; the mind of man has never been found wanting in ways to extract high earnings on credit, despite prohibitions. The idea that a price different from the market price might be just lay behind colonial price controls. These were generally applied in special situations and ordinarily in connection with quality controls of public-service enterprises. Indeed, the absence of attempted price controls by public officials would have been novel in the colonial era.

Similarly, ever since Edward I and the rise of the doctrine of *assumpsit*, persons engaged in any public calling were constrained to serve all who applied, at reasonable prices and competently. Efforts by colonial governments to encourage such competence were specific applications of English law. No one had a right to do business with the public on any other basis. Combinations in restraint of trade by private persons were illegal in common law; Georgia, in the mid-eighteenth century, passed a law that contained the actual medieval words, enjoining merchants against "forestalling, engrossing, and unjust exactions."[44]

In addition to such broad-gauged controls, *market overt* appeared in the New World. (I treat its development in some detail in the penultimate section of this chapter.) According to Blackstone the Saxons would not accept transfer of title in the sale of chattel (except for small sums) without witnesses.[45] The English finessed this problem by appointing certain towns as market towns on certain days of the week and allowing a certain number of fairs. Chattel goods purchased in these market towns on market days were presumed to have been bought before witnesses and so the buyer's title was good. In London every weekday was market day and every shop a *market overt*. The clerk of the market, or whoever "had the toll" of the market, adjudicated in disputes, presided over the merchants' courts (the courts of piepowder), controlled the quality of goods and services offered, and sometimes the prices as well. This is the source not only of the beautiful little market towns of England, but also of Faneuil Hall in Boston, and of covered markets, farmers, markets, and county fairs from the Atlantic to the Pacific—a quaint beginning for retail sales in a country in which every day is market day, night and day, and virtually any location can be the site of retail sales. The exceptions are where local "blue laws" still exist to restrict Sunday transactions. The whole apparatus of *market overt* was brought to the colonies. In the nineteenth century market halls were built across the United States (facsimiles of Philadelphia's market hall apparently being a favorite), as if commerce could be kept within such confines. The Massachusetts law of 1648 suffices as an example of such established markets:

> That there shall henceforth be a market kept at Boston . . . upon the fifth day of the week and at Salem upon the fourth day of the week. And at Linn upon the third day of the week. And at Charleston . . . upon the sixth day of the week. It is also Ordered and hereby Graunted to Boston aforesaid to have two Faires in a year, on the first third day of the third month, and on the first third day of the eight month from year to year to continue for two or three days together.[46]

Such a narrow practice was clearly inappropriate to colonial circumstances. Soon enough special dispensations were made to allow farmers to sell on their farms, and retailers began to appear in the towns, selling out of market areas and on days other than market days. Carl Bridenbaugh, in *Cities in the Wilderness*, points to many examples of retailing in merchants' shops in the seventeenth and early eighteenth centuries.[47] Chancellor Kent observed that the English laws of *market overt* were dying out in the colonies by the time of the Revolution.

This background of control is a major source of municipal licensing, and days and places of provender still are controlled in most cities for different sorts of businesses. While originally controlled market days and times were Norman England's technique of coping with Saxon ways, today the arguments are usually ethical or moral (automobiles may not be sold in Evanston, Illinois, on Sundays), or the consequences of trade-union bargaining (until very recently, no fresh meat was sold in Chicago after 5:00 P.M. or on Sundays). The more things change the more they remain the same.

Specific rules governing colonial business represent an interesting confusion of motives. Governments wanted to have public amenities, such as bridges, ferries, docks, and shipbuilding. Special franchises were granted, giving monopoly rights and subsidies. (Harvard College, for example, was given several subsidies in its early years, including profits from a ferry across the Charles River.) Taxes were varied in order to stimulate desirable businesses. The obligations of tradesmen, together with the exclusive grants of privilege that were customary in England to local merchants (the merchant guilds) or to favored crafts (the craft guilds), produced laws for the control of domestic animals, for weights and measures, and for the grazing and shearing of sheep. Since workmen were to be apprenticed under the Elizabethan *Statute of Artificers and Apprentices* we find rules of apprenticeship in conjunction with quality controls, inspection systems, and price and wage controls. The roles of master and workman, producer and seller, capital and labor, were conflated in this early period of capitalist development. Hence it is not easy to deduce which interests were served, except that in general the laws throughout the colonies seemed to assume that order was maintained by close government control. In a Massachusetts law of 1641 the welfare of brewers, workmen, and the public all seem to be served: "The end no other but good and wholsom Beer be brewed at any time . . . to be sold for the supply of ship or other vessels at sea; and that no oppression or wrong be done to any in this mystery. It is Ordered . . . that no person whatsoever, shall henceforth undertake the calling or worke of brewing beere for sale, but only such as are known, to have sufficient skill and knowledge in the art or mystery of brewing."[48]

The law goes on to say that anyone buying beer that is "unwholesome and useless for their supply" will get his money back plus damages, so an effort was made to give the public an interest in what was otherwise a blatant piece of special-interest legislation. Bakers also were controlled, with prices and bread weights set, and the "Clarke of the Market" empowered to enter bakers' homes in search of short-weighted loaves.

Viewers, searchers, gaugers, wardens, reeves—a small army of inspection personnel—enforced quality controls over production, packaging, and shipping of food and goods. In New England the selectmen of townships were charged with enforcement. Guild monopolies were given (and sometimes refused) in order to raise and maintain the quality of goods and services produced. In Massachusetts and Pennsylvania such quality controls, along with limitations on the number of firms allowed to exist and conditions of entry, intensified in the decades immediately after the Revolution. The rule of *caveat emptor* protected the seller from action by the buyer, but was never meant to sanction business fraud; in the colonial world direct nonmarket controls buoyed up business probity. The typical splitting of fines "one halfe to the Informer and the other halfe to the country" must have had chilling effects upon merchants and manufacturers with butchers' thumbs.

The law also provided for conditions of storage, hiring, delivery, rental, and pawnbroking, all under the English law of bailment. Thus there was little scope for complete originality in American business practices. Indeed, after independence the similarity between American and British commercial practices worked to the new republic's benefit as trade with England became the mainstay of our overseas commerce.

Thirdly, laws that are the direct forerunners of nonmarket control over rates and services of public utilities, common carriers, and other public-service industries extend back into English history. The thirteenth-century law of *assumpsit* charged those in public callings to accept all custom offered, at reasonable rates, and to serve competently. Wherever the idea arose that only "natural" monopolies were the objects of such regulation, it was not medieval England. We know of laws governing common carriers in fourteenth-century England. Taverns and inns also were subject to controls as "public houses" at very early dates. Such enterprises, like markets and fairs, were subject to special laws, and they commonly lay outside normal jurisdictions. In the colonies, to support this point, travelers were not subject to the same restrictions at public houses (for example, those imposed on the Sabbath) as townspeople. It is probable that the medieval passion for order and notions about just price account more for control than disapproval of monopoly. A Massachusetts public utility regulation of 1655, for example, certainly was not motivated by monopoly considerations:

> There being a very great abuse in the Townes of Boston and Charlestown, by Porters, who many times do require and exact more then is just and righteous for their Labours, it is Ordered by this Court. That from henceforth the Select men of the said Townes, from time to time, shall have power to regulate in this case, and to state their wages, as in their understanding shall be most just, and equal, as also to determine what persons shall be employed therein.[49]

In this case number, entry, and price were to be controlled, but no mention was made of quality of service. Its object being price control, this law defended the public interest, except that restriction of entry protected from competition those already in the trade. Such attitudes were common, judging from colonial laws. In Massachusetts, inns were licensed, hours and clientele were restricted, dancing forbidden. The amount of drink consumed per person was restricted. Innkeepers were dissuaded from advancing credit to sailors by a law barring suits for such debts in Massachusetts courts. New York also regulated public houses; in Virginia and Maryland the courts licensed public houses and fixed their rates.

Common carriers were also controlled. In Massachusetts not only were charges fixed, but the ferry service was given priorities—first place was given to medical people "called to women's labours," and magistrates were allowed to travel without charge. Colonial Philadelphia set the rates and conditions for "carters, draymen and porters." The same was true of New York. Jefferson wrote of Virginia: "Ferries are admitted only at such places as are appointed by law, and the rates of farriage fixed." To attract capital, monopoly franchises were granted to operators of toll bridges and ferries.

These practices continued English tradition, and later became American tradition as well. Two such monopoly grants of the early Federal period were momentous: *Gibbons v. Ogden* (1824), the test of the commerce clause, came from New York's grant of a steamboat monopoly to Robert Fulton; and the Charles River Bridge case (1837) overthrew monopoly claims of a state-chartered corporation and was a landmark in the development of laws of general incorporation in this country.[50]

Finally, businesses engaged in foreign trade were never free of control. The doctrines of free trade came not from accepted practice but, from the insights of economic theory. During the nineteenth century, by slow stages of development the British adopted free-trade policies, but other major countries did not follow the British lead. In modern history foreign trade (both imports and exports) has been mainly the province of nonmarket controls by central governments. In England trade was a major source of tax revenue, and from Cromwell onward (1653) trade and the instruments of trade were mechanisms of empire building. The British acts of trade and navigation defined and bound together a world empire, however inefficient they may have been in the allocation of resources within that empire. It was this system, primarily, that Adam Smith attacked in *The Wealth of Nations* in 1776, and that the colonists revolted against.

The British system can usefully be divided into two parts, those laws from 1763 onward that were devised to raise a colonial revenue, and the older basic trade and navigation acts. The first revenue laws started with the Molasses Act of 1733, although it was largely evaded. Between the end of the Seven Years' War in 1763, and 1774, Parliament attempted more direct colonial control. Many of them today are acts well-known: in 1764, the Sugar Act, the Stamp Act, the American Revenue Act, and the Currency Act (prohibiting colonial currency from being declared legal tender); in 1766, the Declaratory Act (declaring parliamentary power to legislate for the colonies); in 1767, the Townshend Acts; in 1770, the Revenue Act; in 1773, the Tea Tax; and in 1774, the Boston Port Act, the Massachusetts Government Act, and the Quebec Act.

Following imposition of such laws, of course, came the American Revolution. In 1774 most of these laws were specified and condemned in the *Declaration and Resolves of the First Continental Congress*, a year later in the *Declaration of the Causes and Necessity of Taking up Arms*, and in 1776 in the *Declaration of Independence*. Taxes were reimposed later by the independent American government, the states were prohibited from issuing money, and the Ohio Valley was ceded voluntarily by the old colonies to the federal government. Revenues were raised from import duties and excises. Thus the "intolerable" laws of the late colonial period were precursors of later and similar American legislation.

The heritage of the other laws, the navigation and trade laws, which lasted from Cromwell to the American Revolution, is even more direct. These British laws closely controlled shipping, ports, and docks. They were congenial enough to the colonists, and indeed were repassed by Congress (slightly rewritten) in 1792 and 1793 and formed our country's own code of navigation. The Navigation Acts are usually dated in 1660, although the date is a bit of British sleight of hand. Legally the Protectorate never existed, so the reign of Charles II began with the date of his father's death and laws of 1660 are dated 12 Charles II. The laws of the Protectorate have no existence in the British constitution. Either they were repassed, or they do not exist.

Cromwell was building an empire of far-flung possessions. The British repassed his 1651 navigation and trade laws in 1660 and enforced them, so that the Massachusetts law of 1645, which provided that "all ships which come for trading onely shall have free access to our Harbours."[51] was canceled in 1661 by a new law imposing the Navigation laws. The Act of 1660 stated that no commodities could be shipped into or out of colonial ports except in English (including colonial) ships whose crews were three fourths English and whose masters were British subjects. English and colonial ships bound to foreign ports could carry commodities, but not those enumerated articles that were reserved for the English market (they could be re-exported). After 1662 only English-built (and colonial-built) ships or prizes of war (which were naturalized) could trade inside the empire. After 1663 direct colonial trade in European goods was illegal. In 1696 the Board of Trade was to review all laws passed by colonial assemblies. The Crown reserved the right to control intracolonial trade. These laws defined the empire.

This control over external trade and commerce was continued by the new republic. As Kent said of our navigation laws of 1792 and 1793, they formed "the basis of the regulations in this country for the foreign and coasting trade, and for the fisheries of the United States, and they correspond very closely with the provisions of the British statutes in the reign of George III."[52] The first tariff act was passed by Congress July 4, 1789 under the federal Constitution, and America's own tradition of free trade, the Massachusetts law of 1645, was forgotten.

Apart from the details of subsequent legislation, one can easily see four enduring consequences of the English nonmarket control system over American trade and navigation: (1) the idea and experience of judicial review, (2) strong admiralty court jurisdiction, (3) effective customs controls, and (4) central government control of commerce between the states.

Judicial review is often considered a unique product of the Federal period, fixed in our system by *Marbury v. Madison* (1803). Yet legal scholars have long acknowledged the eight decades of control by the Board of Trade as the origin, a practice we learned from the English but that was not, however, a part of domestic English practice. From 1696 to 1776 more than 400 laws of colonial assemblies were overturned by the Board of Trade's lawyers as "repugnant" to the laws of England—including Ben Franklin's scheme of 1754 to unite the mainland colonies.[53] The Courts of Admiralty enforced the navigation laws in American waters. In the 1760s and 1770s Americans learned that the American trade could yield a sizable customs revenue, even from low duties, and were not loath to impose such duties upon the newly independent American consumer after the Revolution, with admiralty jurisdiction in the hands of the district courts. Commerce between the colonies had been controlled by the Crown, and the interregnum between 1776 and 1787 illuminated the wisdom of that policy. The colonies, and later the new states, disrupted trade by imposing duties upon each other in the interregnum, a practice that was examined at the Constitutional Convention in 1787. The Commerce Clause was the result.

The Colonial Safety Net

No aspect of colonial social-control methods has had more long-lasting impact than the tradition of local responsibility for the poor, a tradition defended by moral, legal (states rights), and theoretical arguments. Of course, if the poor were to receive public assistance at all in colonial times, the administration would *appear* to be local because of the miniature size of the colonial governments. But even then, local responsibility was the law, and like the tenure in real property, a law in which the colonists had little or no choice.

In 1535 Henry VIII, in a law covering "charitable alms," charged local authorities with the upkeep of the poor. Such had been the obligation of the Church since time out of mind, but now Henry was stripping the Church of its economic power. New arrangements had to be made: "All governors of shires, cities, towns, hundreds, hamlets, and parishes, shall find and keep every aged, poor and impotent person so as none of them shall be compelled to go openly in begging."[54] In this respect modern American cities, like New York, Chicago, Los Angeles or San Francisco are far behind Henry VIII.

The ancient nursery rhyme begins: "Hark, Hark, the dogs do bark / The beggars are coming to town." Begging was dealt with harshly by the Tudors. If there was poverty, the community at large, not individuals, should deal with it; begging was to be abolished. In Henry's law, "a valiant beggar, or sturdy vagabond" would be whipped upon first conviction and then sent to his home parish; the "upper part of the gristle of his right ear" was to be cut off for the second offense, and then,"if after that he be taken wandering in idleness, or doth not apply to his labour, or is not in service of any master, he shall be adjudged and executed a felon." Thus, so far as punishment is concerned, fortunately, our modern cities have advanced some distance from Henry's rule. Private alms were forbidden in Henry's law except "to the common boxes and common gatherings of every parish, upon pain to forfeit ten times so much as shall be given." With that the poor were made the responsibility of local authority. They could not be forced to beg; communal charity would be the rule. Elizabeth amended the law in 1601, still imposing local obligation, and it was this law governing the poor that came to colonial America. Itinerant Quaker preachers with clipped ears who were later executed in Massachusetts were at least done in according to law.

The law's brutality, however appalling, should not mask the principles established. The poor would live in the community's embrace in the colonies and afterward in American communities across the continent. They were not to starve.

The English reformed their own poor laws in 1834, uniting the parish poorhouses into the brutal union workhouses of Dickensian fame. Later on central authority gradually supervened, until the modern national assistance program of the British welfare state nearly eliminated the principle of local control. But in the United States the Tudor principles remained intact. Township relief and the county poor farm remained permanent fixtures, aided in time by private charities, state poor relief (usually after a means test), and finally the Social Security Act, which provided old-age and survivors insurance for some. Disability payments and food programs were added. But federal grants-in-aid continue to be dispensed by local authority, and for masses of the poor, township and county remain the primary centers for poor relief. Herbert Hoover, in resisting pressure for federal relief four centuries after Henry VIII, feared that central government intervention in this matter would undermine the very soul of America, perhaps the most exotic justification ever given to the Tudor regime. But the theoretical argument for local control came in 1819 from the great English master of the "dismal science," David Ricardo:

> Each parish raises a separate fund for the support of its own poor. It is to this cause that we must ascribe the fact of the poor laws not having yet absorbed all the net revenue of the country; it is to the rigour with which they are applied that we are indebted for their not having become overwhelmingly oppressive. If by law every human being wanting support could be sure to obtain it, and obtain it in such a degree as to make life tolerably comfortable, theory would lead us to expect that all other taxes together would be light compared with the single one of poor rates. The principle of gravitation is not more certain than the tendency of such laws to change wealth into misery and weakness; to call away the exertions of labour from every object, except that of providing mere subsistence; to confound all intellectual distinction; to busy the mind continually in supplying the body's wants; until at last all classes should be infected with the plague of universal poverty.[55]

From such terrors did the Tudors save us. The cruelty and brutality that for so long marked poor relief in this country was thus not the result of just sadistic management. In the relief of poverty harshness was deemed a virtue. In Tudor and colonial times poor relief was mixed up not only with the suppression of vagrancy (a crime) but, as noted already, with the compulsory labor that typified the era. A humane tradition could hardly begin there. In any case, local obligation, no matter how mean and brutal, was more humane than the most ready-to-hand alternative, starvation.

The Elizabethan system was introduced in Massachusetts in 1639. As noted, the jails were to be used as places of confinement and labor for the homeless poor. The poor could be sold into servitude; orphan children were to be apprenticed. (Later on, provision was made for mulatto orphans in the South; they were not to be educated or taught trades.) Philadelphia's poorhouse was called, characteristically, the "House of Employment"; South Carolina used the term "work-house." By the 1750s Maryland provided for an almshouse and a workhouse in each county. County courts could sell insolvent debtors into servitude, and church vestries were empowered similarly to dispose of immoral women and their children. Almshouse trustees were to compel the poor to labor. In Virginia, Jefferson said the indigent poor and aged might be relieved in their homes; but, as noted already, compulsory labor in workhouses was the fate of the homeless poor. I will show later how this tradition, born in agricultural and miniature Tudor England and faithfully perpetuated here, would become a millstone around the neck of an industrial American economy struggling to cope with the enormous problems of unemployment and poverty created by the business cycle.

The Financial Heritage

It was from the colonial experience that Americans learned the arts of fiscal management, debt creation, and taxation. As the colonial assemblies gained power, the English system, wherein taxpayers taxed themselves and money bills began in the lower house, developed here. Unlike modern underdeveloped societies, the American colonists were financially sophisticated, and their culture reflected this. For example, they could create and trade in negotiable instruments and use them for credit creation. Three decades before the famous *Statute of Frauds* was passed in England, a Massachusetts law of negotiable instruments in 1647 contained virtually all the defenses against fraud that would be needed even today:

> Any debt, or debts due upon bill or other speciality assigned to another, shall as good a debt & estate to the Assignee, as it was to the assigner, at the time of its assignation; and that it shall be lawful for the said Assignee, to sue for, & recover the said debt due upon bills, & so assigned, as fully as the original creditor might have done; provided the sayd assignment be made upon the backside of the bill or specialtie.[56]

The English rules of seizure of chattel property and distraint for debt prevailed, including protection of the debtor's impounded property. Exemption from debt seizure was granted for capital equipment: "any man's necessary bedding, apparel, tools or armes, neither implements or house-hold, which are for the necessary upholding of life."[57] As previously mentioned, the creation of special franchise corporations was common, and all the English laws of partnerships, jointures, and joint-tenancies were employed. When opportunity arose to use such financial devices, the colonists were ready. A Massachusetts law of 1654 even carried a "gold clause" for loans: "All *contracts and engagements*, for *money, corn, cattle*, or fish, shall be satisfied in kind according to Covenant, or in default of the very kind contracted for, in one of the said kinds, Provided that in such cases, where payment in kind is not made according to Covenant: all just damage shall be satisfied according to bargaine."[58]

But the colonists were really ahead of their time in their handling of paper money. The Crown's effort to control this genie set the tradition that banking and money creation, however loosely governed, would not be as free as other businesses from nonmarket control. The first issue of paper money was in Massachusetts in 1690. The colony had borrowed from its merchant community on tax anticipation certificates as early as 1676. Unable to compensate the veterans of an unsuccessful attempt to capture Quebec, the colony in 1690 issued interest-bearing promises to pay the soldiers. When the government accepted these back in payments, the notes began to pass as money. Other colonies quickly joined in this practice: South Carolina in 1703; Connecticut, New York, New Hampshire, and New Jersey in 1709; Rhode Island in 1710; North Carolina in 1712. Pennsylvania entered the field in 1723, and by 1767 the Quakers overcame their pacific principles sufficiently to make counterfeiting a capital offense.

In 1740 a scheme to issue bank notes against mortgages, the Massachusetts Land Bank, alarmed conservative interests, and a year later the Crown, was prevailed upon to apply the Bubble Act (a law of 1720 prohibiting private joint-stock ventures). Parliament passed a law, "An Act for Restraining and Preventing Several Unwarrantable Schemes and Undertakings in His Majesty's Colonies and Plantations in America," in which triple penalties for violation destroyed the land bank.[59] But its descendants were destined to cover the continent. Eventually Parliament had to act to stop the colonies from declaring their paper money to be legal tender. The colonists had come to understand something, as Ben Franklin put it in one of the most wisdom-laden theoretical statements in the history of economic thought: "There is a certain proportionate quantity of money requisite to carry on the trade of the country freely and currently: more than which would be of no advantage in trade, and less, if much less, exceedingly detrimental to it."[60]

The genie would not be corked. All of the colonies except Georgia had paper issues afloat before the Revolution. Next came Continental currency and the Bank of North America chartered by the Continental Congress in 1781. The chapters of American financial history opened.

Dynamics and Statics of Colonial Institutional Change

Some useful observations can be made regarding the choice of institutions made by Americans in the colonial period. All of the institutions surveyed thus far were implanted wholly or in part from England. In the colonial 150 years, some changed, and some did not. Consider table 2.1. (a) The colonies all began as private enterprises; their charters were their constitutions. By 1775 only Maryland, Delaware and Pennsylvania remained privately chartered. The rest had become Crown Colonies; major change had occurred in the constitutional setup; (b) The conditions of land ownership, the tenure, was unchanged; (c) Except for black slavery, the labor contract had evolved away from force (servitudes) toward voluntary wage labor; (d) Nonmarket controls had expanded with the growth of towns and commerce, and were thus extended in scope; (e) The customs of *market overt* (originally ubiquitous) had nearly vanished and competitive market organization had taken over.

Why was the institutional experience so heterogenous? Some answers are suggested from modern analyses derived from historical knowledge. Lance Davis and Douglass North developed a set of rules

TABLE 2.1
Institutional Experience 1607–1775

Institutions		Experience
a. Constitutions	1	Mergers with the crown
b. Land ownership	0	Rights mainly unchanged
c. Labor contract	1	Moved to competitive system
d. Nonmarket controls	0	Strengthened and expanded
e. Markets	1	Moved to competitive system

Note: 1 = change; 0 = no change.

that explain government as the instrument of choice, instead of private contract.[61] To make extended central power the instrument of choice in colonial America required the prevalence of at least one of four social conditions: (1) a weak private sector, (2) large external benefits enjoyed from existing property rights,(3) indivisible benefits from any proposed changes in existing institutions, and (4) perceived benefits from any changes only redistribute existing wealth. Given any of these four circumstances, they say if no action is taken by government, there will be no action at all. Additionally, Oliver Williamson's work on transaction cost economics adds a very useful constraint: whenever existing institutions are *asset-specific* (can only be used in one location or in a few restricted locations), free contracting between individuals is unlikely to produce satisfactory kinds of economic activity, and there will be motivation to create business firms, organizations, and governments, rather than depend on free contracting.[62] The organizations—institutions of governance—absorb the transaction cost barrier and make economic activity possible.

Apply with me the Davis-North research to the institutions listed in the table. In the case of constitutional transition from individual colony charters to Crown government (a), significant external economies were to be gained. Military power was necessary to deal with foreign powers and the American Indians, and military force was costly for the colonists to maintain independently. As a practical matter the costs of government and defense could be shifted to the British taxpayer by assumption of Crown Colony status. Massachusetts took that route unwillingly, though, and the residual proprietary governments, unprofitable to the Penns and Calverts, probably lingered only for lack of a suitable takeover bid by the Crown. After the British victory in 1763 over the French, when the Crown attempted to shift some of the burdens of government back to the colonies, the American Revolution resulted. In 1787 the victorious colonies produced, in the federal Constitution, another institution to achieve externalities in dealings with foreign powers, Indians, commercial and monetary problems, and most importantly, the conditions for settlement of the western lands.

The land tenure (b) did not change. The technique of ownership, once land was owned at all by individuals as possessory estates, was not specific to any location, but rather was applied globally to the most abundant asset of all, real estate. The laws of land ownership had been set the same in every colony charter. So the technique of ownership could be applied to *any* American land. In this case, by Williamson's rules there is no need to establish any further governance institution to have transactions occur. Enforcement of private

contracts was sufficient government, The Davis-North rules also prevailed: the original land tenure produced large external benefits—law
and order ("quiet enjoyment," as Blackstone put it)—so any benefit
from a reorganization would have been indivisible, and it paid no
individuals to assume the cost of changing the tenure. Only government might have found reason (say, for example, expropriation of all
subsurface mineral rights) to make changes. When it did finally make
major changes, giving land away in vast amounts to railroads and
homesteaders in the mid-nineteenth century in exchange for the performance of settlement services, it was not so much a change as a
reversion to the original model before the first conditions for a land
market existed.

The original colonial labor system—at first mainly servitudes, apprenticeships, slavery—fits perfectly the Davis-North criteria for government as the organizing institution, the instrument of choice. It
had a weak private (i.e., free market) sector. That changed as a domestic labor force grew, generation after generation. Population increased, and a free labor contract "at will" became superior, and
cheaper, than government domination. The labor contract (c) moved
toward a competitive system. The exception was black slavery, of
course; enforced by government, it then was ended by government
action in the American Civil War. With great scale economies and
externalities existing in the system for the benefit of slave owners,
only government action would create any change.

In the use of detailed controls over business enterprise (d), nonmarket controls via the police powers, three of the Davis-North rules
prevail. At the beginning no private-sector alternative existed at all.
Since nonmarket controls were rent-creating, there were external
benefits available to all participants for maintaining, and even expanding, the system. Any changes would be just redistributive (new
entrants sharing the rents with those already established). The costs
of the system being widely disbursed (to all taxpayers and all consumers), and probably unknown, there was no opposition to the system. It remained, expanded, and operates in this country to this day.

Finally, the disappearance of *market overt* (e) follows the Davis-
North rules. At first there were no alternatives. The markets were
established, in time, and place, by the colonial charters. But as the
economy grew in both scale and scope, more transactions over more
kinds of commodities and services, and spread out, spatially, *market
overt* was just the wrong institution. It had developed in the static,
small, rural country of England. It would not work in the fields, and
later forests and mountains of the new world. So even before the
Revolution *market overt* had largely vanished and even in places like

Boston and Philadelphia, long-established public markets came to be bypassed and ignored.

We will see in succeeding chapters, that changes in the economy over time (in the 19th and 20th centuries) yielded further changes in the choice of institutions: in areas like the labor contract, business organization, commodity production, transportation, the old system of nonmarket control reappeared in strengthened form. Even the powerful states rights guaranteed by the founding fathers at the constitutional convention in 1787 would be eroded away as externalities from enlarged central government began to attract politicians, special interests, and voters.

THE WEIGHT OF TRADITION

Thus, during the colonial era virtually every aspect of economic life was subject to nonmarket controls. Some of this tradition would not survive, some would become even more powerful, while some would ascend to the level of federal control. The colonial background was like an institutional gene pool. Most of the colonial institutions and practices live on today in some form, and there is very little in the way of nonmarket control of the economy that does not have a colonial or English forerunner. American history did not begin in 1776.

Chapter 3

CONTINENTAL EXPANSION

> The surveyors shall proceed to divide the said territory
> into townships of six miles square, by lines running due
> north and south, and others crossing these at right angles,
> as near as may be.
> —Ordinance of Congress on Public Lands, *1785*

I N STRICT POLITICAL HISTORY the Declaration of Independence, the Revolution, and the federal Constitution were great watersheds, but from my viewpoint the continuity with the colonial period, not the break, is critical. The nonmarket social controls the colonists inherited and developed were used in the great westward expansion. Words and usages changed, and some heady new developments appeared. But political and social democracy flourished on the ground prepared by the more rigid colonial regime, and laissez-faire economics *with* social control based on the price mechanism achieved a scope in American life it would never know again in our history.

Indeed, anyone who really thinks that American history began in 1776 would have great difficulty explaining how the vigorous young economy of the nineteenth century ultimately came to face the rising specter of federal control power. I submit that in state and municipal laws and practices, and in the unbroken existence of the common law, the old system survived. If conditions changed, if Americans lost faith in the free market and the price mechanism, the old institutional technology of restrictive social control could always be recalled to history's stage. And it was.

At first, though, the colonial experience, which would engineer rapid growth, was put to work with amazing results, and appropriate new institutions were born. Americans showed great ingenuity in developing their vast territorial acquisitions. They found the way to divide up and settle a continent, admit millions of European immigrants into their society, and adapt to the resulting opportunities for economic and social development.

THE LAND SYSTEM: SALE AND SETTLEMENT

How were Americans to take a huge piece of the American continent partly by force and partly by purchase, and then divide it up peacefully among themselves? If history could not answer this question for us, we would be hard-pressed to imagine it. Think of the problems of private-land ownership facing the old Communist empires in the 1990s, and the wonder of the American answer to the question only increases. Our answer lay both in the colonial experience and the ingenuity of the first generations of independent American statesmen.

William Penn had said of governments that they were set in motion like clocks by men. The Northwest Ordinance of 1785 was an extraordinary example. The plans for the survey of the territories were drafted by Jefferson, and they carried the new nation to the Pacific.[1] The new states would be created, and they would be divided into counties and townships, a compromise between Virginia and New England practice. Land could be purchased by township or in separate pieces by individuals. Each township was divided into thirty-six subdivisions, called sections, four of them reserved for government uses. The survey lines were to be in squares, straight with the compass, as in colonial Philadelphia. Following the path blazed in colonial Virginia and Massachusetts, public schools were to be financed from the new land. One section, number sixteen, was reserved in each township for that purpose. The rest were to be sold for not less than one dollar per acre. (The price changed as time passed.) The price was to be "paid in specie, or loan-office certificates, reduced to specie value, by the scale of depreciation, or certificates of liquidated debts of the United States, including interest."[2]

Thus some of the Revolutionary War debt could be used, suitably discounted, to buy land. The Ordinance of 1785 was then supplemented by that of 1787, which, as mentioned previously, settled the land tenures, sales, and inheritances in the territories, and eventually in all the new territory thereafter.

Seen from the perspective of the old English and colonial land laws, the problem's magnitude can more easily be appreciated. Who was to be the "donor," now that the king was gone? What rights did the property owner have, and how could that ownership be transferred, and who could inherit it? The original colonies received their titles from the Crown. How was this right to be transferred unbroken over the hiatus of the Revolution into new jurisdictions? Peaceful and orderly settlement and security for long-term investment for farms, new towns, and cities depended upon successful resolution of these questions.

The problem of the "donor's" identity was solved in theory when the Articles of Confederation were accepted by Maryland in 1781. It was agreed in principle that the colonies with claims on western lands would cede them to the central government. The ordinances of 1785 and 1787 provided the means by which the central government could dispose of the western lands to private ownership, and the new states could step in, filling the place of the central government.

Jefferson's preliminary plan of 1784 for settlement of these lands contained important principles, that would remain in the ordinances of 1785 and 1787. Surveys would precede actual settlement, land would be transferred as perpetual estates of inheritance—the socage tenure, now called fee simple—and land would descend "according to the customs known in the common law by the name of gavel-kind." Moreover, once state governments were established, the lands so held would "never after, in any case, revert to the United States."[3] The donor thus would become the new state governments; there would be direct inheritance by heirs, tenures in fee simple, and inheritance would be by equal division. In 1787 the second Northwest Ordinance set these principles out in full, adding that descent would be in equal divisions in equal degrees of consanguinity, to both males and females and without regard to halfblood. Estates could be sold and willed as in the socage tenure. The laws and customs of prior French and Canadian settlers would be respected, and the double portion of New England and Pennsylvania was dropped.

Robert Dane of Massachusetts, who drafted the 1787 ordinance, wrote of these solutions in a letter to Daniel Webster: "I believe these were the first titles to property, completely republican, in Federal America; being in no part whatever feudal or monarchical."[4]

Dane claimed the inspiration not of Jefferson, but of Massachusetts, yet the basic ideas can be found in Jefferson's 1784 plan. (Since Thomas Jefferson's ideas permeated both the ordinances of 1785 and 1787, his own claim to immortality, based solely upon drafting the Declaration of Independence and founding the University of Virginia, clearly understated his case.) A feat of self-government as remarkable as the Constitution itself, these ordinances were also something of a revolution in human affairs; men were vested with secure property ownership by purchase from governments elected by themselves. That the lands had to be purchased established land-owning capitalism in the new territories, and also determined that the land would be distributed by settled law and not by force of arms, Indian land being the exception.

The emphasis upon land in this history has reason. The first objective of American expansion was simply the acquisition and distribution of land. The legality of the Indian land title posed no more than minimal problems: the moving armed frontier simply beat back the Indians to the final reservations set aside by the federal government for their occupancy. From colonial times purchases of Indian lands by individuals had been discouraged, even outlawed. Primary acquisition traditionally was a government problem, and the government's policies were enforced by soldiers. That moving line of military outposts was noted by Frederick Jackson Turner: "It is possible to trace this military cordon from New England to the Carolinas early in the eighteenth century, still neighboring the coast; by 1840 it ran from Fort Snelling on the upper Mississippi through various posts to the Sabine boundary of Texas, and so it passed forward until today it lies at the edge of Mexico and the Pacific Ocean."[5]

By now, of course, the line has moved far out into the Pacific Ocean. Apart from steady pressure upon the Indians, the land was acquired by war with or purchase from their European overlords, or, in the case of Mexico, by war and purchase. The sequence is familiar. In 1790 the original colonies and their western lands contained 889,000 square miles. The vast Louisiana purchase in 1803 and the territories acquired from Spain in 1819 added 827,000 square miles. Annexation of Texas in 1845, conquest in the war with Mexico in 1846, and the settlement of the Pacific Northwest boundary in 1848 added another 1,205,000 square miles. In 1853 the addition of just under 30,000 square miles by the Gadsden Purchase brought the total to more than 3 million square miles. The Russians sold their rights in Alaska, some 365,000 square miles, in 1867, and the annexation of Hawaii added 4,000 square miles in 1898. The Philippines were an American territory, but they were granted independence in 1946, and it can be assumed that American territorial ambitions finally burned out in the Pacific islands. The lands of the Virgin Islands and the Panama Canal Zone have not been areas of extensive settlement, and Puerto Rico's position is an anomaly. In addition, the United States is scheduled by treaty to hand over the Canal Zone to the Republic of Panama in the year 2000.

These land acquisitions represent nationalist fervor as well as private economic motivation, and it would be fruitless to attempt to determine which factor was decisive. The colonists had hungered for the lands beyond the Appalachians and indeed had begun the westward trek before the Revolution. In fact, the evidence indicates that by the late colonial period settlers faced a shortage of farmland in the older settlements, at least in New England. Economic pressure to move across the Appalachians was real. But valid American titles could only be achieved after a transfer of sovereignty. Initially then, land acquisition was primarily an act of state, as it had been under the old regime. Once land was included within the sovereignty of the United States the problem became one of distribution. The colonial heritage in this matter had been Crown land distribution to actual settlers through intermediaries, townships, proprietors, or colonial governments. Nothing except individual ownership by settlers really made sense unless it was intended that the land be left in its primal state in the interests of the Indians and the fur trade as the Crown seemed to consider with the Proclamation of 1763.

The main distribution of the land was accomplished in essentially three stages: (1) the post-colonial settlement, up to the Land Act of 1800, (2) the era of land auctions, open sales, and public grants up to 1863, and (3) the Homestead Act of 1862, which may be said to have marked the beginnings of a stable government land reserve in what was left of the public domain.

In the first period, colonial practice was followed initially; the system of distribution followed the proprietary land grants familiar from the colonial era. Private companies were granted lands on condition that they create settlements. Once the initial grant was made, proprietors, employing the ingenuity of frontier entrepreneurship, fulfilled the terms of the grant by attracting settlers.[6] The conflicting aims of proprietors and settlers were left to the decision of the marketplace. The settler wanted a farm and the proprietor needed settlers. Grounds for bargaining existed. As early as 1748 the Crown had granted the Ohio Company 200,000 acres beyond the Appalachians, and it was in this enterprise that the young surveyor, George Washington, received his baptism by fire at Great Meadows. His party was beaten in battle by the French and Indians. This action began the French and Indian War, at the close of which, by the Proclamation of 1763 and the Quebec Act of 1774, the Crown attempted to prohibit white settlement north of the Ohio River. Other land companies had already formed, as early as the 1750s, pressing for land grants beyond the Appalachians—Loyal Company, the Greenbrier Company, the Indiana Company, the Vandalia Company; these and more were proprietary companies whose hopes and claims in the empire of the West provided the American Revolution with a commercial background. An omen of the future could be seen in the Indiana Company, composed primarily of Pennsylvania speculators (including Benjamin Franklin), which proposed to open a land office in Pittsburgh in 1768 selling land outright for fifty cents an acre without quit-rents, in lots up to four hundred acres.[7]

Frontiersmen were even more forward, simply cutting their way into the western lands. In 1776 Virginia even sanctioned this break with the colonial past, promising preemption rights to squatters whenever their lands would be placed on the market.[8] In the colonial period such procedures were unknown, but they would be common practice in Federal America. Between the land companies, squatters, soldiers, and speculators, Virginia's lands went fast. The crucial Virginia Land Act of 1779 placed no upper limit on individual land acquisitions, and millions of acres of Virginia's western lands fell into the hands of absentee speculators (Robert Morris held 1.5 million acres; Alexander Walcott, 1 million). As early as 1780 Virginia had disposed of 5 million acres to Revolutionary soldiers, 2 million more to two land companies alone, and, by sales of treasury warrants during the Revolution, had set up claims against an additional 38 million acres.

When the lands were passed to the central government the largess continued. Congress in 1787 granted a new Ohio Company (formed a year earlier) 1.5 million acres north of the Ohio River, and another 1 million acres was granted in 1788 to a New Jersey group. These and later grants, such as the notorious Yazoo Company grant in Alabama and Mississippi, opened the Federal period in an aura of corruption and venality. But there is wisdom in the observation of Marshall Harris that in post-Revolutionary America government corruption may have been a stabilizing influence, giving important men an interest in preservation of the federal system they might not otherwise have had.[9]

Land speculation by private companies was not, after all, a republican invention. It meant that nature's greatest bounty would be subject to powerful political influence so long as great companies were granted lands. Since the companies sold their lands to settlers as quickly as possible, a kinder view is that the weak and impoverished Revolutionary and Federal governments were simply farming out the administrative costs of land distribution. What the government could do—establish an organizational scheme for the new territories—it did in the ordinances of 1785 and 1787. What the government could not do—pair off settlers with land and arrange for payment—it left to its proprietors, the land companies, and the forces of the marketplace. As shown in the previous chapter, the character of the American land tenure and its universality meant that government would need only to enforce contracts once the lands were initially privatized. Ultimately, in thousands of cases, the courts joined in. The outcome of this colonial background was summarized in 1937 by its scholar, Thomas Perkins Abernathy, referring to a Crown policy that was never put in force and the land claims of the original seaboard colonies:

> If the British government had adhered to its policy, inaugurated in 1754, of giving a thousand acres to every actual settler on the frontier, the West would have filled up rapidly with men who needed no other inducement. The wavering, changing colonial policy of England and the unwise legislation of the new States resulted in most of the Western lands falling into the hands of a few speculators. These exploited the lowly settlers who bore the brunt of frontier hardship. Such settlers, not the speculators, were the real empire builders.[10]

What one must bear in mind is that conditions could easily have been worse. Order was maintained; entry was restricted, prices were determinate, and the quality delivered (the American fee simple) was set once the conditions of price were met. The settlers would have been as willing to kill off each other over land rights as they were the unfortunate Indians. Until the Revolution the force of the Crown had kept the settlers partly in check. But once the Crown's control was broken the rush for western land was irresistible. The availability of the land produced a restless urge to tear up roots and move west, and for generations society developed in constant adjustment to this force. Harriet Martineau, writing in the late 1830s, told of her conversation with a congressman:

> He told me that the metaphysics of society in the south afford a curious study to the observer; and that they are humbling to the resident. He told me that, so far from the honour and happiness of any region being supposed to lie in the pursuit of the higher objects of life, any man would be pronounced "imbecile" who, having enough for his moderate wants, should prefer the enjoyment of his patrimony, his family relations, and intercourse with the society in which he was brought up, to wandering away in pursuit of more land. . . . He told me of one and another of his intelligent and pleasant young neighbors, who were quitting their homes and civilised life, and carrying their brides "as bondwomen" into the wilderness, because fine land was cheap there.[11]

The problem was as much maintenance of order as anything else. The colonial heritage at least provided a model, however imperfect, of control of the general outlines by government and by the price mechanism at the actual level of individual settlement.

Once the government achieved some competence it changed policies. Beginning in 1800 government surveys resumed. District land offices were established after 1803, and greater reliance was placed on direct sales to individuals, without intermediaries. Lands were auctioned with a government minimum price reserved. Over time, the sizes of individual plots were reduced, along with prices. Preemption rights were granted to squatters, and after the Graduation Act of 1854 prices of unsold lands were reduced. In 1796 the minimum sale was 640 acres at a minimum reservation price of $2 an acre. By 1832 the minimum plot was as little as 40 acres at a reservation price of $1.25 an acre. Until 1820 partial credit was allowed; after that sales were for cash. Preemption rights were granted to a limit of 160 acres. The process was complex and filled with inequities and fraud. But, given this political framework, it is difficult to imagine how a perfect system could have been devised.[12]

By such means were the lands up to the Mississippi Valley opened to settlement. Between 1790 and 1840 the total American population grew from 3.9 million to 17.1 million. The old settlements—New England, the Middle Atlantic states, and the South Atlantic states—contained 10.7 million by 1840, and nearly 7 million more had settled in the new territories. In a mere five decades more than double the population achieved in the first 150 years had been settled on the land.

From the Homestead Act of 1862 onward, emphasis shifted back to nonmarket mechanisms. Paradoxically, it was free land that began the swing away from the market mechanism. For while the act provided the homesteaders with free land and thus satisfied an old demand of the colonists, the conditions of settlement were controlled by government rules as well as by prices. Homesteads were limited to the squatter limit of 160 acres. Certain improvements had to be made, and five years of continuous residence on the homestead was required (although a cash settlement after six months' occupancy was possible for the more prosperous). In 1873 further nonmarket land acquisitions were made available. In that year the Timber Culture Act allowed homestead lands to be taken out on condition of the planting of trees. In 1878 such lands could again be purchased outright ($2.50 an acre), but in plots of 160 acres or less. Irrigation prospects induced Congress to pass the Desert Land Act of 1877, which allowed lands to be acquired in larger blocks upon condition that water be proved and a specified portion of the land actually irrigated within three years. In 1909 the size of the homestead claim was enlarged to 320 acres in recognition of the semiarid condition of the western states, and in 1916 grazing rights were made available on lands that were useful for little else.[13]

This swing back to nonmarket mechanisms was consistent with past history. At the risk of ignoring the myriad of exceptions, one can discern the general pattern. The colonial regime, with its township distribution, headright grants, quitrents and socage tenures, and long leases with feudal incidents (in New York), can be viewed as pursuing a policy of keeping land relatively scarce, while still encouraging its settlement. The Proclamation of 1763 and the Quebec Act of 1774 are consistent with this general view. Freed from these constraints, the new republic at first mixed tradition with the market and then relied increasingly upon the market. A plentiful land supply rendered a complex social apparatus of distribution superfluous, for straight sales were satisfactory to government and to buyers alike. But when the line of settlement reached beyond the 100th meridian into territories of low rainfall, good land became scarce again, and settlers demanded, and got in the Homestead Act, government rather than free-market land distribution. The money price was reduced to zero, but the government demanded other payments. Land came on fixed, nonmonetary conditions of tenure again.

The Homestead Act marked the reemergence of nonmarket land-acquisition methods in the remaining public domain. Soon to come was the ultimate removal of desirable land from the market altogether in the establishment of national parks, government forests, game control laws, and in a national policy of conservation.

This basic change of attitude has remained to the present day. After the Homestead Act the nonmarket mechanism was relied upon increasingly as the best lands, minerals, and forests were taken into private hands. Three fourths of the private homesteads acquired under the 1862 act were west of the Great Plains.[14] Even under the Homestead Act conditions were hard, and more homesteads failed than succeeded. Where good farmlands were abundant, the government freely sold to private companies and persons. Where the land was less productive, its control was reserved to straight government grants, and title was acquired by nonmarket means.

In the end roughly three fourths of the nation's land area had passed into private hands, and one fourth remained in the collective ownership of government. To have achieved such a distribution with so little bloodshed was a considerable achievement. In cases where bloodshed did ensue, such as in the Civil War and the Indian wars, more than land was involved.[15]

Today, the land area of the contiguous United States is just over 1.9 billion acres. Of this, about 1.4 billion acres are privately owned, and 500 million remain under government control. (In the western states alone, of course, the proportions are virtually the reverse.) Of the lands distributed by the federal government after independence, 29.1 percent were for cash sale, 27.6 percent for homesteads, 21.8

percent went to state governments (to help finance education, internal improvements, conservation, and more), 9.2 percent were for such claims as military bounties, 8.8 percent for railroad subsidies, and 3.4 percent for land entries under later land-settlement acts, such as the Timber and Stone, Desert Lands, and Carey Acts. The federal government actually lost money disposing of the public lands. As a portent of things to come, the bureaucrat as businessman was, at the least, incompetent.[16]

Had the land been used only for farming, this swift disposal of a continental domain might have been less vulnerable to social criticism. But the land was also exploited for its covering forests and its underlying deposits of minerals and petroleum. These were unevenly distributed by nature, and hence so was the resulting income and wealth yield between property owners. However egalitarian the basis of original settlement may have been, the income from real property was strikingly uneven, more so than mere climate and soil conditions would have produced alone. Also some of the crudest agrarian calculations were overturned when semiarid lands began producing oil and the wastelands yielded minerals. Similarly, the growth of industries and cities at relatively few nodal points on the landmass and the selective routes of the rail and road system made the income and wealth distribution still more uneven. These developments would produce demands for government controls as the economy developed, and it became clear that location of ownership, as well as acreage, determined the income and wealth yield of private real property. On the one hand the historian views an impressive social achievement in the mainly egalitarian land settlement during the century and a half after the Northwest Ordinances. On the other hand he sees with some dismay the creation of a universe of new social and economic problems. These problems were augmented by the massive introduction of a new population from abroad.

THE ATLANTIC MIGRATION

Between 1815 and 1914 an estimated 35 million Europeans came to the United States. Americans were long taught that the immigration was an act of charity on the part of our government: "Give me your tired, your poor," as Emma Lazarus put it. This charitable enterprise, however, was a two-way street. Remember that in colonial times immigrants, both white and black, were sold as they came ashore. And their price measured a reality: the potential labor of the new immigrant was valuable. Purchase of an immigrant contract meant the acquisition of a valuable asset whose earlier development had been paid for by someone else. If the price at the dock was less than the net cost of development a capital transfer occurred. Since immigration was usually a desperation "sale" by the owner of the asset—the human being in question—the contract was a bargain for the buyer. As the work of Paul Uselding and Larry Neal shows, probably more than 20 percent of the enormous growth of fixed capital in this country in the nineteenth century can be attributed directly to immigration. Because the cost of preparing the immigrant laborer was paid by someone else, they contend, Americans who exploited that labor had their own resources in equal amount freed for other uses. After the end of indentured immigration, the country received in each immigrant a unit of human capital, essentially free.[17] Immigration was thus a powerful spur to American growth—however charitable it seemed to those who first looked upon the huddled masses yearning to breathe free.

Since the original settlements of Europeans in the New World constituted the transfer of a population as well as the more adaptable parts of its social order, the continuation of large-scale European immigration into the United States after independence is not surprising. For the colonial economy immigration was a lifeline. But until the late eighteenth century the colonial population had remained near the seacoast. The new republic faced a vast empty land with an established tradition of naturalization. Crown practice was to accept non-English immigrants into the colonies who adhered to English law and allegiance. Also, of course, the colonies included French, Dutch, Swedes, and others whose settlements were absorbed by the English. Indian tribes received Crown protection, too, and individual Indians who settled among the whites were sometimes granted lands. The same was true of Negro slaves who had achieved freedom. By the end of the colonial era about a fifth of the white population in the thirteen colonies was of non-British origin. In addition, there were the non-Europeans as well, including over half a million Negroes. The original American stock was a polyglot population.

Still, control of immigration had distinct ethnic overtones. The dominant population, in numbers, was white, Protestant, and mainly of British origin (including Irish). The pressures on immigration control until the 1920s reflected that. Not surprisingly the upsurge of nativism at the end of the nineteenth century revealed the biases of the original stock but with significant exceptions.[18] The end of the legal slave trade in 1808 was no doubt a victory for those who found it morally repugnant. But the end of black immigration was also supported by those who, like Jefferson, deeply believed that whites and nonwhites could not, in the long run, coexist. Jefferson, in his *Notes on the State of Virginia*, was utterly pessimistic about the possibility: "Deep rooted prejudice entertained by the whites; ten thousand recollections by the blacks, of the injuries they have sustained; new provocations; the real distinctions which nature has made; and many other circumstances, will divide us into parties, and produce convulsions which will probably never end but in the extermination of the one or the other races."[19]

The future would test his pessimism. The end of the slave trade stopped large-scale black immigration. Similarly, the Chinese Exclusion Act of 1882 was both a victory for those who feared "Oriental wages" and those who believed that a growing Oriental community would be incompatible with the continued development of established American social life. Such fears were constantly expressed by nativists and were applied to new groups of impoverished immigrants—Italians, Russian Jews and, after the mid-twentieth century, to the massive immigration from Latin America.

Toward the end of the nineteenth century, when the balance of immigration shifted from northern Europe to southern and eastern Europe, nativist pressures built up again, resulting in a bill in 1897, vetoed by President Cleveland, imposing a literacy test. The debates included generous references to Anglo-Saxon superiority, or the "great German tribes"; the new immigrants from southern and eastern Europe, it was held, were not really assimilable. As Sen. Henry Cabot Lodge put it: "The races most affected by the literacy test are those whose emigration to this country began in the last twenty years and swelled to enormous proportions, races with which the English speaking people have never hitherto assimilated, and who are most alien to the great body of the people of the United States."[20]

Similarly, earlier agitation among such groups as the Know-Nothings of the 1850s was propelled by the flood of Irish immigration and the specter of advancing Roman Catholicism.

But apart from ethnic prejudice, largely ineffectual until the early twentieth century, immigration was controlled by the price mechanism, as it mainly had been during colonial times. With the Revolution, headrights had disappeared and convict shipments ended. Slave immigration was legally prohibited in the first decade of the nineteenth century (although slave cargoes apparently came irregularly until the Civil War), bonded indenture ceased to be important, and contract labor never developed into a major source of immigrants. Modern scholarship indicates that the nineteenth-century Atlantic migration was fundamentally a market phenomenon. As the nineteenth-century demographic revolution moved across Europe,

death rates fell faster than birth rates. The result was an unprecedented population increase. Had the industrial development occurred rapidly enough the increase could have been absorbed in Europe—after all, the European countries now have larger populations
than they ever had, enjoying unexampled standards of life. But apart
from Britain, European industrialization was mainly a late nineteenth
and twentieth century development, and the demographic revolution preceded it. Partly then there was a push effect, the result of a
lack of job opportunities within the framework of the European economic community. And partly there was a pull effect of the demand
for cheap labor from overseas European offshoots, the United States,
Canada, Argentina, Australia, New Zealand, South Africa, some European enclaves in Africa, Latin America, and even from heavily
populated Asia. An estimated 50 million left Europe between 1815
and 1914, and the majority of the emigrants came to the United
States. Some immigrants went back to Europe, some left the United
States for other overseas European offshoots, some drifted into overseas countries that were not primarily of European stock. The entire
movement was cyclical, as Brinley Thomas showed in his great work
Migration and Economic Growth, and depended upon the severity of
the push effect and the power of the pull.

For a long time Americans welcomed this immigration, since it
helped to fill up the continent. The nation had a population of 3.9
million in 1790, 31.4 million in 1860, 76 million in 1900, and 100 million by 1915. The immigrants and their descendants had taken part
in one of the most rapid nation-building enterprises known to history, and half of the nineteenth-century population growth came
from the immigrants and their descendants.

The first immigration wave followed the European potato famine
in 1845. The change in magnitude was dramatic. In the five years
from 1831 to 1835 total immigration was 252,000, of whom some
72,000 were Irish. A decade later, from 1841 to 1845, the total was
430,000, with 184,000 coming from Ireland. Then in the five years
from 1846 to 1850 the total jumped to 1,283,000, with 594,000 coming
from Ireland. From 1851 to 1855 there were 1,748,000 immigrants;
693,000 of them came from Ireland. A million and a half Irish arrived
between 1845 and 1860. They were never more than half of the total,
for the potato famine had hit the German states of northern Europe
as well. But the Irish Catholics were the largest single cultural group.
The Know-Nothings demanded a 21-year residence requirement for
naturalization amid discussions of the legions of Rome and the
Grand Army of the Papacy. The Irish never came again in such numbers, but other Roman Catholics did, later in the century when the

great waves of migration out of southern and eastern Europe began. To these were added a mass of Jewish migrants, and the fires of nativism burned hot again.

Ireland was not part of the nineteenth-century European demographic revolution, but was part of a longer-term development. Its population had grown slowly, at a compound rate of about 1.4 percent per annum, and the land that held some 2 million in 1700 contained about 8 million a century and a half later.[21] The economy was mainly agricultural, and when the potato blight struck, Ireland became the first great Malthusian disaster area of the modern world. Joel Mokyr, in *Why Ireland Starved*, estimates that Ireland suffered excess deaths of 1.5 million in the famine years, but emphasizes that general economic backwardness lay at the root of the famine itself.[22]

But soon Germans and others migrating out of northern Europe, including Scandinavians, came to outnumber those from the British Isles in the immigration waves of the 1870s, 1880s, and 1890s. By the 1890s the balance was shifting. In 1889, when nearly half a million immigrants entered the United States in a single year, 75 percent still came from northwest Europe and some 23 percent from southern and eastern Europe. Ten years later the proportions of Europeans were 29 percent from the north and west and 68 percent from the south and east. In 1913, when more than 1 million people entered in a single year, only 15 percent came from the north and west and 75 percent came from the south and east.[23]

These geographic shifts produced the enormous growth in absolute numbers of immigrants: some 4.7 million in the 1880s, 3.6 million in the depressed 1890s, and then 11 million from 1900 to 1913 in the final burst of the Atlantic migration. The purely nativist fears aroused by these immigrant masses, together with the doubt that the country could absorb such continuing numbers, finally produced restrictive legislation. But until then, and throughout the nineteenth century, the country's labor force had been augmented, generation after generation, by this European outpouring and its descendants. The lure of the golden shore, together with the demographic revolution in Europe, had produced the Atlantic migration with a minimum of nonmarket control; individual estimates of relative wages, prices and incomes, and market responses to the ensuing movements of people and resources had done the job.

This achievement, together with the general growth of the economy, supported those who believed that the market mechanism could work prodigies. Against this was the view, growing after the Civil War, that the nation's interests would best be served by an extension of government controls over economic activity. Celebrations of free enterprise were counterbalanced by demands to reform the monetary system, extend government aid to the farmer, raise the tariffs against foreign commodities, impose antitrust restraint, regulate industry, conserve resources, tax the rich, recognize labor unions, and stop the mass immigration. These contrary deductions from the nation's experience introduced a note of bitterness and economic interest into politics in the 1890s and the early twentieth century. The battles that led ultimately to the Wilson reforms, and later to the New Deal legislation, were forming even as the last of the open agricultural frontier was disappearing.

THE NEW SYSTEM AND INTERNAL COMMUNICATIONS

Even though the alliance between government contracts and private enterprise has reached immense proportions in modern times, this happy confluence between public need and private profit is one of our oldest traditions. We saw it in the colonial era. It flourished mightily in the nineteenth-century construction of the transportation system, as it still does today. The basic model was not English but colonial. In England canals and railways were almost entirely built by private enterprise. In the United States, government played a varied and important role. We used governmental power to help organize and release the necessary resources. Contemporaries of the time held that the shortage of capital made such an alliance necessary, that private means were insufficient for such tasks. This may have been true, or partly so, but the continuation of such mixtures into our own times suggests that more was at stake than mere quantity. As demonstrated, government can absorb transaction costs and make economic activity possible that would not otherwise exist. The collective warrant, attained by government seal, involved the general public explicitly in these enterprises and removed the stigma of private gain at the public expense. The system was condemned by Andrew Jackson, after his actions to prohibit federal government aid to local enterprises, as a "plan of unconstitutional expenditure for the purpose of corrupt influence."[24] Direct government involvement made private gain from the exploitation of public resources less objectionable to the electorate and made it easier for organizers to raise public funds.

I have shown that colonial governments commonly granted special franchises to build and operate public utilities, ferries, bridges, docks, and wharfs. Such methods could be extended to surface transport systems. Before the Revolutionary era, there was virtually no effective surface transportation between the colonies. Once independence was achieved, therefore, creation of an effective internal communications system immediately became a priority project. It was natural to follow the colonial tradition, and apart from post and local roads that were mainly built from local taxation and labor services, the first roads were turnpikes built by a mixture of private enterprise and local government assistance, including the legal power to charge a toll. Since land had to be acquired, local government participation was necessary to begin with. But since the cost was locally borne and the benefits accrued to all travelers, contributions to local capital depended upon tolls. The resulting network was piecemeal, charges were high, and the returns were inadequate in most cases. The colonial system of mixed private and government enterprise had been small-scale and concentrated at local points of commerce; long-distance transport clearly posed different sorts of problems.

It was widely believed that a surface transportation system would provide great general benefits, creating external economies, but it was not obvious how the benefits could be captured by individual transportation companies at rates less than exorbitant to individual users. Since the greatest gains, the benefits accruing to the whole public, were in fact unmeasurable, it was also natural that a general contribution via taxation would be appealing to most sections of the community.[25] Moreover, since each local community viewed itself as competitive with its neighbors, it was also natural that enthusiasm would be generated once any community launched a campaign for internal improvements that would divert commerce in its own direction and away from its rivals.

The obvious solution was a federal system of internal communications, and with Albert Gallatin's blueprint of 1808, the Gallatin Plan, a truly national system of internal communications became a possibility. Gallatin's proposals called for federally financed roads and canals connecting the major waterways from New England to Georgia and into the interior. His cost estimate, including aid to certain purely local projects, was $30 million, an amount equal to half the national debt of the time, or more than three years' total federal expenditures. The system was never built by the federal government.[26]

Presidents Madison and Monroe both favored internal improvements, but believed that the Constitution did not warrant such undertakings by the federal government. Madison argued, in a message to Congress on October 23, 1811, that "no objects within the circle of political economy so richly repay the expense bestowed upon them." Yet he vetoed a bill passed in the Congressional session of 1816–17 to distribute funds (derived from profits of the new Bank of the United States) for that purpose. Monroe, in a long and rambling message on internal improvements of May 4, 1822, thought the advantages of internal improvements to be "incalculable," and stated that "It cannot be doubted that improvements for great national purposes would be better made by our national government than by the governments of the several states." But after a long examination of Constitutional powers, he held that they were inadequate for such purposes. He proposed that the Constitution be suitably amended. This was never done, and when Andrew Jackson vetoed the scheme for the Maysville Road in 1830, the campaign for a federal program came to an end. Some federal funds (under $2 million) had been appropriated to support canal construction between 1824 and 1828, and the National Road reached into Ohio and eventually into Illinois before it was turned over to the states through which it passed. But the large parts of Gallatin's plan failed to receive federal support.

Carter Goodrich, the greatest modern student of the subject, thought that regionalism in Congress was largely responsible for the failure of federal action, that the political representatives of each state and region were jealous of the external benefits that a truly national system would make available to other regions.[27] By the 1820s this regionalism, which would eventually produce civil war, already was clearly evident. In particular, the tendency for westerners to support protective tariffs in order to acquire eastern votes in support of internal improvements was anathema to the South. But as time passed, representatives of the eastern states, where roads and canals were being built by local enterprise, had little enthusiasm for federal expenditures on similar projects in other areas.

Failure at the federal level illuminated the essential nature of the problem. Since the objectively measurable (or estimated) benefits of a transport system were local, the primary support for action was also local. The relative unprofitableness of the turnpikes was quickly overshadowed by the prospects of canals and these, in turn, were dwarfed by the magical aura that surrounded the first railroads. In these, entrepreneurial motivations produced dramatic results. The historian is left only with the question of whether the community, through its political leaders, exploited private enterprise by subsidies that produced an overall social gain larger than the total direct costs, or whether private businesses exploited the public to acquire, by subsidy and franchise profit-making enterprises on a scale beyond the reach of purely private capital.[28] Since capital, in this sense meaning sheer financial power, was the resource in short supply, it is not surprising that mixed enterprise was the result. Transaction costs were too high for a free-market solution. In my exposition of social control a nonmarket solution was called for. As noted earlier, political involvement—government's blessing upon enterprises that expropriated the public domain in the form of land grants—was perhaps an additional necessity, if only for insurance against possible political reactions.

Not that private enterprise was not tried. Two canals, the Santee, completed in South Carolina in 1800, and the Middlesex, built from Boston to Lowell in 1803, did not receive public financial aid. It was the Erie Canal, completed in 1825, however, that focused attention upon mixed enterprises between state or local government and private business as the way to build internal improvements.

Canal enterprises were already under way elsewhere, including Maryland and Virginia, but the Erie was the spark that launched the great internal improvements mania of the 1820s and 1830s. Between 1817 and 1825 some 363 miles of the Erie were constructed under legislation of 1817. It was entirely a New York State enterprise, as efforts to enlist federal aid had failed. In 1823, the shorter Champlain Canal had been opened. Both it and the Erie were initially profitable, and Erie bonds quickly passed into foreign hands—over half by 1829—a portent of things to come, as foreigners became heavy investors in the developing of mixed private and public canal and railroad system. The initial outlays on the Erie were $7 million, and toll collections totaled $1 million even before the canal was completed.

More canals were immediately begun in New York, and other states followed: Pennsylvania started the Mainline in 1826 in an effort, by a complex system of locks and traction (ultimately rail links), to integrate the eastern part of the state with the Ohio Valley. Further south, the Chesapeake and Ohio, started in 1828, was financed in part by the federal government, the state of Maryland, city governments, and private sources alike. Across the Appalachians, canal systems were begun in the late 1820s in Ohio, Illinois, and Indiana, using land grants, state bond issues, and special canal taxes. Total canal mileage reached four thousand miles before enthusiasm shifted to railroads. For the most part the system of mixed enterprise was relied upon. There were a few small, privately built canals, mainly in Pennsylvania coal regions, and they were largely profitable undertakings. But for the most part state and local government was relied on to reduce capital scarcity during the great canal boom. When the enterprises failed financially, and most did, it was state credit that was put in jeopardy. About 68 percent of all canal investment between 1815 and 1860 came from public sources.[29]

The greatest single case of nineteenth-century mixed enterprise in America was the railroad. The evidence has been sifted by modern scholarship and the nature of private and public financial mixing is most interesting. Very generally, the private element was strongest in the initial construction phases when the estimated profit potential was largest; public participation tended to rise wherever profit prospects fell. As already noted, this pattern can carry two interpretations. In the first, the private entrepreneur is seen as a risk averter, who uses governments as risk-absorbing substitutes for private capital whenever potential profits are reduced. In the second interpretation, expansion-minded government leaders co-opted private capital into railroad construction cheaply (smaller government participation) when profit potentials were higher. In the first instance the private sector seeks rent creation by manipulating the government. In the second the government creates a rent as a bait to entice private capital. Albert Fishlow's work on antebellum railroads tends to support such generalizations. Thus, in the first railroad construction boom of the 1820s (Fishlow dates the period 1828–43), when the innovation was new, the first trunk lines were reaching out, and there was relatively limited experience, governments put up a third of the investment costs. In New England in the 1840s and in the major middle western states in the 1850s, where freight potentials were higher, private capital was more dominant as lines were built into areas already settled. In the middle western states the extent of public support may have been less than 10 percent of total construction costs. But at the same time, in the South, where freight potential was not so high, governments absorbed some 50 percent of the total costs.[30]

This pattern was partially obscured by a separate problem, the massive defaults of state-supported enterprises in the late 1830s and early 1840s that ultimately led states to severely restrict direct participation in railroads, canals, and other internal improvements. This adds a further barrier to believable generalization, since it could have been the case that, by the first interpretation, private capital was forced into the open by failure to secure state funds after the financial imbroglios ended the first railroad boom.

Overall, more than 25 percent of the total railroad capital stock of a billion dollars had come from public sources, mainly state and local governments in the antebellum period. The 3.7 million acres of public land granted to the Illinois Central Railroad in 1850 was the largest single federal contribution. The Illinois Central Act changed this pattern. After the Civil War, when the transcontinental lines were established across the sparsely settled plains, mountains, and deserts, government's share of the mix rose again, although temporarily. But now it was the federal government that granted more than 100 million acres of the public domain to the railroads, and, in addition, loaned the Union Pacific half the cost of its construction.

As the railroad system matured, or was shaken down and rationalized in succeeding financial crises, and as the capital investment increased after the 1860s, public entities', direct role was reduced. At the end of the 1880s, according to Goodrich, public funds allotted for new construction were "negligible."[31] Railroads, despite their checkered financial history, had become prime financial assets, and they no longer needed direct public participation.

But just as the railroads achieved sufficient strength to forego government support, they began to draw government regulation. Beginning with the Granger acts of the 1870s the users of railroads demanded control of rates and services, a form of control, in keeping with our country's common-law heritage. As the railroad system emerged from its own tradition of a mixed public and private enterprise system, its privileged position as a collection of chartered corporate franchises made it liable to a different kind of public, or government, control. With the Interstate Commerce Act of 1887 the railroads began their careers as federally regulated carriers. The career became a permanent one. In addition to their liabilities under common-law rules governing franchises and common callings, the railroads were now tarred with the populist opprobrium of monopoly, and eventually, in the breakup of the Northern Trust in 1904 (argued in 1903, decision in 1904) and the Southern Pacific in 1912, the railroads contributed famous landmarks to the development of antitrust law.

From start to finish, counting corporate charters and special franchises (even for roads financed mainly by private capital), government played an important role in railroad history. First it supplemented the shortage of capital in those areas where public funds were needed. Then, as the railroads themselves became a relatively scarce resource—for their massive expansion amplified their influence in the growing economy—government imposed public controls on them. As the railroads succeeded and became more indispensable, their services could become more expensive—too much so, the Populists charged.[32] I will examine shortly how the emerging regulatory control of railroads was associated with a larger movement of social withdrawal from the full consequences of the market economy as the new American industrial system expanded after the Civil War.

Because of the hopes of its promoters and the widespread fears of its powers, the railroad dominated the national scene as did no other nineteenth-century innovation. Consider the raw statistical facts. At the end of 1830, with only the Baltimore and Ohio in operation, there were twenty-three miles of railroad line; in 1930, nearly 430,000 miles of railroad track were in operation. Some 260,000 miles of that were main lines and about 300,000 miles could be described as main track, backed up by nearly 130,000 miles of yard track. The construction came in waves, with apparent major peaks in 1841, 1854, 1872, 1879, 1902, 1906, and 1910.[33] Economists have long been fascinated by this prodigy of American history, for so many precedents—in finance, management, federal land grants, labor relations, public control, and technical spinoffs, to name a few—were associated with the construction of the roads. As Robert Fogel has shown, some considerable exaggeration accompanied such associations, but the fascination was real.[34] Also, the railroads were always mixed up with politics; the legislative consequences made major contributions to the emergence of antitrust legislation and tradition.

Such an enterprise, opening up overland interregional trade on a new basis within the country, affecting all classes of people and cutting across state lines, was bound to invoke public participation and control. From the beginning, local business interests were deeply involved in railroad promotion, since the routes, yards, depots, and branch lines of the railroads brought with them new business, often at the expense of towns not favored with railroad service. The impact of the Erie Canal, which had diverted interior trade to New York, was not lost upon community leaders in other major cities. Despite efforts to construct canal systems elsewhere, the railroad would make it easier to overcome the disadvantages imposed upon seaboard states blocked from the interior by natural barriers. Favorable charters of incorporation, state and municipal subsidies and financial participation, grants of land, and tax privileges—all became standard devices of public participation in the early railroads.

Baltimore's Joint Committee on Internal Improvements of 1836 showed an acute understanding of the issues at stake. Baltimore had already authorized expenditures of city funds on the B&O as early as 1827. By 1836 the position was urgent: the project, the Committee said,

> calls for the efforts of our men of business, property holders, capitalist and municipal authorities in the adoption of measures for a prompt, vigorous and active prosecution of the various works of internal improvement. . . . It is perfectly evident to every mind that upon the course that is now pursued must depend the issue of the question of whether the city of Baltimore is to be reduced to a place of comparative insignificance in a commercial point of view.[35]

As it turned out, Baltimore engaged more than $20 million of municipal funds in various Maryland railroads in the nineteenth century, most of it before the Civil War. The state of Maryland also participated.

In fact, before the Civil War, railroads from Maine and Vermont to Florida and westward to Missouri benefited from the assisting hand of state and local governments. Sometimes direct government representation in management followed, an unwelcome innovation to the private interests. Apart from short railroads in the coalfields, nearly all railroads were partly financed by state and local governments before the Civil War, and even Vanderbilt's "free enterprise" New York Central included amalgamations of companies started by mixed public and private efforts. But apart from land grants, the federal government's direct participation was relatively small before the Civil War.

Federal government grants of land to the states to support internal improvements had begun in the 1820s. A combination of factors shifted the emphasis to direct federal aid for railroad construction. The depression of the late 1830s and early 1840s witnessed severe financial strains among the states, including widespread default on state and local bonds issued to help finance internal improvements. In the revulsion against state support for such enterprises, the legal authority to participate was eliminated in some cases, and sharply curtailed in others. Canal and railroad interests were sold off to private parties.

By then the balance of public participation was shifting to the federal sector and the federal land grant. In the 1820s the federal government granted more than 3 million acres of public land to subsidize canal construction. Between 1836 and 1849 some 22 million acres of federal land were granted to the states to support improvements. With the Illinois Central grant, in 1850, the federal government established the precedent that was to characterize the building of the transcontinental lines—direct subsidy from the public domain.[36] Alternate sections were given on each side of the track, on condition that they be settled (shades of the colonial land grants), and compensation was made in the form of other land where track-side land was not in the public domain. In total, the Union Pacific received 23 million acres; the Northern Pacific, 44 million acres; and the Atlantic and Pacific, 23 million acres. In addition, the state of Texas (where the U.S. government owned no public land) gave some 27 million acres to railroad construction after the Civil War.

Further direct money grants were made by states, especially in the Reconstruction South. (Goodrich estimated the total public aid for railroad construction at about \$350 million between 1861 and 1890.) But the *proportion* of public aid was far less than in the antebellum era, and most of it came before 1873, when less than a third of the country's ultimate maximum mileage had been built. As the railroad system grew, the direct public subsidy fell; private capital now filled in, despite the sometimes appalling financial record.[37]

The extent of government and state control of this vast mixed enterprise varied in place and time, but, according to Goodrich, the general pressure was for domination by private interests. Since the railroads were creations of the state (and rents were created accordingly), it is not surprising that conflict between their managements and the public resulted in public regulation. Such was the common-law tradition, such was the colonial tradition, and such would soon be enshrined in court decisions and federal laws. The form of social control that found little support was that of complete reliance on the price mechanism, on the free market. When the railroads became strong enough to no longer need further public aid, "the people," through their governments, imposed regulation. Nonmarket controls were persistent in U.S. railroad history and have remained so. Whether the railroad and the country would have been better off to let straight free-market processes emerge is a relevant and interesting question, but one whose answer history alone cannot provide.

The Change of Scale: Business and Labor

Westward expansion meant that new states and legal jurisdictions began with a thinner veneer of colonial-style nonmarket control than had existed in the original colonies. State regulations had to be re-created (although judges could impose common-law restrictions in court actions). State laws therefore tended to differ in detail from each other, just as had the controls of the colonies.

At the same time, some of the original control apparatus had weakened or nearly died out. Established markets and monopoly controls in trades were not well suited to the commercial and industrial world of modern America. Indeed, as Carl Bridenbaugh found, retail selling and the traveling salesman appeared early in the first American cities and were found to be more effective ways of conducting trade in the American setting.[38] Clerks of the market, and the whole apparatus of established markets, with their market halls and separate legal practices, became rare. They slowly disappeared along the expanding frontier.[39]

Property laws were mostly set by colonial practice, the Northwest

ordinances, and the new state constitutions. The amount of real innovation was small, and indeed it has been held that, because American lawyers studied Blackstone and Kent and because few law
schools existed in the antebellum period, by 1860 American law was
more like the England of colonial times than it had been in 1776.[40]
Part of the old business law, *caveat emptor* ("buyer beware"), had
proved to be infinitely flexible in frontier conditions. *Caveat emptor*
now protected the seller as the law of established markets had protected the buyer. The paper money of the antebellum banking system
and the traveling salesmen of the Yankee trader era must have
greatly eased the loosening-up of the commercial system. The day of
the guild merchant was gone.

Nevertheless, all business activity remained in the grip of the common law, even where there were no specific statutes in the new
states. So the frontier lawyer, such as a Lincoln, studied his Blackstone, Kent, and Story as guides to universal rules of behavior in
Anglo-American society. Any interested reader, by a perusal of Kent
or Story, can quickly appreciate the power of legal continuity in the
new republic. For example, in the famous contract case of *Dartmouth
College v. Woodward* (1819), the state of New Hampshire was not allowed to overturn a patent granted by King George III. His rule must
have been upheld to cement the entire settlement of property in this
country before 1775. The English law of contract was a rigorous behavioral rule that was not to be questioned; it was a legal axiom. The
same was true of most of the tradition. Consider our old friends from
colonial times described in 1826 in Kent's *Commentaries*: Innkeepers,
"In New York, and throughout the Union, inns and taverns are under statute regulation."[41]; Sellers of liquor in New York, "no person
who has not at the time a license to sell strong or spirituous liquors
or wines, to be drunk in his house, shall put up any sign indicating
that he keeps a tavern."[42] The carters, draymen, and carriers controlled in medieval England and in colonial America had their direct
descendants, now called common carriers. The rules had not
changed: "As they hold themselves to the world as common carriers
for a reasonable compensation, they assume to do, and are bound to
do, what is required of them . . . and [if they] are offered a reasonable and customary price; and they refuse without some just ground,
they are liable to an action."[43] And again, "In New York, the English
common law on the subject of . . . common carriers has been fully,
explicitly, and repeatedly recognized in its full extent."[44] The entire
corpus of the common law of contract, bailment and agency that was
brought to the colonies continued in the new republic.

Similarly, the specific nonmarket controls of the colonies—controls over business in terms of number, entry, price, and quality—continued in the original states. Louis Hartz concluded that in Pennsylvania such controls were even extended in the Federal period; for example, in 1835 a law was passed regulating, by inspection, the quality of goods to be exported from the state, including flour, fish, beef, pork, lard, flaxseed, butter, and biscuits. Business licensing flourished as a primary source of state revenue. Such control was not questioned because "its legitimacy was taken for granted in terms of the earlier mercantilist tradition of the colonial period."[45] Oscar and Mary Handlin, in *Commonwealth*, wrote that Federal Massachusetts continued the colonial systems of licensing and inspection and of controls over business of all sorts. Manufactures and processed foods were inspected. Informers were still used to spot violations, and fines were still split between informers and the courts. Monopolies (for example, window-glass manufacturing) were still enfranchised and protected. Lawyers, indeed, demanded a system of licensing to protect their interests. Mill rights were given out as monopoly grants.[46]

One sees in all this the continuity of economic life and controls over it, straight through the Revolutionary era into modern America. But change was admitted too. Mechanic lien laws were an example of this. They appeared in Pennsylvania as early as 1803, and eventually became common in the other states. Kent thought the remote origins of these laws could be traced in the common law of agency and bailment, but the laws were new on the statute books. In 1826 Kent wrote: "It is now the general rule, that every bailee for hire, who by his labor and skill, has imparted an additional value to the goods, has a lien upon the property for his reasonable charges."[47] These were democratic measures, recognizing explicit property rights of workmen in their labor, altogether fitting the spirit of Jacksonian America.

As new forms of business developed that seemed to require regulation by the old measures, special commissions, as of old, were created to regulate them. They evolved into permanent public service commissions: in Massachusetts, before the Civil War, there were permanent commissions governing "banks, insurance, railroads, education, charities and pilotage."[48] Such forms of control were destined to achieve a power of enormous magnitude when they were adapted to the needs of the federal government itself a generation later.

Alongside this continuity of nonmarket control the new experience of freer economic life in the westward expansion was creating an acceptance and tradition of its own, which made the old rigidity of controls an uncomfortable garment to the emerging business community. Ultimately the two traditions, old and new, control and laissez-faire, would provide the basis for continuing ideological and legal conflict. The Handlins saw this problem in Massachusetts as early as 1860. Writing within a metaphor of real property, they defined it thus:

> It was as if, imperceptibly, all the familiar metes and bounds that marked off one man's estate from another vanished to leave a vast and open space, familiar, but with the old landmarks gone. Somewhere, everyone knew, the state could act directly, somewhere it could legislate as arbiter, and somewhere it had no place at all. But where one field ended and another began, no one knew; the master map was not yet drawn. . . . In practice, a society that found "a disposition in the people to manage their own affairs" also witnessed a remarkable extension of government interference with the lives of its citizens.[49]

Hartz quoted a Pennsylvania law of 1781 that asserted it to be "the duty and interest of all governments to prevent frauds, and promote the interests of just and useful commerce."[50] Modern economic development from an ancient legal mold would later be fruitful of conflict between control and freedom.

Change was not only in form, but in magnitude as well. Nowhere would this be more vexing than in the old idea of the privileged corporation, which was to become a common, and eventually, dominant form of economic organization.

The rise of manufacturing industry and the great expansion of corporate business organization powered the modern social ascendance of the American business community, its practices, and its values. The modern corporation is the greatest organizational innovation in the history of American business. It is essentially a multiple partnership. It is also a legal creature existing by sovereign power, and it, and not its components (for example, the owners), has both authority and legal obligation. In older English corporations, such as chartered towns, the sovereign's delegation of power and special privileges, freedoms, or concessions, was explicit. The power to create corporations was originally a Crown power in England, later shared by Parliament. The colonial governments were Crown corporations, and for the most part the creation of corporate powers under those charters was a prerogative of the royal power in the colonies, although there was also a certain amount of participation by colonial assemblies. With the outbreak of the Revolution, these assemblies were succeeded directly and immediately by state governments, and the power to create corporations passed directly to the states. They were the direct and immediate successors to the Crown before the federal Constitution was adopted.

After that, the federal government held the power to create corporations concurrently with the states, but for a long time it was diffident about using it. Before the Civil War the only two corporations chartered by Congress were the First and Second Banks of the United States. In the antebellum period, thousands of corporations were created by state legislatures with special-action charters—one charter at a time for a specific purpose.

The special-action charters of legislatures were no real innovation, even if before the 1870s they appeared almost on an assembly-line basis. Americans moved from special-action charters, with structure and function prescribed by legislation, to general procedures for incorporation without specific legislative act. General powers left the specific form and structure of the corporation (and changes therein), size, and place of business to be determined by the entrepreneurs.[51] That was a revolution indeed, and it represented a response of the political organization at the state level to business needs. So much was this the case that historians have viewed the development of general incorporation laws with considerable suspicion, even though they contained less possible ground for corruption than the special-chartering procedures.

Rarely does one find a major institutional change favoring a single interest without the development of subsequent remedies against abuses. The community at large was not without reactive powers. After the state laws of general incorporation in the 1870s and 1880s produced powerful new corporate forms—such as trust and holding companies with unlimited financial powers—the dormant powers inherent in the commerce clause of the federal Constitution were brought to life by the Sherman Antitrust Act of 1890. The Congress had used this power to create the transcontinental railroads during the Civil War.

The Sherman Act, however feeble and misdirected its initial enforcement by the courts, was potentially a powerful control of the corporate form of business organization. Although a proprietorship could equally well be part of a combination in restraint of trade, corporations were the chief objects of antitrust enforcement when the Justice Department finally turned away from its initial targets, the labor unions. From the Sherman Act through the Securities and Exchange Commission Act of 1934, this social control continued to develop, and corporations have been kept under legal rein, however loose. True, the English preceded us with general laws of incorporation (1863), but all the evidence indicates that our corporate laws were the product of our post-English history. As James Willard Hurst emphasized in *The Legitimacy of the Business Corporation*, "in this area of life we did not borrow much from anyone else."[52]

Before a federal policy evolved, corporate development was left to the states, with federal intervention coming from the Supreme Court, notably via *Dartmouth College v. Woodward* (1819), which established the corporate charter as a contract, and *Bank of Augusta v. Earle* (1839), which set up rules for interstate operation of corporations and established them in law as entities with legal domiciles. A portent of more control came in the sinking fund cases in 1879, validating the Thurmond Act of 1878, which ordered that 25 percent of the net earnings of the Union Pacific and the Central Pacific railroads be set aside to repay federal construction loans. Then as now, federal aid gave rise to federal control. As Chief Justice Morrison Waite phrased it, the Act was "a reasonable regulation of the affairs of the corporation and promotive of the interests of the public and the corporations."[53]

By that time pressures already were building to produce social counterweights to corporate business enterprise. The states were already moving away from special-action legislation for specific corporate charters, and in the direction of general incorporation.

At first general powers of incorporation were granted such nonprofit enterprises as churches, libraries, and fire companies. But other areas of economic life slowly were included. New York provided general incorporation for manufacturing-enterprises as early as 1811. Connecticut had a general act of incorporation in 1837. In the revision of the New York state constitution in 1846 more liberal rules of general incorporation were specified. Other states followed the New York lead, and despite the continued mass of special-action charters, the movement toward general laws of incorporation grew. With it came state competition for the business of granting corporate charters. In 1875 New Jersey eliminated maximum capital restrictions and then in 1888 allowed its corporations to do all their business outside the state, opening the sluice gates to holding companies and giant mergers. Delaware joined in the charter-issuing competition in 1890.[54] State specialization in the creation of corporate charters explicitly for nationwide business activity is an excellent example of manipulation of state government for the benefit of private interests, rent creation by government power. The object was to create options to nonmarket control powers limited by state boundaries. The Delaware or New Jersey corporation operating in Illinois or Colorado had advantages local corporations could not get.[55]

The advantages of the corporate form already had been identified with monopoly by 1890—although the *Charles River Bridge v. Warren Bridge* (1837) case had established the state's freedom to incorporate competing franchises if it pleased. But the tradition of English law, which held that sovereign control (or at least the potential for it) went with a franchise, had continued in colonial times, and the corporation was never really safe from control, even if its charter left great areas of freedom of action. States had entered the business of regulating, and during the Civil War had begun direct federal regulation, involving the railroad companies, under the war powers. In 1874 Congress attempted to set up a board of commissioners to regulate the railroads under the commerce clause, the bill passed the House, but not the Senate. In 1878 an auditor of railroad accounts was established in the Interior Department, and another bill to regulate common carriers passed the House (but again failed in the Senate).[56] In the spring of 1877 the Supreme Court had reported *Munn v. Illinois* (and the other Granger cases) a landmark decision that signaled a new expression of concern for the public welfare in the far-reaching economic changes of an increasingly integrated transport, industrial, and commercial system. The transcontinental expansion of the nation's social and economic institutions had passed the stage of euphoria, and new problems were now pressing for solutions as the era of heavy industrial growth dawned. In the next sixty years, from the 1870s to the 1930s, the network of public control of business developed to an extent that was scarcely known in American history except in its colonial beginnings.

The closing of the frontier also effectively marked the closing of the time when economic activity within the overall frame of the American social system expanded with the expectation of automatic freedom from nonmarket control beyond the traditional areas. Small beginnings, like the enforcement of the power to regulate interstate commerce in *Gibbons v. Ogden* (1824), ultimately would grow into an overpowering panoply of government intervention. The effective beginning of this new phase came with agrarian unrest and the rise of the new industrial system in the 1870s. It was then that the states beyond the Appalachians began to legislate new controls over business, and it was out of that legislation that the *Munn* decision came and a new chapter of American history opened. By the time the Supreme Court had stanched the flow of laws motivated by *Munn v. Illinois* the commerce clause had become the basis of an all-enveloping system of nonmarket controls.

Changes in labor's status came with economic expansion, as can be observed in the appearance of mechanic lien laws. Special problems arose concerning the person whose property was the labor of his hands. Both indenture and slavery passed through the Revolutionary period intact. Indenture died out when the states refused to continue imprisonment for debt. It took the Civil War to end slavery. But remaining were the anomalous problems of a social class of workers, inferior in law and tradition in colonial times, whose main property, human exertion itself, could be sold only by individuals not in concert with one another. Even protection of skills in guilds withered under the heat of economic and social change. The organizational equivalent of the business corporation was the labor union, and its position in law remained ambiguous until the twentieth century. Herbert Hovenkamp points out that had the labor unions incorporated themselves, the differences between their treatment by the courts and the treatment of business would have been less obvious. An agreement to raise prices arrived at jointly by the owners, directors, and management of a single corporation was not considered a conspiracy because they were the acts of agents of a single legal person. But. "A joint decision of laborers working for a single corporation . . . was conspiratorial because each laborer was a distinct legal person."[57] Refusal by the unions to incorporate, and thus to expose themselves to inspection (and possibly control) by the incorporating power, would lead the unions into conflicts that might otherwise have been avoided. For example, the efforts to establish by strikes and boycotts a market value for the collective property of union members, work rules and union wages, might more easily have been achieved by monopoly powers created by incorporation.

In the early history of the labor movement it is difficult even to know what was meant by the word *labor*. A special interest, identifiable as a labor interest, could only exist once a differentiated functional role came into existence. To make matters worse, from the seventeenth-century establishment of guilds or guild-like trade associations in colonial America to the end of the eighteenth century, quantitative evidence about American guilds is almost lacking. Part of the problem was the conflation of the roles of merchant, manufacturer, and laborer in a single person, so that a strike, like that of the New York bakers in 1741, is hard to classify. The bakers refused to bake bread at the price set by municipal authority, but it was a refusal of the masters, who also were sellers of bread, not a strike of workmen against employers.[58] Other early trade associations seem to have involved a similar conflation of roles. It was only in the strike of the Journeymen Cordwainers of Philadelphia against the master cordwainers (leather workers) in 1805 that were clearly differentiated the roles between employer and employee. The Journeymen Cordwainers were held to be a criminal conspiracy by the court; seventeen such conspiracy trials involving efforts to form labor unions preceded

Commonwealth v. Hunt in 1842.[59] In that landmark decision it was held that a mere combination of laborers was not in itself a criminal conspiracy. One long-held rule of the common law was ended: "We think, therefore that associations may be entered into, the object of which is to adopt measures that may have a tendency to impoverish another, that is, to diminish his gains and profits, and yet so far from being criminal or unlawful, the object may be highly meritorious and public-spirited."[60]

Commonwealth v. Hunt introduced a deep logical inconsistency into our industrial life that may be understandable on moral grounds, but not in terms of economics. The courts would come to define certain activities as legal under the Sherman Act if they were engaged in by business, but illegitimate if performed by combinations of workers. In section 6 of the 1914 Clayton Act an effort to escape this anomaly with the statement—"the labor of a human being is not a commodity or article of commerce"—only made matters worse, since labor in reality is a service, sold like any other article of commerce. Other laws regulated labor accordingly, and the courts only added to the confusion by upholding such laws. When, finally, the National Labor Relations Act of 1935 established collective bargaining by federal power, the contradiction was merely made official.

Following *Commonwealth v. Hunt* the American labor movement began a period of vigorous, and largely futile, organizing activity. Before the Hunt decision trade unions had attempted to achieve concrete reforms, such as limitation of the working hours of women and children, passage of mechanic lien laws, reform of schools, and collection and payment of strike benefits, and they did agitate successfully for a ten-hour day for government employees. These actions were guided by the National Trades Union, which did not survive the Panic of 1837. As industrialization, factory labor, and urbanization progressed, attempts by labor to improve its position in society developed apace. Although intricate, and involving diverse trends, including cooperatives, uplift unionism, and straight craft alliances, the movement inevitably embraced politically ambitious organization on a national scale, which culminated in 1869 in the loosely defined Knights of Labor. These activities seemed to mirror general economic development. The history of labor organization shows a movement without any unifying sense of direction, tossed by the changing tides of national life. The only consistent theme one sees in the era from the 1840s to the end of the 1860s is an apparent realization of the advantages of national organization, but unifying issues were political and moral rather than economic. Hence the Knights of Labor appeared as a logical blind alley. Little survived the early unions, apart from a clear divergence of identification between employer and employee (and even that was blurred by the amorphous Knights). A long-lasting form of organization had to wait for the final thrust of idealism represented by the Knights of Labor, which faded out in the 1890s in the face of competition from Samuel Gompers and the American Federation of Labor, a business union organized "in the imitation of capital." Before then labor partook of a smorgasbord of panaceas for all the ills—Greenbackism, Populism, free silver—that swept the country after the Civil War.[61]

The record of unionism before the AFL is a full one, but it is one in which cohesive national power was not achieved, and despite *Hunt*, organized labor found no respectable place in American life. The union was not the same as the guild, and since American society had become less tightly organized and less subject to communal control, the unions of the nineteenth century were not impressive innovations. It is questionable whether organized labor had a more effective place in American society in 1891, at the time of the Homestead Strike, than it did a century earlier in 1794 when the Journeyman Cordwainers were organized. Such was distinctly not true of business organization in the nineteenth century. It was transformed in structure and in the scope of its power by the corporation. It would require control by the federal government to redress the imbalance.

Money in the New Republic

Once the Revolution began the Americans pursued with vigor their two really original colonial innovations, paper money representing the government's debt capabilities and private bank credit based on mutual debt exchanges, which was also money, but represented private indebtedness. The American Revolution was financed in small part by taxes, and in large part by debt. The Continental Congress authorized an issue of bills of credit in June 1775 "for the defense of America," and an epochal currency depreciation began. The initial authorization was for only $2 million valued in "Spanish milled dollars" in denominations of one to twenty dollars. By 1779 more than $260 million of this currency had been issued. In 1777, $1.25 Continental would buy $1.00 in gold; by April of 1781 it took $167.50 Continental to buy the same $1.00 of gold. At the extreme limit of depreciation, in 1781 the Continental currency was worth only 1/1000 of its original exchange value against gold. Oddly enough the rise in real output was such during this period that the increase in prices was only about 200 percent in the period of maximum inflation, from 1775 to 1779. The colonists had long known that a rising money supply and rising prices tended to be related to each other. But this was more than desirable. Attempts to abate the inflation by means of a more conservative paper issue (one new dollar exchanged for twenty old dollars) in 1780 had some success, but imported goods, paid for by loans from the French and the Dutch, absorbed some of the liquidity.[62]

When the new republic was organized under the federal Constitution in 1789 the government had to dig out from the Revolutionary financial debacle. The job was surprisingly easy. Washington's Secretary of the Treasury, Alexander Hamilton, funded the Revolutionary debt (backed by a sinking fund) at about $77 million.[63] Debts of the states were mostly assumed by Congress, and customs were levied and collected. In 1791 a central bank, the Bank of the United States, modeled after the Bank of England, was chartered by Congress for twenty years. Its charter involved political compromises that moved the capital from Philadelphia to the Potomac swamps. As the bank's capital was both publicly and privately held, there was plenty of room for political compromise. By August of 1791 U.S. bonds sold above par in Europe, and by 1795 the foreign debt was paid off. Prices had fallen more than 50 percent from 1781 to 1791, and the Revolution's purely monetary effects were past.

By 1791 the two conflicting financial interests of the colonial era— paper money and private banking—were on the surface again. The new federal Constitution had forbidden the states to issue their own currencies, thus succeeding where the Crown had failed since 1690. But in 1781, Congress acceded to the design of Superintendent of Finance Robert Morris and chartered a private corporate bank, the Bank of North America, thus undoing the English law of 1741 against "Unwarrantable Schemes and Undertakings." The bank could issue money; Americans now had the beginnings of a commercial banking system. Banks chartered by the states could issue their own notes— paper money—so the restraining effects of the constitutional prohibition on the states was weakened. Indeed, modern research shows that the state legislatures deliberately chartered note-issuing banks to circumvent the federal constitution.[64] In addition, under the twenty-year charter given the Bank of the United States in 1791 Congress had imposed a control over the note-issuing powers of the commercial banks. By 1811, when the charter ran out, the Bank of the United States had, by all evidence, admirably managed its affairs. It had not only administered the government's day-to-day finance, but also had competed for business with the state-chartered banks, and disciplined them by returning their notes for collection in gold or silver coins. The bank's recharter therefore was vigorously opposed and died under the tie-breaking vote of the vice president in the Senate.[65]

As in colonial times, coins were in short supply, and inflationists joined bankers in opposing any extension of the bank's charter, which they rightly saw as a form of potential control over the money supply. The problems underlying the bank's recharter were to bedevil American finance until the Federal Reserve System was launched in 1914. They were only partially resolved then, and are not absent today from American life. They were the same problems involved in the colonial paper money issues and the Massachusetts land bank scheme. Wages and prices tend to rise when money is plentiful. Both situations are favorable to the interests of manual workers, farmers, and debtors in general. Those who lend money, on the other hand, are favored if prices and wages are stable or falling, other things being equal. The former people tend to be inflationists, the latter financial conservatives. Jackson vs. Biddle, Resumption vs. the Greenback Revolt, Bryan vs. McKinley—the underlying economic problems represented by the political battles of American history could not be eliminated by any magic wand of policy. The issue was, and is, a matter of whose interests the financial system should favor. The question is rooted in economics, the answer in politics.

Even the problem of a coin circulation was not solved by independence. Once freed of British restrictions the Americans launched into disasters of their own making. By the Mint Act of 1792 the coinage was to be bimetallic, an inherently unstable system. The mint was to buy an ounce of gold with fifteen ounces of silver. European gold prices were higher, so the newly minted gold coins were shipped out of the country. The new silver coins, shiny and well made, were acceptable in trade for heavier and cruder Spanish coins in the Caribbean; so the silver coinage was exported and the Caribbean silver imported as bullion to trade for both gold and silver. The new republic very shortly had no coins of its own in circulation, and had to rely on foreign coins, mainly English and French, for small purchases. In 1834 an attempt was made to remedy this situation by raising the gold price to sixteen ounces of silver, but the gold discoveries of the 1840s and 1850s raised the exchange price of silver, and it disappeared from circulation again. Bank notes of less than a dollar were printed to make small purchases. In the 1870s silver prices fell sharply as new mines came into production in the West, and gold coins became relatively expensive. The Silver Purchase Acts of 1878 and 1890 brought silver to the Treasury but drove the gold out. The results of these efforts to "do something for silver" helped empty

President Cleveland's Treasury to the extent that by 1895 he was forced to borrow from private bankers to maintain lawful specie payments from the Treasury. Heavy balance of payments surpluses after 1896, gold discoveries in Alaska and South Africa in the late 1890s, and finally the Gold Standard Act of 1900, which eliminated official bimetallism, finally blotted this particular form of monetary folly from American life. It had given our history a legacy of madcap monetary economics.[66]

The coin problem, which defined the national monetary standard, was merely the tip of the iceberg. After all, internally most business was financed by credit in the form of debt instruments. A bank note is a bank liability. A deposit account is a bank liability. A bill of exchange is a commercial liability. Apart from coins, money is essentially debt. The volume of debt instruments of all kinds outstanding at any time was more directly the product of overt policy than was the circulation of coins. Just as the inflationists agitated for a federal currency issued against the increasingly abundant silver after the Civil War, they favored freely issued paper money from the beginning.

Until the period between 1838 and 1863, neither party gained a clear-cut victory. No sooner was the Bank of the United States gone in 1811 than the country found itself at war again with no ready method of financing it. After the war with England ended, Congress promptly attempted to remedy this deficiency. Relying upon past experience, it chartered a Second Bank of the United States in 1816. Again the bank was modeled after the Bank of England; it did both private banking business and managed the government's day-to-day financial needs. Ownership was both public and private. The bank competed with private banks and, in its branch drafts upon the central office, created its own currency. By presenting private bank notes to their issuers for payment in specie, the bank imposed monetary control.

Accordingly, when President Jackson attacked this "money monopoly" in his veto message on the premature recharter attempt by Congress in 1832, he echoed the complaints of the private banking community. The Second Bank was no monopoly, but it was the largest bank in the country and was in a position of power and control. By 1834 there were 506 state-chartered banks with total assets of $419 million. In that year the Second Bank of the United States had total assets of $75 million and outstanding loans and discounts of $55 million. In 1832, loans and discounts were over $66 million. So the Second Bank was a relative giant. When Jackson let the government's funds at the Bank run out and began making government deposits in the state banks, he moved the financial system away from central bank control and toward a more competitive system, if numbers alone could be taken as a measure of competition. The man was hardly consistent. By virtually paying off the federal debt, Jackson eliminated part of the reason for having a central bank, and might have encouraged a net increase in the money stock. Similarly, the government deposits in state banks doubtless supported a higher volume of loans than they did in the Second Bank. But his Specie Circular of 1836, demanding payment in gold or silver for purchases of government lands, was hardly an inflationary move.[67]

It should be emphasized that efforts to control money emissions by state banks also existed in the private sector. In the Suffolk System, inaugurated in Boston from 1819 to 1821, and in the New York Safety Fund System of 1823, constraints were imposed upon state bank note issues. Until 1838 state banks had been chartered only by special legislative acts, and even afterward, in the "free banking" era, reserve requirements were commonly specified by state law (with success in Louisiana, the only state in which the banks stayed open in the 1857 financial crisis). But generally, the fall of the Second Bank of the United States may be taken as a long-run victory of the backwoods paper-money enthusiasts in league with the more sophisticated commercial bank expansionists, whose intellectual origins all dated from the colonial era. From 1836 until the Civil War there was no central control, and the banking system moved increasingly toward purely market controls over money issues. By 1861 there were more than 1,600 state-chartered banks, most of them issuing their own money in various denominations, and thousands, perhaps as many as 10,000, different kinds of bank notes were in circulation. Since the federal Constitution prohibited the states from issuing bills of credit, and the notes of state banks were obligations of state-chartered institutions, there was considerable legal opinion (denied by the Supreme Court) that state bank notes were in fact unconstitutional.

By 1861 paper currency readily acceptable at face value was in relatively short supply; the system was a national scandal and an international joke. The paper-money advocates had prevailed for more than two decades; but nationwide financial panics in 1837 and 1857, together with one of the deepest and longest depressions in American history (with a trough in 1842), hardly were evidence that free emissions of paper money alone could solve all economic problems. In fact, the modern monetarist might argue that not enough money had been printed. From 1836 to 1860 the trend of prices was downward, with a slight rise in the early 1850s. Despite the absence of central-bank control, bank assets and notes issued had in fact lagged behind the growth of other economic indicators. Total bank deposits from 1836 to 1860 rose from $190 million to only $310 million; note issues from $140 million to $207 million; and total assets from $622 million to $1 billion. Since population had more than doubled, rising from 15.4 million to 31.5 million in the same period, there was actually less bank money per capita in 1860 than there had been in 1836. From 1840 to 1860 the real net national product had more than doubled.[68] Two decades of free banking had scarcely produced the inflationists' millennium. But it had produced an utterly chaotic currency system.

With the banking acts of 1863 and 1864 establishing national banks, we began the swing back to nonmarket control of the monetary system, which, however slow and uneven, has been relentless to the present day. After independence the banking system had moved irregularly away from nonmarket control, chiefly through the struggle of state-chartered banks for greater freedom. The demise of the first two central banks were landmarks along that route. The free-banking era after 1838 was the ultimate triumph of free-enterprise banking. In 1863 and 1864, with the senators and congressmen from the rural South temporarily absent from Washington, Secretary of the Treasury Salmon Chase, under the impetus of wartime necessity, was able to establish a uniform bank-note issue. A third of the national banks' capital was to be invested in government bonds (thus pressing the banking system into wartime finance). A tax placed upon the note issues of the state-chartered banks in 1865 ended that episode in American history. On the other hand, the $450 million in greenbacks, United States notes issued by the wartime federal government, gave the paper-money advocates a fillip and a model that clouded American politics for years. The Confederate paper money was simply canceled by the Union victory, thus aiding the continued circulation of the federal paper. As Charles Calomiris emphasizes, this successful flotation of federal fiat money was of doubtful constitutionality; however, it worked.[69]

Uniform accounting and reporting procedures and legal cash reserve requirements imposed government rules on national bank operations. By example they influenced the whole system. The state-chartered banks made a comeback as the nation increasingly adopted checks and deposits as currency substitutes. This "money" represented the combined credit of the bank and its depositor, and the assets of anyone who endorsed such instruments while passing them as current payments to others. The state-chartered banking system grew again prodigiously from a low of 247 banks in 1868 to 20,346 by 1914. That year the combined assets of state-chartered banks were

$15.9 billion, compared with $11.5 billion for the 7,518 national banks. Severe monetary crises struck in 1873 and 1882, but it was the sequence of panics in 1893, 1903, and 1907 that finally produced agitation for more rigorous control, and ultimately the Federal Reserve Act. The regulations and example of the national banking system had been an element of nonmarket control, but with the Federal Reserve System the nation's banking, for the first time since 1836, was potentially back under the thumb of a central bank. Even though the Federal Reserve Act specified an "elastic currency" as its object, the system soon enough imposed banking restraints that resembled those of the Second Bank of the United States.

In the cases of money and banking it is remarkable that a pattern related to economic reality should emerge at all, since these two subjects are as infected by fanatical belief as is any theological dogma. Yet the history before the Federal Reserve Act does show fairly distinct phases, to some extent overlapping each other. This is not surprising, however, when you consider that the economic interests behind monetary expansion and restraint then were as real as they are today. The expansionists tended to favor a free-market control, and the conservatives favored other devices, such as central banking and direct government regulation. The question in nineteenth-century American history is what real economic interests were served by conservative dominion in banking beginning in 1863 and culminating, perhaps, with the Gold Standard Act of 1900. In the following chapter I will show that the coalition of forces that imposed nonmarket controls on other parts of the economy at the end of the nineteenth century and in the early twentieth century were not at all obvious allies of the forces of monetary conservatism.

In the monetary system as in all other parts of the economy the legacy of nonmarket controls influenced future growth. Apart from money, land, and foreign trade, however, the controls after independence remained for many decades primarily at local and state levels—in the courts and in everyday business life—but not in the power of the federal government. Then, in the last quarter of the nineteenth century and the first two decades of this century there was a great change, and the federal government emerged as the dominant force in nonmarket control over the economy. The reasons seem complex, but in terms of the initial discussion in chapter 1, the main pattern of this change will be seen to be simple enough. Control gained the upper hand over the new laissez-faire at the federal level because powerful groups rejected the decision of the free market regarding the ownership and distribution of economic power.

Chapter 4

THE FIRST REACTION

> Every contract, combination in the form of trust or
> otherwise, or conspiracy, in restraint of trade or
> commerce among the several states or with foreign
> nations, is hereby declared to be illegal.
> —*The Sherman Antitrust Act, 1890*

Revulsion Against the Free Market

Probably no period of American economic history has been more difficult to understand than the four decades between the panic of 1873 and the First World War. In virtually every facet of the nation's economic life the patterns that had slowly evolved in the decades after independence experienced radical changes. Agriculture neared the end of its great geographic expansion, and despite the rise in domestic food consumption and an unprecedented export trade, the American farm sector became the source of demands for fundamental federal government intervention. The transportation sector saw continued expansion of railroad mileage, but public complaint about the nature and price of the resulting services gave rise to direct public regulation, first at the state and then at the federal level. The corporation became more pervasive in manufacturing and distribution enterprises, and public resistance to the resulting aggregates of economic power ended with antitrust legislation and a host of controversial and precedent-setting court cases. The rising structure of modern business was met head-on by control legislation at all levels—at the federal level with a meat inspection bill and finally the Pure Food and Drug Act of 1906. Business practices were subjected to federal control generally by the establishment of the Federal Trade Commission in 1914.

The growth of per capita income was accompanied by agitation for a graduated tax on incomes. There had been a temporary income tax in 1864; a tax imposed in 1894 was thrown out by the Supreme Court on constitutional grounds, and there followed a successful initiative that ended with the Sixteenth Amendment, adopted in 1913. The banking system was subjected to increasing criticism as it changed and expanded to accommodate the new industrial economy. A more systematic federal control was imposed in 1914 with the reappearance of central banking in the United States in the new Federal Reserve System. The unprecedented exploitation of national resources produced a conservation movement. The Reclamation Bill of 1902 began extensive government controls over the extractive industries. Attempts by governments to regulate wages, hours, and conditions of labor, together with basic innovations in the American labor movement, were entangled in a web of conservative court decisions as the labor force grew apace with general economic expansion.

Wherever one turns in this complex history, American society seemed to be turning in its tracks, away from familiar patterns of behavior and toward uncharted regions of federal control. Alterations in income distribution between economic sectors due to fundamental economic change were considered to constitute a breakdown, or an imperfection in the market, by those adversely affected. The appeal to control to "correct" the new conditions set federal nonmarket mechanisms in place on a permanent basis, reducing the price system's power to allocate resources in response to the market's choices. The resulting correction was apparently more satisfactory to the public than the previous condition of more extensive market freedom, no matter how poorly the nonmarket-control mechanism performed. One only rarely sees in American history any popular demand to return to the free market once an apparatus of nonmarket control has been established. Either one must assume a general acquiescence in nonmarket control or, following the analysis of Lance Davis and Douglass North in *Institutional Change and American Economic Growth*, argue that interests vested in the new control system were effectively more powerful than any others in contention for the levers of power.[1] *Some* group benefited and protected its own interests, it is usually charged, by gaining control of the nonmarket mechanism itself. The great exceptions to the rule were wartime controls, but even those left a residue of historical change, if only in a greater willingness to turn to nonmarket social control the next time similar problems arose.

Why have Americans demonstrated such a long-term distaste for the free market? In every case a long list of answers is available. But since the movement to nonmarket control was a national phenomenon, and not merely a matter of special circumstances in a few extraordinary cases, the social scientist naturally casts about for some equally general explanation of this turn of events. Numbers tell an interesting story in aggregate, but numbers are evidence, not explanation. The frontier phase was ending in the last quarter of the century, and in the four decades leading to 1914 the urban industrial economy came into existence. There was a decisive shift in the balance of economic power away from the agrarian population, which had always dominated American economic, political, and social life, as may be seen in table 4.1.

In this time period, the farm labor force did grow, but far less than did the nonfarm labor force. Agriculture's value of output more than doubled, but nonfarm output grew by a factor of seven, and the share of national income going to agriculture fell behind that of manufacturing. Immigration, together with natural increase and domestic migration from the farms, had filled the cities with an industrial labor force. The urban population, a mere 10 percent of the total in 1870, was 42 percent of it by 1910. In 1870 there were no cities of over a million inhabitants and only 1.6 million lived in cities whose population exceeded 500,000. By 1910 8.5 million lived in cities of more than a million, and another 3 million lived in cities of the second rank. The nation's industrialization, as in England and Western Europe, was producing a "harvest of cities." With the rise of an urban society came a new constellation of economic leadership and political power. This change lay at the root of the turbulent political life of the period.

Since our own life as an industrial nation parallels in so many ways the European experience in the proliferation of nonmarket control, it would be easy to pass the whole question off as a somehow natural development. Such an argument, in fact, was developed by Karl Polanyi in his book *The Great Transformation*.[2] To him the whole idea of the self-regulating market as society's major social control mecha-

TABLE 4.1
Product, Distribution of Income by Sector, Gainful Workers Employed, 1869–1916

	Gross Domestic Product Annual Averages in Prices of 1929 ($ Billions)			Distribution of National Income[a] (In Percent)			Gainful Workers Employed[b] (Millions)		
	Total	Farm	Non-farm	Agric.	Mining	Mfg.	Total	Farm	Non-farm
1869–78	11.6	4.1	6.8	20.5	1.8	13.9	12.9	6.8	6.1
1912–16	62.5	10.1	49.8	17.7	3.3	20.8	37.4	11.6	25.8

Source: *Historical Statistics of the United States*, series F 44-48, F 34-43, D 36-45.

[a] Percents in line one are averages of 1869–79 figures; percents in line two are averages of 1909–18 figures.

[b] Figures in line one from 1870 census; figures in line two from 1910 census.

nism was simply "utopian." His ideas are not specific to American economic history, but are suggestive of certain general characteristics of western industrialization that were shared in the American experience.

Guidelines to the material that follows in this chapter are derived from the discussion in chapter 1. First, there is no doubt that a heavy political element hangs over this economic history and is inseparable from it. Just as one expects profit-maximizing businessmen or groups to move in upon externalities created by change in the economy, so one expects vote-seeking politicians to exploit every advantage. Economic change produces political issues, and the electorate must choose among political positions whose remote origins were economic and conceivably subject to straightforward economic solutions originally. What actually happens in politics is something else altogether, and since so much political thought is or becomes utterly irrational, it is well nigh useless to seek for more theory to explain it. Political slogans are rarely rational programs for effective solutions to problems. Politicians know their business—how to get votes; "talking sense to the people" has rarely been a blueprint for electoral victory, as any survey of American political history effectively demonstrates. In the American democracy politicians may lead, but they also follow swings in public opinion, and sometimes surprising initiatives appear in the political sector that reflect, usually in a distorted way, economic realities that have given rise to public agitation. The same is true of the courts, although to a lesser extent, since there the devotion to precedent, the internal logic of legal exegesis, presents certain effective barriers to radical change in court-sanctioned behavior and in legislation that can pass through the sieve of constitutionality. As Stephen Mueller wrote concerning this: "In its powers of adaptive change, law is perhaps slower than other institutions of social control. Because of this tardiness, it becomes a social force tempering the mold of change with the conservatism that legal procedure and delayed deliberation require."[3]

Second, the work of Davis and North provides a useful searchlight on behavioral innovations, especially where new combinations were profitable consequences of economic change that introduced external economies and imperfections in markets and in the transmission of knowledge.[4] Finally, the public reaction may readily be understood from our discussion in chapter 1. Whenever important sectors of the body politic begin to lose advantages formerly available from given lines of endeavor, agitation for nonmarket control appears to preserve or restore the situation. This has been the American experience. Hence the dramatic rise in the capital-output ratio in the period from 1870 to 1914 (reflecting the great investment in the fixed plant and machinery of the new industrial economy and the rise in the return to capital relative to labor) could be expected to induce more vigorous attempts by labor to hold or improve its position outside the individual wage bargain. In fact, the labor movement turned away from the uplift unionism of the Knights of Labor after 1886 and embraced the hardheaded bargaining unionism of Samuel Gompers and the AFL, with a vigorous gesture toward revolutionary unionism in the International Workers of the World. Similarly, the shift of income shares away from agriculture was accompanied by the Populist revolt. Foreign trade apart, the scheme appears to be symmetrical: American industry, now moving into the abundance flowing from a new technology, assumed the mantle of the frontier individualist, the squatter mentality, demanding a free rein internally. Machines, factories, electric power, railroads, Wall Street—there was a new frontier of infinite dimensions, and the new frontiersman wore a silk hat.

These guides to analysis will prove useful, but excessive faith in such explanations is not warranted. It is the nature of historical theorizing that its apparent explanatory power appears to grow as its simplicity increases. Reality is more complex; much of the development from 1873 to 1914 was not touched by such ideas, and the history of our adoption of nonmarket social control in modern forms was only beginning, considering where it has since gone. Specific and nonrepeatable historical events were crucial. That complicates the problem of historical understanding, as there is no general way to deal with such historical externalities as, for example, the importance of personality factors among the great political and economic leaders, or the consequences of European harvest failures in solving our balance of payments problems in the late 1890s and, at the same time, shifting political debate away from radical solutions. One can theorize, but one cannot ignore exceptions to postulated results.

Generally, political agitation for federal control correlated with periods of economic malaise, which were temporary. But in subsequent expansions much of the political residue remained. Thus, it is something of a sour joke that the period of American economic history that produced the most rapid real long-term growth rates we have ever experienced also should have been a prolific seedbed for nonmarket control over economic life.[5]

As I will show in this chapter, each separate subversion of the price mechanism's consequences seemed justifiable to contemporaries in the prevailing conditions, and they may have seemed to be adequate solutions to problems. The long-term outcome could not be foreseen. For example, one is saddened now to read of the origins of the Interstate Commerce Commission (recently dubbed "an elephant's grave-yard of political hacks"), an agency intended until recently, says Milton Friedman, "to protect railroads from competition by trucks."[6] The commission resulted from a secular crusade, and the potential regulatory power of the commissioners was greatly feared. As Senator George Hoar of Massachusetts said at the time: "You give these men power over the business of great towns and great cities and great classes of investments—a power which no Persian satrap or Roman proconsul was ever entrusted with."[7] Yet, as Davis and North point out, such is the logic of public regulation that the imbalance of economic forces creates an external economy that makes its capture profitable to those regulated. Achievement of such a capture, logical to firms in regulated industries, damages the public at large and ultimately makes hash of the independent regulatory agency as a non-market control operating in the public interest. Hence North's baleful comment: "A continuing dilemma of regulatory agencies is that they can become vehicles whereby the regulated regulate the regulators, in the interest of the regulated—rather than that of the public."[8]

The study of federal regulation is a sad one, especially when one considers the hopeful beginnings that so many times seemed to end as government-sponsored price-fixing cartels like the now defunct Civil Aeronautics Board, an agency whose actions were more effectively and flagrantly against the public interest than straightforward private monopoly might have been. The experience with outright public ownership has been equally disheartening and Milton Friedman, at least, argued that, "if tolerable at all, private monopoly may be the least of the evils."[9]

I am now concerned with origins and will treat the long-term outcomes later. Just as those who fought for federal establishment of collective bargaining in the 1930s could not foresee the industrial hijacking developed by the industrywide strike (in which the general public's agony is used as the bargaining fulcrum in industrial conflicts), so the founders of the regulatory commissions could not foresee the long-term consequences. The political system transformed public complaints into electoral issues, the courts ruled on the resulting legislation, and an apparently permanent edifice of federal control began. Expanded by the exigencies of war, depression, cold war, and stagflation, that edifice still rules today. (I shall show later that the deregulation of the 1970s and 1980s was largely a paper dragon.) It is odd indeed that the period roughly dated between 1870 and 1914 should have been viewed as the triumph of American capitalism, when it marked, in fact, the political beginning of nearly ubiquitous federal control. The extensive free-market capitalism of 1870 now looks like an exotic species, as extinct as the dodo. The economy was indeed transformed between 1865 and 1914,[10] but 1914 saw an elaborate system of federal control that did not exist at all in 1870. The American economy, hurled headlong into an astonishing epoch of economic change by the forces of industry, came out not only with a productive capacity equal to the major European nations combined, but with the market mechanism constrained in ways unknown by those who lived in 1870.

AGRARIAN UNREST AND THE DEMAND FOR FEDERAL CONTROL

Between the Civil War and the Bryan candidacy of 1896 the farmer's belief in his own distress was crucial to the swing of sentiment away from free-market economics. The farmer and his family remained a numerical majority having political power until the First World War. Even if that power was on the wane, farmers tried to influence government. To the farmers the free market's benefits were considered too costly to bear. The Populist demands for basic changes were a rejection of the free-enterprise capitalism that largely had carried the nation since independence. That these policies were called reform should not mislead where economics is concerned. What was at stake was private control over productive resources with only the price of mechanism as social control.

The sequence of Greenbacker, Granger, and Populist groups—the farmer protest movements of the late nineteenth century—long has been tainted by the aura of the funny-money schemes associated with their names.[11] From 1864 to 1896 prices moved downward, with only temporary cyclical interruptions. Wholesale prices fell more than 50 percent, but basic crop prices, such as wheat and cotton, experienced declines on the order of 70 percent. No doubt the incidence of this price fall was uneven, hitting the inefficient farms hardest. But most farming is relatively inefficient, and the numbers of farmers must be considered as well as the justice of their cause. The farmers, no longer able to move to new and more productive western lands, believing themselves overcharged by industry and the railroads, discriminated against by the financial system, and cheated by the politicians, raised a standard of revolt against the consequences of the free market. The famous Populist demands and formation of the People's party were the results. As John D. Hicks emphasized in his *Populist Revolt* six decades ago, the Populist demands comprised the wave of the future.[12] Moreover, since Hicks wrote before the

1930s and the New Deal, he knew only a part of the Populist influence.

What he did know was impressive enough. Direct election of senators, suffrage for women, and the secret ballot were Populist demands that became law. In economics the Populists were radical, and much of their economic program ultimately became law. They demanded government mortgage loans on their land and loans with stored crops as collateral. If the banks would not consider agricultural real estate as prime collateral, they wanted another agency to do it. If the market did not consider stored crops worthy collateral for short-term credit, the farmers demanded that government step in. The demands were met, but most times not until a generation after they were made. From the viewpoint of the late twentieth century, that lag does not seem to be as important as it was at the end of the nineteenth century. The deed was done. The land banks, organized under the 1916 Farm Loan Act, made mortgage loans; and a host of crop-loan agencies, through federally sponsored production credit associations (including the Commodity Credit Corporation in our time), linked crop storage and credit. The Populist belief that paper money could represent real things other than precious metals or government bonds was a throwback to colonial ideas. Land could generate money, crops could, and in the Populist sub-treasury schemes the federal government itself was to create legal tender and lend it against crops in storage.[13] In less direct fashion, after all, such is the modern practice.

Similarly, the Populist demand for fiat money issues to raise prices was accommodated by the 1914 Federal Reserve Act, in theory, and has been more than fulfilled by several generations of American governments, although the scheme has not kept farm prices from falling in cyclical depressions. Even in the depressed 1930s, however, farm prices did not sink back to earlier levels. Let it be noted that the Populist demands in 1891 and 1892 that paper money issues should be on a per capita basis were ultimately echoed by respectable economists like James Angell in the 1930s, or such contemporary luminaries as Milton Friedman. One wonders if government regulation since the 1930s was not perhaps more than the late nineteenth-century farmers would have wanted. The same is true of their demand for a graduated income tax. The perennial demand for free coinage of silver at sixteen-to-one produced successive silver purchase acts, and the demands for postal savings and better schools for the mass of children were met.

Other Populist demands were never met, or were met only in part. For the platform of the 1892 Omaha Convention, the People's Party of America demanded nationalization of the railroads and telegraph lines. These forms of enterprise were put under regulatory agencies instead, although in other countries, such as the United Kingdom, railroads and telegraph systems have long since been nationalized. (In the Thatcher regime of the 1980s, the telephone service was put up for sale to private investors, along with other nationalized industries, in an attempt to stop the hemorrhage of H.M.'s Treasury that the publicly-owned enterprises generated.)

The Populists demanded a century ago that land should be withdrawn from the market and reserved for actual settlement and for conservation: "The land, including all the natural resources of wealth, is the heritage of the people."[14] They demanded an end to alien ownership and to speculation by railroads and other corporations. By then private land speculation had fallen upon leaner times after the high plains were reached by settlers. Earlier legislation, such as the Timber and Stone Act of 1878 and the Desert Land Act of 1877, did encourage actual settlement, and the subsequent withdrawal of land from the market (The General Revision Act of 1891) in the establishment of national parks and forests and the withholding of minerals and oil reserves from the market partly met the Populist demands. By the early twentieth century, with the Forest Service and the Reclamation Service in existence, more than 300 million acres, an area larger than the land holdings of the original thirteen colonies, had been withdrawn from entry altogether. Obviously, the Populist statement "we oppose any subsidy or national aid to any private corporation for any private purpose"[15] was not going to enjoy much recognition in an economy of the sort implied by the Populist demands. But their position was illogical in any case; they were not free-traders pure and simple, and tariffs are, in fact, indirect subsidies. The Populists opposed free immigration and agitated with organized labor for restrictions. In 1882, Congress barred certain kinds of undesirable immigrants, the first such law to pass Congress. In succeeding years, efforts to bar illiterates were stopped by presidential veto three times. Finally, the 1921 National Quotas Act ended the great nineteenth century free transfer of European human capital, which had been such a powerful external influence on the American labor market and economic growth. The Populists also urged abolition of the national banking system, whose members were not allowed to make mortgage loans against farm real estate. The objection was partially met in the 1914 Federal Reserve Act, which enabled member banks to accept that species of collateral.

Hence the Populist demands were far more basic and portentous than was implied by the Populist caricature as a hayseed money crank. The basic Populist demands were for creation of a more congenial economy than the one they had experienced. It can be said, too, that their movement, as the last of the agrarian movements that followed the collapse of farm prices after the Civil War, represented a reaction to an unfavorable shift of income and power, as previously noted. Those who have written of the agrarian revolt have often emphasized such factors.

The Populists also raised complaints about railroads and corporate power. Railroad rates were too high relative to farm prices, they said, and the new industrial corporations had excessive power and influence. The Populist platform of the 1892 Omaha Convention was a long enumeration of such complaints. The nation faced "moral, political and material ruin." The government was corrupt in all its parts, including "the ermine of the bench." Business was bad, labor impoverished, and the land and its wealth concentrated "in the hands of capitalists." There had been Pinkertons at the Homestead strike in 1891, so private armies were excoriated. The maldistribution of income and accumulation of "colossal fortunes" were decried. One memorable sentence from the Populist platform, probably referring to railroad construction and protective tariffs, reads: "From the same prolific womb of governmental injustice we breed two great classes—paupers and millionaires." The charge built up finally, with the usual convention rhetoric, into a robust expression of the "paranoid style" in American political life: "a vast conspiracy against mankind." Civilization itself was at stake.[16] The Populists won no presidential election, but they won other elections; for governors, senators, and congressmen. American capitalism had somehow spawned a massive opposition that had either to be crushed or accommodated. Wherever the Populist invective touched a vulnerable point, what inevitably had to be sacrificed for social peace was the free-market allocative mechanism.

How justified the agrarian unrest was between the Civil War and the turn of the century has been the subject of much historical writing, largely inconclusive. Just now the weight of opinion is with the agrarians. It may change again. It makes little difference, since the agrarians believed in their own distress and were consequently able to change the economic system. Frederick Jackson Turner neatly expressed the innate contradictions the Populist movement represented. Their commitment to free-market capitalism was only as extensive as the supply of easily accessible land. Their reversion to older ideas of government control was not remarkable from their viewpoint:

Taken as a whole, Populism is a manifestation of the old pioneer ideals of the native American, with the added element of increasing readiness to utilize the national government to effect its ends. This is not unnatural in a section whose lands were originally purchased by the government and given away to its settlers by the same authority, whose railroads were built largely by federal money and governed by the national authority until they were carved into rectangular States and admitted into the Union.[17]

Whereas the Populist demands were largely met in the long run, efforts of the earlier agrarian groups were far from barren. Legislative price control arose with the Granger Laws of the 1870s. The doctrine of valid government control enunciated in *Munn v. Illinois* paved the way for later use of the commerce clause to establish the ICC and the Sherman Act and the continued development of that power.

The importance of the *Munn* doctrine lies not in its immediate consequences, but in the fact that *Munn* opened the door to an extension of nonmarket controls whenever circumstances warranted such action. The background of *Munn* lay in conflicts between railroad companies, their customers, and state governments, whose actions had created the railroads. From the 1830s onward there had been state controls of varying degree over railroads, even, in New England and then elsewhere, through state regulatory commissions.[18] The common-law tradition allowing such controls had never been relaxed or questioned. Regulation of common callings had continued, varying from place to place. During the 1870s Iowa and Wisconsin passed laws prescribing maximum railroad charges; Illinois and Minnesota set up railroad commissions. These laws and the controversies surrounding them, occurring in the general aura of farmer unrest in the early 1870s, formed the background of *Munn*. Because the Granger movement was in full flood in the 1870s the laws were called the Granger Laws, and six cases concerning these laws went before the Supreme Court in the fall term of 1876.[19] The main argument against the laws was that the Fourteenth Amendment's due-process clause protected railroads and other businesses from arbitrary state regulation, especially rate fixing. The *Munn* case itself did not concern railroads, but rather rates charged by grain elevators, yet it was chosen by Chief Justice Waite to define the law in all the cases. The decision, called ever afterward the *Munn* doctrine, stated that any private property whose use becomes of public concern, becomes "clothed in the public interest" and may be regulated by government in our legal system.

The *Munn* case set several hares running.[20] First, it reaffirmed the customary regulatory power of government; second, it added the doctrine of generalized public interest to potential control of a wide range of property; and third, it raised the issue of monopoly. Before these ideas were absorbed by American capitalism through court action and by legislation, the new structure of federal controls had arisen. In the *Wabash* case in 1886 the Supreme Court ruled that only Congress had the power to control interstate railroad business, and Congress began the process of assuming that power.[21] The ICC was established the next year, but effective rate-making power was not given to that Commission until the Hepburn Act of 1906, after the Court ruled in *Smythe v. Ames* that reasonable freight rates had to return a reasonable profit to capital, and it was finally left to the ICC to establish what reasonable really was. It never found out. Monopoly was dealt with in 1890 in the Sherman Act, and the idea that other businesses clothed in the public interest remained liable to state control was contested in the courts until the *Nebbia* case in 1934, when it was held that such criteria need not exist for government control to be imposed; such was inherent in the sovereign power of government. In his own way Chief Justice Waite had argued the same in the *Munn* case, but had added the public interest doctrine to justify his opinion. It is commonly charged that he had led American constitutional law on a wild goose chase, since regulatory power had always existed. The real question one wants to ask is: Had it not been for *Munn* what route would the rise of nonmarket regulation of giant enterprises have taken? Was it inevitable? Justice Holmes said of the *Munn* doctrine in 1927 that "the notion that a business is clothed with a public use is little more than a fiction intended to beautify what is disagreeable to the sufferers."[22]

All of this is after the fact, and in 1876 might not have seemed so clear as counsel for the defense thought. Moreover, fifty years of *Munn*-style legislation and litigation suggest that the problem was not all that simple.

In its constitution of 1870 (Article 13), Illinois assumed the power to control grain storage charges at public elevators and railroad properties. Under this power Illinois passed a law in 1871 setting rates. Munn and Scott, who owned a grain elevator, refused to take out a license to operate a public warehouse, and, moreover, their charges were higher than the official rates. In the resulting lawsuit, *Munn v. Illinois*, the U.S. Supreme Court upheld the state of Illinois, together with the other state regulatory laws, in a decision handed down in March 1877. Chief Justice Waite, delivering the majority opinion, argued that the powers of Parliament had devolved upon the states after the American Revolution, apart from those specifically given to the federal government in the Constitution. The powers of the states included the traditional economic controls, commonly embodied in the "police powers." Such powers had been used

> in England from time immemorial, and in this country from its coloniza-
> tion, to regulate ferries, common carriers, hackmen, bakers, millers, wharf-
> ingers, innkeepers . . . and in so doing to fix a maximum of charge to be
> made for services rendered, accommodations furnished, and articles sold.
> To this day, statutes are to be found in many of the States upon some or
> all of these subjects; and we think it has never yet been successfully con-
> tended that such legislation came within the constitutional prohibitions
> against interference with private property.[23]

Waite knew his history well, and went on to discuss cases of controls, weights of bread, carriages, cartage, commission rates of auctioneers, all held within the traditional grip of nonmarket control. He then cited an essay written in 1670 by Matthew Hale, an English jurist, who figured twice in our history: once as judge at witchcraft trials in England, which Cotton Mather said served as explicit models for the Salem trials, and then in the *Munn* case. Lord Hale discussed the nature of private and sovereign rights in the difficult cases of ports, harbors, and wharves. In his paper *De Portibus Maris*, Hale argued that such properties, even if privately owned, could become of public consequence, and as such, "affected with a public interest."[24] They no longer were *juris privati*, but became *juris publici*, which Hale defined in his book *Analysis of the Law* as things that "are common to all the King's subjects."[25] Waite went on in exegesis of Hale: "When, therefore, one devotes his property to a use in which the public has an interest, he, in effect, grants to the public an interest in that use, and must submit to be controlled by the public for the common good . . . he must submit to control."[26]

Such had been the case in England, Waite found, and in the United States in common law. The power to regulate was inherent in the common-law rule that charges must be "reasonable." Moreover, the Munn and Scott enterprise, connecting rail and lake transport, stood astride the very "gateway of commerce," charging a toll, and thus had monopoly powers by virtue of its location.[27] Although Waite is not often given credit for the analogy, he may well have considered that a grain elevator on Lake Michigan was strictly comparable to the "wharf and crane" that Lord Hale offered by way of illustration.

Justice Stephen Field, in dissent, realized the limitless potentiality of Waite's decision and argued that it was an attack on property and a license to regulate the prices of everything "from a calico gown to a city mansion."[28] He was right. It took until the 1930s to whittle the *Munn* doctrine away, and by then such things as gasoline, fire insurance, milk, theater tickets, and more had been singled out for price control by state legislatures. A long legal road lay ahead after the *Munn* decision. By a generous refreshment (and perhaps, it has been charged, an overdose) at the fountain of seventeenth-century common law, Chief Justice Waite had "transformed the whole course of the American law of price regulation."[29] Field became the guru of a doctrine, substantive due process, that elevated the sanctity of private contract to a judicial cult.[30] Both Waite and Field were sent packing in *Nebbia* in 1934.

Any history of nonmarket control of American economic life must come to grips with *Munn*. It is clear that the *Munn* doctrine could have had revolutionary consequences for American capitalism. State regulatory laws regarding railroads were cut short, but business could be clothed with a public interest by legislative edict; here a fundamental split appeared in the Supreme Court between conservatives like Chief Justice William Howard Taft and, later, Justice George Sutherland, who fought to restrain the state legislatures, and liberals like Justice Oliver Wendell Holmes Jr., who argued that legislatures were not restricted regarding control of business. Taft had the best platform when the Court overturned the Kansas Industrial Relations Act of 1920. The Kansas act had declared food processing, clothing manufacturing, fuel production, and other basic business activities to be affected with a public interest and therefore under state control. The act also controlled wages in those industries. In the test case, *Wolff Packing Co. v. Court of Industrial Relations* (1923), the Court overturned the Kansas act. Taft argued that if such controls could be imposed by "mere legislative declaration" then "there must be a revolution in the relation of government to general business."[31] Four years later, when New York State declared theater-ticket scalping to be clothed in the public interest and regulated ticket prices accordingly, Justice Holmes, in a dissenting opinion, said that the *Munn* doctrine was superfluous and that the New York law (overthrown by the majority) should be upheld. Price regulation by states did not require such an extraordinary legal argument as Lord Hale's essay; rather, Holmes said: "The truth seems to me to be that, subject to compensation when compensation is due, the legislature may forbid or restrict any business when it has sufficient force of public opinion behind it."[32]

In the end Holmes was right, but so was Taft, and the *Munn* decision was destined to change the relationship between government and business. *Munn* put the Supreme Court's stamp on the idea that in American capitalism, private property was subject to government regulation even if that property had not benefited from a special license or franchise, or was subject to eminent domain. The Supreme Court narrowed down the *Munn* doctrine over the years, incurring obloquy both for usurping legislative power when state laws were struck down and for turning the courts into an ideological arena by favoring laissez-faire: it had made a "choice . . . among competing schools of economic thought," as Justice Holmes put it in *Lochner*. Despite all this, the *Munn* idea persisted. World War I had provided more precedent for direct government control, and in the 1920s the Court fought doggedly against *Munn* doctrine legislation coming up from the states. Taft had been correct, and American capitalism was compromised by *Munn*. In 1933 New York fixed the minimum price of milk on the ground that milk production was affected with a public interest. In the resulting test, *Nebbia v. New York* (1934), the Court upheld the New York law, but said: "It is clear that there is no closed class or category of businesses affected with a public interest."[33] That is what Holmes had said in his dissent to *Tyson v. Banton* (1927), New York claimed that theater-ticket scalping was an enterprise clothed in the public interest. There was no retreat from this incursion against the rights of property to be free of public control, only a broadening of regulatory powers. It was a paradox that in their victorious battle against *Munn* the Supreme Court conservatives loosed a far more ambitious regulatory doctrine in *Nebbia*. It put the power of the regulating colonial governments on the federal level three hundred years after its Massachusetts beginnings.

The Granger cases were mainly concerned with state regulation of railroads. It was here that the *Munn* decision pushed another constitutional issue to the fore. Since Chief Justice John Marshall's decision in *Gibbons v. Ogden* in 1824, the commerce clause had not been imposed in a regulatory fashion for more than half a century. With *Munn* the state legislatures were regulating commerce. Railroads, by their nature, were involved in commerce between the states. It was only a matter of time before the federal government would be forced to assume permanent active intervention in railroad affairs. The railroads simply attracted legislation and regulation. Too much land, too many interests, too much government was, and had been, involved in them from the beginning.

Even though the creation of the Interstate Commerce Commission in 1887 seems the logical result of the *Wabash* case, which eliminated the basis of state railroad regulation under the *Munn* doctrine, the general background is important. The celebrated abuses of the railroads, charged with monopoly, exploitation, fraud, corruption, and worse, are a well-known part of American history of the period. There is no doubt that such was the widespread belief at the time, and hostility to the great new innovation, or at least to its management, was real. The federal government had given more than 100 million acres of public land to build railroads, and it was claimed that the railroads' charges were excessive as well as discriminatory. The milieu of the Granger laws favored direct control of some sort. Moreover, it is argued, the railroads themselves favored federal control over that of state legislatures. The railroads, along with other corporations, had claimed protection under the Fourteenth Amendment's due-process clause. Corporations had become legal beings with rights of legal domicile via *Dartmouth College v. Woodward* and *Bank of Augusta v. Earle* in the early years of the century, and from 1868 the Fourteenth Amendment had protected "persons" from loss of property without due process of law. In 1886, in *Santa Clara County v. Southern Pacific Railroad* the beings of *Dartmouth College* were held to be in fact legal persons. Appeal to the federal power on those grounds was an escape route from state control.[34] The railroads also were motivated by the developing legal doctrine of "concurrent power": unless Congress acted, the states could regulate matters even of national concern—such as interstate rates—that impinged upon the affairs of the states. There could be no power hiatus under this doctrine.

Attempts before 1887 in Congress to create such regulation had been unsuccessful. After the *Wabash* case, those efforts, however fruitless, seemed justified. Something appeared to be gained by all relevant interests from government regulation. Hence the public, the railroads themselves, and factions in Congress had all prepared themselves when the time came for a federally established power to regulate nationwide common carriers.

The hand of federal control of railroads had been visible since the Civil War, when the Union government had taken over some railroads, authorized new construction, and made loans and grants of land for it. During the war, Congress had authorized construction of the Union, Central, and Northern Pacific railroads. Federal land grants and loans were made, and scandal had followed the Union and Southern Pacific. In reaction, the Thurmond Act of 1878 had required that 25 percent of the Union and Central Pacific railroads' net earnings be put into a sinking fund to retire their indebtedness to the government. Upholding the act a year after the *Munn* decision, Chief Justice Waite held such federal intervention to be reasonable. Field, a dissenter in *Munn*, also dissented in the Sinking Fund cases: such federal intervention would "create insecurity in the title to corporate property."[35] Events had nearly overtaken Field, even then. In 1873 the House considered federal establishment of a board of commissioners of commerce to control railroads. A year later a bill to regulate railroads with a board of nine commissioners actually passed the House, but not the Senate. In 1878, the year after *Munn*, Congress established a railroad accounts auditor within the Department of Interior—a title later changed to commissioner. There followed more direct attempts to legislate. In 1878 the Reagan Bill, regulating interstate commerce and railroads, passed the House but failed in the Senate. The next year more bills were attempted, but failed. In the years between *Munn* and the *Wabash* case, state regulation earned for the entire period the label "extreme states rights period."[36]

In 1885 Senator Shelby Cullom of Illinois succeeded in convincing a select committee of the Senate to "investigate and report upon the subject of regulation of transportation by railroad and water routes in the United States." The committee's report, known as the Cullom Report, was released in January 1886; in October the *Wabash* case was reported out of the Supreme Court. This set the stage. It would now be federal legislation or nothing. Cullom's bill, which contained regulation by commission and which had already been considered once, was now debated again, and this time passed. In the House the Reagan Bill was reconsidered, and passed. The two bills were referred to conference, and the Interstate Commerce Act was the result.[37] Thus, the Interstate Commerce Commission came from a lengthy and complex historical development involving an entire spectrum of social forces, the law, the railroads, and the people and their political representatives.[38] What is more, the act fell back on the language and tradition of the common law and of ancient uses. If Chief Justice Waite could be criticized by his colleagues for introducing the "antiquities" of English legal history into modern America by dragging in the ghost of Lord Hale, what of the Interstate Commerce Act? The language of section 1, that all rates must be "just and reasonable," goes far beyond Lord Hale into the mists of English history, as does the whole notion of the common carrier, a special class of business automatically subject to regulation in the common law of England.[39] If its detail met the needs of modern America, the general philosophy of the act was blessed by the usage of centuries.

Even though it took years of litigation and legislation before effective rate regulation was lodged in the ICC, it was inevitable that such would occur, once the initial step had been taken. Americans were not willing, after the Revolution, to overthrow their system of law, and hence the patterns of the colonial settlements and their English ancestors were renewed by fresh application as the country developed. Thus it was not excessively novel to introduce a seventeenth-century English common-law doctrine en masse into nineteenth-century America, as was done with *Munn*. In any case, as Professor Harry Scheiber's research has shown, Lord Hale's doctrine had been applied extensively in state courts before it was taken as the rule in *Munn*.[40] The 1887 act setting up the ICC was not more than a huge version of a New England town-control ordinance. Nor was it illogical. First, control of the service and of the charges of common carriers was an ancient common-law tradition, both in England and America. It is inconceivable that this power would not have descended upon the railroads, even without *Munn*. Second, the power of price control was a commonly exercised police-power prerogative of governments and was inherent in the commerce clause of the constitution. Third, the railroads were special-action franchises, government creatures with the power of eminent domain from their very beginnings, and as such were exercising delegated powers of sovereignty. Such enterprises had no real defense against regulatory power since, in effect, they were an arm of government—they had the power to take private property by eminent domain.

Such general considerations seem clear enough, but after the fact. Congress was wary of granting federal control powers, and did it only piecemeal; the courts resisted inroads into private capitalism implied by the rate-making power, and then participated in this control over the fruits of private ownership. The definition of "just and reasonable" rates had been left to the ICC initially. Until 1897 the ICC heard complaints and set maximum rates it considered to be just and reasonable. Adverse court decisions in 1896 and 1897 eliminated this part of the commission's power. In 1889 the Court concluded in *Smythe v. Ames* that reasonable rates must include reasonable profits.[41] In 1906, after a period of confusion, the Hepburn Act explicitly gave the commission power to set maximum rates within a specified procedure. But where were such powers to end? An inventive population continually produced new means of communication that involved the transport of economic goods; information, for example. In 1910 the Mann-Elkins Act extended ICC controls to telephone, telegraph, and cable services. Other legislation was necessary to strengthen the commission as its powers extended into the heart of business practice. Accounting rules had to be made uniform, the power to subpoena had to be created, penalties imposed, and rules made concerning appeal and enforcement.

Wisdom was not immediately available, and parts of each legislative expansion were doomed to failure; for example, the Commerce Court established under the Mann-Elkins Act. In 1913 Congress passed an act ordering that rates be set on the basis of a fair return to asset valuation. But how much were a railroad's assets worth? The commission was enlarged, and specialized divisions were set up as the control obligations multiplied. In 1917 the ICC was given power to regulate railroad car-pooling under the Esch Act. The commission's powers had been extended earlier to Pullman cars, lounge cars, and refrigerator cars. Special legislation was required to cope with the rate-discrimination practices that the railroads had perfected to exploit their markets. During the First World War the government took over the railroads, and as a result of this experience, the Transportation Act of 1920 gave the ICC more control over terminal management, securities issues, abandonments, mergers, and construction. Rates were equalized between roads, with the inevitable consequence that, for the sake of equity, profits had to be redistributed between high- and low-cost lines (the "recapture clause"). To make matters even more complex, in the *Minnesota* and *Shreveport* cases in 1913 and 1914, and later in the Wisconsin passenger fares case of 1922, the Supreme Court ruled that the ICC had power to regulate intrastate as well as interstate rates of common carriers. The Hepburn Act had also made pipelines common carriers and subject to regulation, a natural concomitant of railroad regulation, since the two forms of transport were competitive. Water transport was also partially under ICC regulation from 1887 onward and became more so by a long evolution of experiment and legislation.[42]

This sort of history of bureaucratic growth and development can be extended at great length, as the work of I. L. Sharfman shows.[43] The example is instructive for the historian. Even the briefest description of the ICC's early history demonstrates how a simple mechanism of nonmarket control quickly became complex and unwieldy. Such should not be surprising. Production and distribution of goods and services involve an infinity of decisions. The market mechanism encapsulates these in the price bargains of all individuals. The administration of the price mechanism is essentially decentralized to the smallest units. Specific regulation means that rules must be made to fit unnumbered individual cases. The ICC, our first major federal regulatory body, was established in response to public clamor against the abuses of monopoly power of the railroads and to centralize the control at the federal level. It seems logical when one reads the accounts of 1887 and before. But what followed acquired an appalling complexity, and fairly quickly too, as the nonmarket control, specific to specific cases, had to be extended repeatedly to become effective, and to embrace the interests of the public, the courts, the regulated industries, and the ICC itself. Even with the best performance, this kind of nonmarket regulation would have to be cumbersome. In our political and legal system, scope existed for all concerned to make the regulation complex, and so it became. In 1966 Mark Green reported that handling the 270,000 rate proposals filed each year, the ICC conceivably had jurisdiction over 43 trillion possible rates.[44] It is not surprising that charges against the ICC include complaints that its decisions are tardy.

Regulation of common carriers led to nearly ubiquitous control since competing modes of transport left free could underbid the regulated forms. Hence commission control spread throughout interior forms of transport: pipelines, waterways, cables, telegraphs, telephones, and trucks. When air transport developed, a separate agency was created to embrace that, as was the case with radio and television. The result of an initial foray into direct and specific regulation in 1887 was that as technical advances transformed our methods of transport and communications, an enormous apparatus of regulatory power developed alongside them. Since the regulation involved intricate control and rate-making procedures, the regulated industries came to be largely exempted from the antitrust laws.[45]

The 1887 act had said that rates should be just and reasonable. The wisdom of Solomon would not suffice to carry out this charge in a giant modern economy. As the primary sources of expertise were the regulated industries themselves, those industries assumed increasing power over the regulatory apparatus.[46] Such has been the surprising harvest of the 1887 act. What seemed simple at first developed a complexity that staggers the imagination. Yet in a peculiar way, this Gargantuan apparatus of control faithfully mirrors the original models: the English and colonial American villages, with their ordinances and viewers and searchers, enforcing the ancient powers of government control over common callings. The thing gives one pause. A country such as ours, devoted to the common-law pattern of life—legislation followed by court test—probably could not have done it any other way. To some extent the system we have, then, was imposed upon us by history. The term *path-dependent* from computer jargon applies.

As a reaction to the agrarian revolt, which aimed at railroads and corporate power in general, the ICC was fairly limited in scope. A more far-reaching kind of nonmarket control came in 1890 in the Sherman Antitrust Act—again, an idea of initial simplicity that was destined to become an intellectual labyrinth.[47] Antitrust control is general, and indeed, as Kayson and Turner estimated, by the late 1950s less than 20 percent of national income, that is, income generated in this country, was free of antitrust control.[48] The advantage of general over specific control of the regulatory agencies is that, within the rules of the game, entrepreneurs are relatively free in their pricing and service strategies. They are only regulated as regards combination, not as regards either the quality or price of service or product. Far more scope is given for the price mechanism to operate within the restrictions set by control. Decisions tend to be economic decisions, not responses to administrative rules, and can therefore still be efficient in the economist's sense of that word: profits can be maximized with respect to costs in the factor market and in demand conditions. The problem is enforcement. Since antitrust cases are commonly tried in the law courts, and the Justice Department is the main source of regulation, the possibility of capture of the regulatory body by the regulated is, or should be, nil. But changes in products and technology together with innovations in business practice are a constant strain on the Antitrust Division. In U.S. history it has usually been efficiency, measured by low prices, that has been the symptom of undue economic power. The great English economist, Alfred Marshall, thought this would be the normal tendency of the free market, as efficient entrepreneurs drove the inefficient to the wall.[49] But Marshall expected that mortality rates, together with the tendency of succeeding generations to be more feckless, would hold down the long-term threat of monopoly based upon entrepreneurial efficiency. He lived in a world of proprietorships and partnerships. With the corporation, ownership is indeed removed by mortality, but management need not be, as it can be constantly replenished. There need never be a respite.

The Sherman Act represented new phenomena in American life, just as did the ICC. In the latter case it was new forms of transport on a massive scale; in the former, giant enterprises, primarily in manufacturing and finance. The corporation was the target for Populist wrath. The event was foreshadowed in President Cleveland's annual message to Congress in 1888: "As we view the achievements of aggregated capital, we discover the existence of trusts, combinations, and monopolies, while the citizen is struggling far in the rear, or is trampled to death beneath an iron heel. Corporations, which should be the carefully restrained creatures of the law and the servants of the people, are fast becoming the people's masters."[50]

With the Sherman Act of 1890, the Clayton Act of 1914, and the Federal Trade Commission Act of 1914, the Congress of the United States made a radical, and curious, departure in economic history. Whereas the ideas behind *Munn* and the ICC were hallowed by experience and the common law, such cannot really be said of antitrust legislation. To be sure, some common-law precedent was found, but it is not convincing; as nineteenth-century lawyers themselves pointed out in court, in common law only unreasonable restraints of trade were held to be illegal.[51] In the Sherman Act the word is *every*, which came to be understood as *all*, with the specific exemptions of regulated industries, trade unions, and the individual exceptions that make up the morass of antitrust case law. The courts have tried in vain to find a consistent interpretation.

The antitrust laws gave rise to a secular religion regarding American capitalism that is interesting, since the clear implication of antitrust enforcement, from my viewpoint, is that the economic factor, which had become scarce by the late nineteenth century, was competitive capitalism itself! Trust-busting became, *ipso facto*, a virtue, in order that the sensitive plant, the competitive system, be nourished. Left to itself, it was believed, American capitalism would become merely an economic oligarchy of giant corporations. Justice Harlan Stone said as much in his dissent in a *Munn* doctrine case, *Ribnik v. McBride* (1928), concerning a New Jersey law imposing controls over fees charged by private employment agencies. He placed laissez-faire and the competitive system in a surprising juxtaposition, one of mutual *incompatibility*. He argued that, in fact, interference by the courts and other control agencies must maintain competition by setting up rules of the game, or else manipulate and control the game itself, laissez-faire, whenever it produced monopoly power as the natural outcome of competition.[52] Herbert Hoover would later express a similar view: "In my philosophy the anti-trust acts had emancipated and protected the American people . . . from the vicious growth of *laissez-faire* economics inherited from Europe. . . . European industry with its uncontrolled *laissez-faire* had grown into a maze of cartels, trusts and trade restraints the result of which was to stagnate improvements in favor of price and distribution controls."[53]

Similarly, when the Northern Securities Trust was broken up under the Sherman Act in 1903 because that organizational masterpiece of James J. Hill, Edward Harriman, and J. P. Morgan had lessened the sum of competition among the railroads, Oliver Wendell Holmes, dissenting, noted the shift away from antitrust to protection of competition. The Court had reasoned "as if maintaining competition were the expressed object of the Act. The Act says nothing about competition."[54] Americans wanted both; they wanted the efficiency and stability of big business and the freedom and flexibility of competition. As Herbert Hovenkamp demonstrates, around 1890 the law provided Americans with justification for both. The evolution of legal and economic theory held that some restraints of trade were legal, and some were not, that competition both embraced many kinds of collusion, and also did not. The latter interpretation came from developing technical ideas in neoclassical economic theory that condemned every kind of market that was not in a state of perfect competition as not being competitive at all. The wild confusion of the early legal actions under the Sherman Act were thus inevitable. Different judges believed different versions of competition and restraint of trade.[55] It would take decades to sort it out, even to the extent that such clarification was achieved.

Some historians have written as if monopoly in the late nineteenth and early twentieth centuries was an aberration within the dynamic world of competitive capitalism. The development of the antitrust tradition implies the opposite: that American capitalism is normally a world of structured economic power in which competition is ever endangered and that competition cannot survive in this world unless it is constantly protected from market forces.

Moreover, it is clearly implied that competition leads to monopoly, so too much competition is also a bad thing; it is ruinous and destructive, unfair, and it must be forbidden. This seeming illogic, an inherent part of the world of antitrust, represents a fundamental shift in American thought, or at least seems to. Insofar as we can tell, there was not extensive or publicly expressed doubt about the virtues of competition between the Revolution and the Civil War, apart from protective-tariff arguments; and there, since the protectionists usually won out, it would seem that Americans were certainly opposed to one kind of competition—foreign.

It is often said that Americans lost their faith in competitive capitalism in the 1930s when the system clearly malfunctioned. But the Sherman Act alone shows that doubts were there much earlier. If, as some have suggested, Congress never meant for the act to be enforced, that it was merely a sop to Populist sentiment, history played an unfair trick. Subsequent legislation merely reenforced the non-market control over the price mechanism in the name of antitrust, or for the sake of the preserving of not-too-much competition, as in the case of the Robinson Patman Act of 1935 and the subsequent state fair trade laws that legalized price-fixing by manufacturers.

Now, it must not be supposed that an irrational system is an undesirable one to most people. Many desirable things are in some sense irrational. Moreover, what was irrational to some was rational to others. In a recent paper Gary Libecap shows that some of the moving spirits of the Sherman Act knew precisely what they were doing: they were attempting to rein in the power of large business organizations in the interests of the more numerous, and politically effective, small businesses of the country. The appropriate methods had just been applied in meat inspection legislation adopted to slow down the growth of the great Chicago meat packers who were using refrigeration to make a national market for themselves.[56]

The Americans obviously preferred the halfway house of antitrust to the full blast of the price mechanism, or to more rigid nonmarket control mechanisms beyond those imposed by commission-style systems like the ICC, or to the direct police-power controls such as those embodied in *Munn*-doctrine legislation. The Sherman Act and its amendments and supplements placed competitive capitalism within legal constraints beyond those derived from the traditions of its colonial and English past. There is little evidence that the people object to this constraint. There has been no great movement to repeal the antitrust laws.

Section I of the Sherman Act, quoted at the beginning of this chapter, ruled all restraints of trade illegal. Section 2 said that monopolies, or attempts to create monopolies, were misdemeanors. William B. Hornblower, writing in 1911 in the *Columbia Law Review*, said that the Sherman Act had been carefully constructed, debated, and amended by the best legal minds in the Senate: "One would have supposed that if ever a statute would prove to be unambiguous, intelligible and enforceable, this would be that statute; yet it is safe to say that no statute ever passed since the foundation of the government has been the subject of more difference of opinion or the cause of more perplexity, both to judges and lawyers than this same statute."[57]

Yet, by that time the beginning of the antitrust tradition was in place. In 1899, in the *Addyston Pipe* case, the Court held that price fixing by cartels was illegal, and, in later cases, that no rule of reason could be applied to price fixing (as in the common law of England). In 1904 the *Northern Securities* case made trust-busting a respectable substitute in cases of large firms where evidence of actual monopoly practice was lacking. The Northern Securities Trust was broken up, in part because President Roosevelt desired that such action be taken. In 1911 a more substantial monopoly business, Standard Oil of New Jersey, was ordered dissolved. These landmarks were probably obscured to contemporaries like Hornblower by events such as the *E. C. Knight* case in 1895, in which the government's case was lost against acquisition of competing firms by the Sugar Trust, or the *Addyston Pipe* case, in which part of the price-fixing ring involved achieved its goals by merger. The use of the Sherman Act against labor unions during the Pullman strike in 1894 had raised further questions about the Sherman Act. It had been Hornblower's opinion that strict application of the Sherman Act would "produce chaos in the business world."

Business was put under additional reins in 1914 by amendments to the Sherman Act: the Clayton Act and the Federal Trade Commission Act. The Clayton Act prohibited price discrimination if the result was held either to substantially reduce competition or to create monopoly power. The Clayton Act also stated (section 6) that labor was "not a commodity or article of commerce," and that labor organizations were not to be held as "illegal combinations or conspiracies in restraint of trade." Since interpretations of the Clayton Act were left to the courts, there remained a long future of further legislation and rulings before established unionism could comfortably exist in the American economy. The Clayton Act, "labor's Magna Carta," was not quite that in fact. But the act did specify as illegal such practices as price discrimination, tying contracts, acquisitions of stocks in competing companies, and interlocking directorates.

In 1914 the recent past had included one of the most sensational periods of antitrust and antimonopoly feeling. Two presidents, Roosevelt and Taft, had molded vociferous antitrust politics into effective electoral power. Congress had also entered into this profitable attack on big business with such well-publicized investigations as the Stanley Committee's probe of U.S. Steel, and the Pujo Committee in 1913 investigating the money trust. The Clayton Act and the Federal Trade Commission Act both reflected such political realities. With Woodrow Wilson and his New Freedom in the White House and surviving progressives and reformers of the Populist period in the seats of power (William Jennings Bryan was Secretary of State in the first Wilson cabinet), an era of new federal nonmarket constraints on American capitalism was inevitable. Both the Clayton Act and the Federal Trade Commission Act were responses to the demand to put teeth into the Sherman Act. The Federal Trade Commission began in that atmosphere, and started a vigorous series of interdictions of business practices restrained only by the courts, which were more conservative. The FTC, charges Gilbert Montague, was a case of "multiple impersonation," assuming the roles of "complainant, jury, judge and counsel."[58] Its coercive power lay in its cease and desist orders against unfair practices, and it was subject to constraints only by the courts, together with its own internal rulings on its own investigations. The five appointed commissioners had a permanent staff, and the FTC could hold investigations and seek enforcement of its orders in the courts.

Hence between the Granger cases and the 1914 antitrust legislation state legislatures, Congress and the courts had warranted and promoted three distinct kinds of nonmarket controls over American business: controls at the statehouse level under the *Munn* doctrine, permanent federal independent commissions under the commerce clause in the ICC and the FTC, and Executive initiatives authorized by the Sherman and Clayton acts. There also were other laws under the general police powers, such as the Import Tea Act of 1897 and the Food and Drug Act of 1906, which represented public reactions against abuses by business. But scale changes of business agglomerations in the post-Civil War era lent particular importance to the common-law and commerce-power controls. They were reactions to presumed failures of laissez-faire and *caveat emptor*—crudely, every man for himself and let the buyer beware. The concentration of economic power in industry, transportation, and finance represented by such new giants as Standard Oil, United States Steel, the great meat packers, the railroad companies, and the centralization of financial power associated with the rise of Wall Street have traditionally been considered the focal points of agitation. And indeed, such companies as these in expanding economic sectors quickly became targets for investigation and regulation once the necessary powers and agencies had been erected.

Overtly the complaint against big business was that its services and products were not only too expensive and unfairly priced, but that changes in the economy's structure had given big business monopoly or quasi-monopoly powers. The latter could not be countered by individuals on the demand side of the market, so federal intervention was called for, and it came to be viewed as a panacea. The price mechanism had failed to allocate scarce resources fairly.[59] The developing economy was becoming increasingly interdependent. No western frontier of cheap, rich land was available as an alternative. A rapidly growing urban population with major portions of economic life placed by federal power under nonmarket control was part of a new conception of economic life in which Americans regarded unsatisfactory performance by industry as a license for government intervention. (The day would come when they felt the same about job security.) Since this expanded government power was permanent, those who participated in the politics of discontent in the decades after the Civil War succeeded better than they knew. The social contract of the American democracy was changed, and by 1914 business enterprise had entered an era of controlled, if unstable, capitalism. More than merely the physical frontier was gone.

LORD BRYCE AND THE FIRST REACTION

James Bryce, writing in the *American Commonwealth*, was perplexed by the growth of nonmarket control in the United States.[60] He thought its origins came from sheer hubris. The man on the street was not frightened of government power, he had no conception of *der Staat* as the Europeans knew it—"a great moral power the totality of wisdom and conscience and force of the people, yet greater than the sum of the individuals who compose the people."[61] Bryce saw that Americans had little regard for such things. In the United States it was the individual citizen who mattered, almost alone:

> In America . . . even the dignity of the state has vanished. It seems actually less than the individuals who live under it. The people . . . inspire respect or awe, the organism is ignored. The State is nothing but a name . . . administrative machinery. . . . It has no more conscience, or moral mission, or title to awe and respect, than a commercial company for working a railroad or a mine; and those who represent it are treated in public and in private with quite as little deference.[62]

In that case, what then motivated American society? Bryce said there were beliefs so universally held among nineteenth century Americans as to be axiomatic. They were:

1. The right to "enjoy what he has earned," and the right to free speech are "primordial."
2. Sovereign power comes *only* from the people.
3. Governments, officials, government employees ought to be kept in check by law, by each other, and by the "shortness of the terms of office."
4. Whenever a given government function may be discharged at any level, then the local government should do it "for a centralized administration is more likely to be tyrannical, inefficient and impure."
5. Two men are wiser than one, twenty wiser than two. The will of the majority is the source of political wisdom and justice.
6. The less government the better.[63]

A people who believed this would seem to be a poor candidate to support the growth of big government. Yet the majority did support it. Why? One must have some sort of an explanation for such a momentous contradiction. Bryce argued that there were two sources of belief in the virtues of laissez-faire: the sentimental and the rational. The American in the street, he said, had only sentimental attachment to the doctrine, "the desire of the individual to be let alone, to do as he pleases, indulge his impulses, follow out his projects." That was easy enough to accommodate; it was, after all, not more than the mind of the squatter. As for the rational ground, that took study; it came from the minds of great (mainly English and European) thinkers. "The [rational] view, incessantly canvassed in Europe has played no great part in the United States; or rather it has appeared in the form not of a philosophic induction from experience, but of a common-sense notion that everybody knows his own business best, that individual enterprise has 'made America,' and will 'run America' better than the best government can do."[64]

Logic is forever, but sentiment changes with circumstances, and when the world of the squatter on the land vanished, those now settled on the land wanted to control those who still believed in laissez-faire, the rising industrialists and financiers to whom the squatter mentality made sense; for those with access to resources from the remaining public lands, or to laborers coming right off the immigration ships, squatter ideals still made sense.

The seedbed of government intervention was the state legislature—a point that modern students of government growth never can seem to understand. The agrarians controlled the state legislatures in most states. Bryce believed that Americans, so used to creating governments, had no fear of them. Americans were in a hurry to build the country and were impatient with social and political evolution. What did not come from free-market contracting could be, if desired, created by legislation. Americans wanted to solve problems right away. Besides:

> There are benefits which the laws of demand and supply do not procure. Unlimited competition seems to press too hardly on the weak. The power of groups of men organized by incorporation as joint-stock companies, or of small knots or rich men acting in combination, has developed with unexpected strength in unexpected ways, overshadowing individuals and even communities, and showing that the very freedom of association which men sought to secure by law when they were threatened by the violence of potentates may, under the shelter of the law, ripen into a new form of tyranny.[65]

So lay on the controls.

Americans, Bryce contended, did not fear government: "They may strip it tomorrow of the power which they have clothed it today."[66] Theory—reasoning from logic why enlargement of the state power might become permanent and threaten the Americans' great creation, the nineteenth century free-market economy—frightened no one. "Economic theory did not stop them, for practical men are proud of getting on without theory."[67] Besides, the new controls were always said to benefit "the greater number" at the expense of the minority—the vulgar democratic notion of justice, truth and beauty. So they plunged in. Bryce ends his essay, "Laissez Faire," with a long list of control legislation imposed at the state level by the state legislatures. (Municipal ordinances would have vastly multiplied his list.) Bryce marvelled at the ubiquity of state nonmarket control measures, which he said far exceeded anything known in the

1890s in Europe. He considered, in point of fact, American state legislatures to be trailblazers of the world in the creation of government interference in free markets: "The policy of state interference as a whole has not yet been adequately tested. In making this new departure American legislatures are servicing the world, if not their own citizens, for they are providing it with a store of data for its instruction."[68]

It is obvious that not many members of state legislatures read Bryce in the 1890s, and more obvious that modern scholars who think the New Deal and the crises of the twentieth century *caused* big government also are innocent of Bryce's insights. He knew us well.

THE CENTRAL BANK RETURNS

The Populist rage was directed at finance as well as at transportation and industry. But since much of the financial system already operated under controls, the appeal for more regulation could hardly promise fast or easy success. The national banks, with a third of total deposits, already were under federal regulation. The state banks were under various controls, so their deficiencies, however extensive, were not due to absence of control. Innovation was called for. The problem with American banking was rooted in its basic vulnerability: a fractional reserve banking system is illiquid; the depositors cannot be paid if deposits are withdrawn en masse. Even in England where, under the gold standard and the Bank of England Act of 1844, nineteenth-century banking had reached the apex of monetary science, financial troubles were not absent. In the long years of their Great Depression, 1873–96, a period corresponding roughly to our own age of agrarian unrest, prices had fallen year after year, unemployment was endemic, relieved only by large-scale emigration, and long-term economic stagnation taxed the theories of economists, bankers, and statesmen alike.[69]

In the United States, conditions were held to be even less desirable. Stability had never been a leading characteristic of the American monetary system. The severe banking panics of the antebellum period had been superseded by the suspension of specie payments during the Civil War. In the decades that followed there seemed much to complain of. The new National Banking System aroused the bitter antagonism of the farmers, and decade after decade they called for the familiar nostrums: a return to a system of expanded fiat money, free silver, and the sub-treasury system. Then in the 1890s the United States Treasury itself was barely able to meet its specie obligations.

President Cleveland called upon the hated moguls of Wall Street to get European gold for U.S. government bonds sold at rates held to be a scandalous giveaway. The various silver purchase acts not only failed to cause prices to rise (as true believers in the silver interest had hoped), but the Sherman Silver Purchase Act of 1890 had provided for automatic conversion into gold of Treasury notes that had been issued to purchase silver at a price subsidized above the market. This caused the famous "endless chain," wherein silver purchases drained the Treasury of gold. Financial panics and periodic mass bank suspensions had continued, with severe dislocations in 1873, 1893, and again in 1907. There was financial pressure in other years. In addition to minor periods of stringency, there was the sensational stock market panic of 1901 and the Northern Securities Panic, which had led Morgan, Hill, and Harriman to set up the giant Northern Securities Trust. There was a long list of bankruptcies and scandalous insolvencies in the railroads and corruption in the new insurance empire that led to the revelations of the Armstrong Committee in New York and to demands for stronger controls over that industry. The state banks had recovered from the loss of their note issues following establishment of the national banks, and had grown again in number, power, and instability. The Gold Standard Act of 1900 had ended officially the long national attachment to bimetallism, and that too was a source of unhappiness to the cheap-money interest.[70]

After the dust of the 1907 panic settled, the country's leaders began casting about for some method of imposing order upon the financial system. There had been no central bank since 1836. In times of panic the Treasury had attempted, with only limited success, to shore up the system by depositing money in key private banks. But the Treasury had insufficient powers to create credit-money. Issuance of clearing-house certificates in New York to meet that city's payrolls in 1907 pointed to a Populist-style remedy, one in keeping with American ingenuity in the creation of paper money. Accordingly, the Aldrich-Vreeland Act of 1908 empowered bank currency associations to be formed across the country to issue such "money" against their own assets in times of emergency. It also established a National Monetary Commission, a body whose report in 1912 proved to be of great importance, as it led directly to a more comprehensive system of money control. The power to create money according to need was demanded, and with that possibility came the appearance in 1914 of the country's third central bank, the Federal Reserve System. This time the country went back to originality in a big way. The original Federal Reserve System was established with twelve central banks.[71]

What should be understood regarding our country's return to central banking in 1914, and its mixed career afterward, is the contradictory nature of central banking itself and the utter lack of agreement in any sense about its *raison d'etre*. The idea of easier accommodation for business, and a bank of last resort for the banking system, is congenial to those who would borrow and to those who would have need of large amounts of readily available credit in times of emergency. But how much credit should there be? If the central bank can create money, how much should it create? Great issues were in the balance: investment, wages and employment, the price level, and the social impact of debt. The issues were the same as those faced by the colonial monetary experimenters, and the lines of battle that were drawn represented the same interests. The Populists had demanded the creation of legal tender of not less than fifty dollars per head. Little attention was paid to that. The most prestigious available paradigm, the Bank of England, was not of great use either. Privately owned and controlled, the Bank of England had long since ceased even to attempt to follow the ideas of those who wrote its organic law, the Bank of England Act of 1844. By that law a country's money supply should be primarily gold coin and notes representing bullion deposited in the central bank. The amount of both should be determined by movements in the balance of payments, representing the ultimate consequences of consumer sovereignty. The 1844 Bank Act, modeled after a plan written in the early 1820s by David Ricardo, was the clearest statement of nineteenth-century gold standard principles. The act had proved awkward in the crises of 1847, 1857, and 1866, and the governing body of the Bank of England had learned to operate with considerable discretion and to circumvent the Bank Act should trouble arise. In any case the congressmen, after the panic of 1907, had probably seen enough of the gold standard's automatic workings.

A great issue was at stake, one that had been fought out in England in the years before the passage of the 1844 act: Was there to be discretionary power to determine the money supply? The act of 1844 was an effort to reduce such powers to the minimum. Under the logic of that legislation, the level of economic activity was to be closely controlled by the price mechanism. Flows of specie through the balance of payments determined bank reserves and, perforce, all else. The effective social control was consumer preference. No government body was to have power to mitigate, or to stay, those decisions of the markets. Lord Overstone, whose ideas, following Ricardo, were embodied in the 1844 Bank Act, believed that occasional brutal financial contractions were necessary to purge the economy. The Bank of England was simply a fulcrum, expanding the money supply as gold flowed in, contracting it as gold flowed out. In this hypothetical world any central banking power to create money on paper assets would actually thwart the price mechanism. Hence only in extreme circumstances, as in the crises of 1847, 1857, and 1866, were provisions made for money creation against government debt to relieve financial pressure. Similarly, if a central bank were to create any level of money supply, to satisfy any nonmarket criteria of any kind, the price mechanism would be sabotaged. Hence the Bank of England rarely played a leadership role, having learned to live within the legislative corset given it in 1844.[72] The Americans wanted something more, an "elastic" currency that expanded with the needs of the times. Compared to the pure gold standard embodied in the act of 1844, almost all American proposals seemed the rankest heresy.

The National Monetary Commission Report of 1912 contained a long catalog of our banking system's deficiencies. The commission recommended establishment of a National Reserve Association, groupings of commercial bankers nationwide divided into fifteen districts with mixed control between banking and other business interests. The federal government played a minimal role. The commission said that its banker-dominated bill was "essentially an American system, scientific in its methods and democratic in control."[73] The proposal was in fact a virtual facsimile of Senator Nelson Aldrich's suggested *Plan for Monetary Legislation*, published the previous year.[74] The emphasis was on maintenance of maximum private power. When the Democrats swept into office with Wilson in 1912 they took over the proposed legislation, and the resulting Federal Reserve Act was signed by Wilson in December 1913. Most of the Aldrich bill's basic ideas remained in the Federal Reserve legislation: the country had multiple central banks, bound together by a governing body in Washington; ownership of the System was still private, and even though the Federal Reserve Board members in Washington were presidential appointees, and the Secretary of the Treasury and the Comptroller of the Currency were ex officio members, the district bank officers were nominees of the local banking fraternity. Compared to the Aldrich bill, the Federal Reserve System contained a strong mixture of political ingredients. But it was still not a government bank.

The Federal Reserve System began operations in 1914, a bank for bankers, doing no direct business with the public—a major departure from the First and Second Banks of the United States. Despite disclaimers that the United States had no tradition to build on, the opposite was true and helped to make the new system a partial success from the beginning: (1) a traditional acceptance of paper-money creation prevailed, (2) the national banks were compelled to become the nucleus of the new system, (3) the tradition of noninterest-earning central reserves of Boston's Suffolk System of 1828 was co-opted, and (4) the staggered reserve requirements of the various-sized cities that had existed since the National Bank Act, as amended in 1887, were also adopted. All of these formed the bricks and mortar of the new system. It had originally been thought, according to Professor Elmus Wicker, that a body of political magnitude, such as a regulatory commission like the ICC, had been created and that the Federal Reserve Board members held the hierarchical and ceremonial status of assistant secretaries—a matter of great importance amid the rustic bureaucratic punctilio of our capital city.[75]

No sooner was the new system organized than it was immersed in the complexities of wartime finance and committed to policies that were destined to compromise its freedom from Treasury influence.[76] There still was no real power of initiative in the day-to-day management in the original system. Money could be created on the basis of approved securities, but who was to decide the really basic issue: How much central bank money was there to be? As it turned out, the solution was partly found after the war by Benjamin Strong, governor of the New York Federal Reserve Bank, J. P. Morgan's trusted helper in the 1907 panic, and leader of the New York banking community. His Open Market Investment Committee, in operation from 1923, was the origin of modern central banking operations in the systematic direct purchase and sale of government securities for monetary policy reasons. Before that date the system simply tried to accommodate itself to the government's enormous fiscal needs, absorbing government securities in order to help give the patriotic Liberty Bond drives the patina of success.

Once the Open Market Committee began massive purchases and sales of government securities, using the combined reserves of the twelve District Federal Reserve Banks, there was a new power in the land. President Wilson's "assistant secretaries" had a day-to-day power potential over the realities of economic life greater than the president himself. Since Governor Strong was in the private sector of the Federal Reserve System (the New York Bank is owned by the member banks of the Second District) the System's independence from direct government control acquired a status that had not been foreseen. In the 1930s Strong's creation, the Open Market Committee, was to be taken over by the political appointees, the Federal Reserve Board, and in so doing they not only took the real power but acquired independent stature as well. Marriner Eccles, the Utah business polymath and "brains of the New Deal," was responsible for the changes when he wrote the Bank Act of 1935.[77]

The Federal Reserve System imposed controls over bank reserves, accounting procedures, and management, produced a uniform currency, cleared checks and collections on a national scale, handled government finance, and in most respects improved American banking beyond recognition. However, the Federal Reserve System was not designed simply as an efficiency device. It was charged, in its charter, to make the currency "elastic," that is, to vary its amount with the needs of business. That was supposedly the motivation of monetary policy; the Open Market Committee was merely a part of the means to that end. If the object of monetary policy really is to provide an amount of currency that will satisfy business demand without disturbing the general price level, and the Federal Reserve System is the only vehicle to achieve this, then the System is a failure today, and has been since its inception. There is no such thing as a neutral central bank policy. If the idea of the elastic currency, on the other hand, was to enable the nation's banking system to be mobilized to influence economic activity—for whatever purpose and at whatever level—then the System is a partial success. It could hardly be more, since the question about monetary policy—to what end?—is not answerable except in the usual platitudes about stability or, as Federal Reserve Board Chairman William McChesney Martin put it, "leaning against the wind." If that policy means anything at all, it means that the Fed should resist whatever the flow of economic activity is at any time, presumably, to oppose excesses. Benjamin Franklin had said it better than has any Federal Reserve official.

In 1914 there was even less wisdom than we have today about monetary policy and how to make the banking system more effective and reduce the impact of financial panics. The latter was not achieved by the Federal Reserve System, as the events of 1921, 1929, 1933, and 1938 would show. Demand for banking reform had been endemic. It was believed that our banking system was economically harmful, as the National Monetary Commission said in its report: "We have made a thorough study of the defects of our banking system, which were largely responsible for these disasters and have sought to provide effective remedies for these and other defects, in the legislation we propose."[78] Federal control simply had to be tried, they believed. What was not understood was the complexity of business fluctuations and the magnitude of *real* economic contractions represented by the large-scale financial panics—or, for that matter, the amount of elasticity the currency would really need if expansion were to be based upon money supply only. The thinking that went into the Federal Reserve Act was naive, even ignorant, by present-day standards.[79]

The 1913 Federal Reserve Act was a product of the upheavals of the previous four decades; it seemed destined to exist no matter what its intellectual justification. What the system became, though, was the product of subsequent events. The quasi-Populist origins were soon enough forgotten, and central-banking control replaced such ideas as the currency associations. The Federal Reserve System would attain gigantic powers; it is a pity it was so inconsistently managed for so much of its existence.

INSTITUTIONAL IMPACT OF WORLD WAR I

The material in this section is both complex and crucial to our understanding. Before the 1980s it was not given much prominence in conventional histories. Indeed, if this book were merely a descriptive history, this section, which centers on the First World War, would be a separate episode. But in certain crucial respects the development of our social control structure in 1917 and 1918 was a continuation of the changes wrought by the agrarian radicals, the Populists, and their successors in the Progressive movement of the early twentieth century. The latter essentially capitalized on the preceding decades of upheaval. In the 1930s we experienced a major shift to new ground, but the New Deal was in turn largely inspired by the experiences of World War I.[80] So many historical strands are here intertwined.[81]

The growth of federal control after 1914 spread from events that are usually treated as separate phenomena, external to normal economic life, but that had far-reaching permanent consequences: the First World War, the depression of the 1930s, the Second World War, and the Cold War. Arguments connecting these things causally have been partly convincing, but they are not entirely satisfying intellectually. It is possible, by extended argument, to see the depression of the 1930s as a consequence of World War I and the failure of adjustment afterward; to see the changes wrought by government control in the Second World War as a partial continuation of the New Deal; to see the post-1945 economy as a combined legacy of the New Deal and the war; and then simply to trace the continued expansion of government and its control powers and institutions under the impact of the Cold War as merely linear extensions of recent American historical experiences.

Let me digress a moment by way of illustration and examine two fundamental examples of this sort of historical continuity: the federal budget and, very briefly, the Employment Act of 1946, which will get a fuller treatment in the next chapter.

The establishment of federal budget power in the executive branch removed from private decision making part of its power to produce disequilibria that must be adjusted by fundamental realignment of productive factors and their prices. Boom-and-bust was wasteful of men and resources, but, as Professor Schumpeter emphasized long ago, such was the method whereby capitalism advanced.[82] Once the federal receipts and expenditures became items of managerial control, the power to manipulate was created, and as such, was bound to be used when the men and circumstances warranted such use. The Employment Act of 1946, which obligated the federal government to interfere with the consequences of the price mechanism to "promote maximum employment, production, and purchasing power," was a license to eliminate precisely those evils that Schumpeter thought were necessary to make free-market capitalism efficient. The act was vague, to be sure, and provided plenty of latitude for policy flexibility, but in fact, since 1946, unemployment, stagnation, and/or inflation have been chargeable to the federal government itself—a far cry indeed from old-time capitalism. The government was willing, as in the roman numeral phases of the 1971 Nixon economic program, to regulate prices and wages by its version of the colonial selectmen, the Price Commission and the Wage Board. The results were hardly impressive.

I will treat these matters in detail later. The point I want to emphasize here is that the wars of our century made such expansions of federal power possible. Federal power could attempt decisive solutions to economic problems that the price mechanism handled only by protracted adjustment processes. It was in this way that executive budgetary control and the full employment obligation were established.

Both Congress and the executive branch long had resisted attempts to establish highly organized budgetary procedures before the Bureau of the Budget was established with its own director in 1921. It was Wilson's wartime regime that finally made palatable, under the Republican Harding, that which had been looming since 1905 when Theodore Roosevelt's Keep Commission advocated reform in the expenditure process. Taft's sample federal budget in 1914 was ignored by a hostile Congress, but the idea of planned government budgets was gaining increasing support at the state levels, by actual adoption, and in national politics through party platforms. A vast federal expenditure increase, from $761 million in 1915 to a peak of nearly $19 billion in 1919, and an increase in the federal debt from $970 million to $25.2 billion in the same period had been accomplished primarily through expansion of the executive power. Such realities softened resistance to a centrally focused federal budgetary process.

Similarly, the American business community had continued its resistance to the New Deal innovations. But the euphoria of wartime release from the political and social tensions of the 1930s, the realization of government economic power in wartime in conjunction with the comprehension of this power that came from the new Keynesian economics, together with the desire of the Roosevelt-Truman administrations at the Bretton Woods negotiations to make a dramatic commitment to postwar stability—all of these combined to create that strange postwar atmosphere of optimism. Yet it was lingering fear of another depression, and trust in the panacea of government power, that made the 1946 act possible.

In both cases it may well be that the psychological influence of successful war efforts merely accelerated the inevitable: that Americans would have acceded in any case to centralization of power in the executive branch of government. But one wonders about that too. After both world wars there was intense pressure from the private sector as well as within government itself to dismember the federal straitjacket of direct control. But the force of such commitment to the free market and to decentralized economic power was diluted by the willingness to tolerate a residual of expanded power in Washington. In addition, there was the increased readiness, born of wartime experience, to call up direct government control in the event of future economic problems, both in the interwar years and after 1945. The heady experience of the war power in central administration made a return to aggregative nonmarket control devices less painful psychologically on each successive occasion for American capitalists, and in truth the vulnerability of all taxpayers to their 1040 tax forms must have reduced enormously the willingness to resist. The aura of the national emergency made American capitalists increasingly supine, as in August 1971, when President Nixon almost casually imposed the direct authority of the Executive Office over the lives of millions to facilitate his pursuit of inflationary policies without accepting the obvious consequences. By 1971 the leaders of the American economy apparently could accept direct controls with barely a whimper. In later administrations, the idea of the national security state made resistance to expansions of military and foreign aid programs (more that a quarter of which were for direct military purposes) politically unwise.[83]

War, and preparations for it, have been the most dramatic and steadily recurrent act of state for Americans in this century, and, like the citizens of the Roman Republic, we have gradually become hardened to it. In addition, of course, modern war directly engages the industrial and agricultural economies and is extremely profitable for those who neither fight nor have their gains taxed away—top businessmen, corporation executives, and political leaders. The direct legacy of war—the dead, the debt, the inflation, the change in economic and social structure that comes from immense transfers of resources by taxation and money creation—these things are obvious. What has not been so obvious has been the pervasive yet subtle change in our increasing acceptance of federal nonmarket control, and even our enthusiasm for it, as a result of the experience of war. As early as 1920, Secretary of the Treasury David Houston saw the issue clearly:

> The first impulse of many was to turn to the Government and especially to the Treasury, as the sole instrumentality for full economic salvation. This disposition, well developed before the war, was reinforced during hostilities by practices of the Government which became necessary for the successful prosecution of the war. It is this disposition, rather than self-aggrandizing efforts of Federal departments to extend their functions, which is the main explanation of mounting Federal budgets and of centralizing tendencies frequently criticized.[84]

Another seventy years would see no change of direction in this regard.

Such considerations shed a clearer light on the events of World War I and their connections both to the past and the future. The tremendous wave of reform that swept out of the Populist and, later, Progressive movements and that underlay Wilson's New Freedom, produced the federal control legislation exemplified by the Clayton Act, the Federal Trade Commission Act, and the Federal Reserve Act. This was decisive movement toward federal nonmarket control and not only represented dissatisfaction with the first wave, the *Munn* doctrine state laws, the ICC, and enforcement of the Sherman Act, but set the stage, both psychologically and structurally, for the massive intervention that came with the mobilization effort during the First World War.

There was then a concatenation of historical trends centered on the two Wilson administrations that must be considered simultaneously. The first administration was the capstone of the revulsion against the free-market capitalism that had come after the Civil War with the first formations of giant enterprises. The resulting agitation against trusts, monopolies, and big business in general produced the triumphant

Wilsonians and the New Freedom. Then came the wartime experience: direct controls over production, intervention in the bargaining process over wages, control of the railroad system, outright federal government organization and ownership of corporate businesses, and development of extraordinary financial linkages between the federal treasury and the new Federal Reserve System. The future crowded in closely upon the past.

The momentum of the Wilsonian reform movement continued to burst open solutions to long-deadlocked economic problems even before war actually came. Of particular import was the Adamson Act of 1916, which established the eight-hour day in railroads. This was the beginning of the end of the free wage bargain in industry. In contrast, the courts and Congress had both held that interstate commerce could not include actual production, and in *Lochner v. New York* in 1905 the Court ruled against a New York law limiting employment in bakeries to sixty hours a week, arguing that such a law interfered with the freedom of contract guaranteed by the Fourteenth Amendment. The Court also stopped Congress from interfering with other areas of wage employment, such as child labor. In *Hammer v. Dagenhart* (1918) the Court overturned the Child Labor Act of 1916, because labor performed in manufacturing was not interstate commerce and was not subject to congressional control. It was 1941 before the Court reversed this case. Reform of wages, hours, and working conditions was thus stalemated, with child labor in manufacturing industry sanctioned. The courts stuck with *Lochner* through the 1920s, but allowed exceptions. Finally in the 1930s the old doctrines were mainly swept away and federal government claimed and was granted ubiquitous power in the wage bargain. It was the Adamson Act of 1916 that started this long and irregular movement away from the ideal of the wage bargain as a market-directed bond between the employer and the individual employee. A railroad strike threatened; the government did not want it and settled the issues under the commerce power on the premise of national emergency. It was as simple as that. Thus vanished decades of careful legal construction. The federal government entered the place once occupied by the selectmen of the colonial townships. However wrongheaded, it had been the policy to keep the federal government out of the wage bargain. The Adamson Act was an example of a phenomenon that became ubiquitous: direct federal government entry into the private economy for reasons of national interest.[85]

Wilson's wartime government conducted a national mobilization of men and resources on a scale never seen before. Direct controls of all sorts were imposed by Congress and by the Executive under war powers. National emergency became the catch-all justification for extension of federal power into the private economy. From my viewpoint the actual wartime controls are largely irrelevant, since they represented no logical product of economic evolution; essentially the government decided to regulate whatever it wanted, and proceeded to control its existence. The wartime controls are interesting for other reasons, though: the number of precedents they set for peacetime nonmarket controls.

The federal apparatus began its wartime growth with the National Defense Act of 1916, which enabled the armed forces to expand, and the Shipping Act of 1916, which formally created a merchant marine under a United States Shipping Board empowered to regulate maritime commerce. A centrally focused bureaucracy began with the Army Appropriations Bill of 1917, in which provision was made for a Council of National Defense composed of various cabinet secretaries with an Advisory Commission to do the leg work. In his message of May 19, 1917, Wilson asked Congress for power to control prices and production, adding, in genuflection to the free-market tradition, that "The last thing that any American could contemplate with equanimity would be the introduction of anything resembling Prussian autocracy into the food control in this country." He produced the Federal Bureau of Investigation instead.

The resulting legislation, the Lever Food-Control Bill of August 10, 1917, was a prime vehicle of federal control during the war; its provisions were so wide-ranging that by 1919 Attorney General Alexander Palmer had his Intelligence Division (including the young J. Edgar Hoover) searching out "foreign radicals" under its auspices. At first even Lord Hale was conscripted, and the proposed legislation was justified because food production was clothed in the public interest. This well-worn path to nonmarket controls was not needed as the war powers became universally accepted. The Lever Act prohibited the destruction or hoarding of necessities and provided for a licensing system to control the flow of food and fuel supplies (with penalties for excess profits). Factories could be taken over for national defense and commodities requisitioned. The President was given power to set a minimum wheat price, thus partially acceding to long-time agrarian demands for federal intervention in the markets and setting a famous precedent for subsequent federal control of agriculture.[86]

Under the Lever Act, Wilson created the United States Food Administration and appointed Herbert Hoover to head it. There followed a successful control program of meatless and wheatless days. The act's provisions for direct production and price controls were the bases for establishment of the United States Fuel Administration, with Harry Garfield appointed as administrator. This agency fixed coal prices, purchased on its own account, controlled deliveries, and set up its own standards for labor relations. There were heatless days and Sundays patriotically spent without gasoline. The Food and Fuel Administrations were destined to be models for New Deal agencies in later years. As the network of agencies proliferated, the need for consolidation arose, which was met by the Overman Bill early in 1918. The War Industries Board, originally under the Council of National Defense, was made an independent branch of the Executive Office, with Bernard Baruch installed as its chairman. By then Commander-in-Chief Woodrow Wilson was nearing the peak of his authority, and he said simply of the board, in an executive order of May 28, 1918, that it was "to act for me and under my direction." Baruch's organization directly fixed prices to be paid by the government and set production priorities; its authority seems never to have been challenged.[87] Murray Rothbard may be correct when he argues that the WIB was so dominated by business executives creating their own deals via the government's new powers there was nothing to challenge.[88]

The government went directly into business with an innovation, the government-owned corporation, a co-option of one of American capitalism's most successful institutional developments. This piece of pseudo capitalism was destined to play a critical role in the future. There were precedents, of course: both the First and Second Banks of the United States were originally partly government-owned, the Federal Reserve System was a hybrid of private ownership and government control, and the railroad in the Canal Zone was an outright government company. The Emergency Fleet Corporation was set up under the Shipping Act of 1916 to mobilize shipping. It was incorporated under the laws of the District of Columbia, and went into shipbuilding on a massive scale. There followed the United States Grain Corporation, incorporated under the laws of Delaware, with its stocks mainly held by the government, except for private holdings sufficient to qualify private individuals as directors. The Grain Corporation bought grain and other commodities free of day-by-day congressional scrutiny. The United States Housing Corporation was established under the laws of New York and was headed by the Secretary of Labor. It condemned land, built houses for defense personnel, and provided a precedent for later federal entry into the private housing market in peacetime. On April 5, 1918, the War Finance Corporation was established to subsidize and underwrite bank loans to war industries—it was the forerunner of the Reconstruction Fi-

nance Corporation, President Hoover's desperation device to bail out
banks and railroads a decade later and was an innovation that was to
prove almost infinitely useful as a method of indirect government
control. With these and similar corporations, traditional preserves of
private capitalism were initially opened up to federal control under
the stress of war. Subsequent administrations of both political parties
owed Wilson a great debt for his pioneering ventures into the pseudo
capitalism of the government corporation. It enabled collective enterprise, as socialist as any Soviet economic enterprise, to remain
cloaked in the robes of private enterprise and thus to acquire political
neutrality in an ideologically hostile environment.

The most famous wartime entry of government into the private
economy in the Wilson era was, of course, the government takeover
of the railroads. This was done in a way that presaged the Gulf of
Tonkin Resolution in 1964. Under the Army Appropriations Act of
1916 the government was empowered in time of war "to take possession and assume control of any system or systems of transportation."
Senators involved in its passage later claimed that they envisaged the
possible need to move troops to the Mexican border. Wilson waited
until Congress had abandoned Washington during the Christmas of
1917 and then took over the railroads, as of December 28, by executive order. On January 4, 1918, Wilson appeared before Congress to
ask for the necessary legislation to endorse his actions.

The government's railroad venture was to have enormous long-
term consequences, even though the railroads were turned back to
private control after the war. In the first place, Wilson's action rees-
tablished the government's direct interest in transportation beyond
that implied by the creation of the ICC and the various Sherman Act
prosecutions of railroad mergers. Second, many of the deadlocked
issues of labor relations up to 1914, first breached by the Adamson
Act, were now handled directly. Wages were raised, and equipment
and rolling stock pooled. As the government became the largest single employer of labor, its policies were widely noted by all parties.
Under the President's Mediation Commission, headed by the Secretary of Labor, collective bargaining was encouraged. A War Labor
Board was established with representation for management and labor sitting side by side. The board supported unionization. After the
Supreme Court upheld the "Yellow Dog" contract (a pledge not to
engage in union activities) in *Hitchman Coal and Coke v. Mitchell* in
1917, the board resisted enforcement of such persecution for union
membership. The government took over the telegraph lines for the
duration when Western Union refused to reemploy men discharged
for union activity, and a strike threatened. When states passed laws

against union organizers, U.S. attorneys were ordered to supply defense.[89]

When, in the Transportation Act of 1920, the railroads were handed back to private control, extensive new peacetime controls over them were given to the ICC, including supervision of securities issues, equipment uses, terminal facilities, rates, construction, and abandonments, and in the recapture clause, efficient railroads were made to share profits with less efficient roads to make possible uniformity of rates. In the Railway Labor Act of 1926 a mediation board was provided, as during the wartime experience. The wage bargain was finally heading for a new kind of public control after decades of labor violence, and the experience of government as employer and manager in the First World War was the prime reason for it. As will be shown in the next chapter, it could hardly be shown that society was naturally moving in that direction by the evidence of the Court's rulings until the *Jones and Laughlin* case in 1937 established the Wagner Act with its National Labor Relations Board. It was the experience of wartime emergency powers that led to permanent federal involvement in the wage bargain.

The economic historian must feel a sense of frustration in dealing with such institutional changes wrought during the First World War. The forces involved were hopelessly entangled between previous peacetime developments and the exigencies of war powers—purposefully to some extent. There can be no doubt that Wilsonians used the occasion of war to carry through many of their reform ideas, as well as to enhance the defense effort. Much that came from it was thus only obliquely related to the main strands of history before 1914. The dam at Muscle Shoals, a point of origin for the Tennessee Valley Authority, was originally a project launched by the Defense Act of 1916, and only later became our greatest conservation effort. The conservation program before 1916 had little to do with Muscle Shoals. On the other hand, in 1918 Congress passed the Webb-Pomerene Act, sponsored by the Federal Trade Commission, so that American firms would not have to compete with each other in foreign markets. The long-term result was the international oil companies and their cartel, which cut short U.S. foreign oil supplies in 1973 and 1974, and 1979. This was hardly in the spirit of the 1914 legislation establishing the FTC, but Webb-Pomerene certainly was a true reflection of the protectionist-monopoly spirit that motivated much of big business. The war was a crucible into which many strains of American economic and social life were poured to structure the kind of society that could produce a military victory.

As in all our wars, a deposit of permanent historical change was left behind when peace came. When Harding called for a return to normalcy and ended the state of war in 1921, he was calling spirits from the deep. American society could not go back to 1914. Those parts of the war experience that would prove useful in the future would not be forgotten. The entire episode was clouded at the end by Wilson's desperate battle for his treaty and his unwillingness to give up the war powers that had made of the U.S. presidency that omnipotent office with which we have become so familiar. The Senate and the House opposed him successfully and gained lasting opprobrium from historians in so doing. But with our own modern experience of Vietnam one sees through sharpened vision the U.S. military mission to Armenia disguised as transport and economic experts, and Wilson's request on May 24, 1920, for the United States to accept a League of Nations Mandate in Armenia, in central Asia.[90] Congress was still jealous enough of its independence and suspicious of Executive ambitions to engage in great and dramatic adventures.

In the end normalcy reigned for a little while. But the members of the War Industries Board were in Washington soon enough to help establish Roosevelt's National Recovery Administration. It was Hoover himself who called back into life the War Finance Corporation as the Reconstruction Finance Corporation. The Lever Act's Fuel Administration was to reappear as the National Bituminous Coal Commission, and then as the Bituminous Coal Division of the Interior Department, setting also the precedent for the Interior Department's control of domestic oil production through the Texas Railroad Commission. Experience with federal wage setting would be a background for minimum wage laws, and government management experience paved the way for the Railway Labor Act of 1926 and the Wagner Act of 1935. The wartime housing agencies would reappear in the New Deal and in later administrations in which a government role in the nation's housing market came to be accepted. The Shipping Board was transmogrified into the United States Maritime Commission.[91]

So the exigencies of the First World War produced a selection of federal nonmarket social controls to join those that appeared with the agrarian revolt after the Civil War. New economic crises in the 1920s and 1930s would be the source of further innovations in capitalism, American style.

Chapter 5

THE SEARCH FOR STABILITY

> I conceive, therefore, that a somewhat comprehensive
> socialisation of investment will prove the only means of
> securing an approximation to full employment; though
> this need not exclude all manner of compromises and of
> devices by which public authority will co-operate with
> private initiative.
> —*John Maynard Keynes, 1936*

The New Deal in Its Historical Context

It should be apparent that nonmarket controls established between 1933 and 1938 did not constitute a social revolution. It simply was not. The New Deal was a continuation, an acceleration, a great augmentation of an historical trend in an extreme economic crisis.[1] Since the Civil War, interested groups had successfully used the political mechanism in order, by changes in law, to transfer segments of economic activity from control by the price mechanism to various nonmarket control agencies, which were increasingly becoming the American government. What became apparent was the hydralike nature of the nation's economic problems. New problems arose as old ones were solved or controlled, and frequently enough the solutions and controls themselves created new problems. The great natural endowment had given the heirs of colonial America the physical wherewithal to escape from privation, but the institutional framework could not ration out the social product in proportions and time sequences that could obviate social and political discord.

Those parts of the social product that were rendered relatively scarce (considered excessively expensive or difficult to obtain in real terms by special interests) by changing combinations of productive forces became the objects of nonmarket control. Since property and incomes were unevenly distributed, because of inheritance, unequal innate abilities, or the external fortuities of aggregate economic change, including technological change, American capitalism produced social unrest as well as economic abundance—measured in aggregate. There remained rich and poor, and the cycles of dearth and plenty provided grist for the mills of politics and consequent legislative fallout. Nonmarket control was coming to be accepted widely as a panacea long before the catastrophic economic collapse of American capitalism in 1929–33.

Accordingly, the New Deal was largely a traditionalist reaction. In an institutional sense, more regulatory bodies and more ubiquitous laws governing specific activities were seen in America not for the first time in the 1930s. Even the attempted cartelization of industry in the NRA codes under government sponsorship was a page, on a gigantic scale, from the texts of nineteenth-century capitalism. Pierpont Morgan, organizer of private "community of interest" agreements, would have recognized the industrywide agreements on output, wages, prices, and investment as old friends clothed in the raiments of federal power. He (like Henry Ford and, later, the Supreme Court) might have considered those codes to be "not legal." But even that opinion came from historical experience and antitrust tradition.

I do not mean to deny the New Deal's very real achievements. I even agree with William Leuchtenburg that Roosevelt's character was a crucial determinant, and that without him "the history of America in the thirties must have been markedly different."[2] The question is how markedly it would have differed. The Nuclear Regulatory Commission and the National Aeronautics and Space Administration, after all, are as much descendants of institutional precedent—the First and Second Banks of the United States, the Panama Railroad, the government-organized and owned "private" corporations of the Wilson regime—as they were of the New Deal. The permutations of the menu of nonmarket control devices were available to Americans even without Roosevelt's services as chef. It is inconceivable that the national reaction to the Great Depression of the 1930s would have excluded a further proliferation of nonmarket economic control. Such was developing, even in the 1920s, both under *Munn*-doctrine state laws and attempts, mainly unsuccessful (like the Haugen-McNary bills, to be discussed later), to change the private-government mix in American capitalism via the political mechanism. Hoover's Reconstruction Finance Corporation not only was a portent of further innovations, but was, actually, the War Finance Corporation of 1918 reborn. More remotely, the New Deal's social legislation had precedents back to colonial times and beyond—the Fair Labor Standards Act of 1938 had an ancestor (albeit with different sympathies) in Elizabeth's *Statute of Artificers and Apprentices*, whose long life embraced American law and practice in the colonial settlements. American history, and the wisdom (and unwisdom) derived from it, did not begin in the 1930s. In February 1933, *before* FDR's inauguration, Marriner Eccles presented to a shocked Senate Finance Committee a list of policy recommendations that now can be seen as an outline of the New Deal to come. But as Eccles later wrote, with bitterness, his ideas about compensatory federal finance were never really accepted before the 1930s became history.[3] The wartime experience, together with the fundamental changes implied by the Keynesian revolution, coalesced in the Employment Act of 1946, which marked a fundamental shift in the notion of governmental responsibility.

Federal responsibility for the maintenance of a satisfactory level of economic life *was* a radical break with tradition.[4] Some, like Eccles, hoped for it in the thirties, but it was not until 1946 that a majority of Congress went along. This was a legacy, but it was not New Deal policy. Hopkins, Tugwell, and Eccles did not represent any congressional majority in the 1930s.

What happened in the 1930s was such an institutional failure that the very rudiments of economic life came to be scarce, in the sense I have used, and jobs, agricultural, and industrial production, and the whole supporting social and financial apparatus became candidates for nonmarket control. If no amount of real outlay of physical energy can acquire a job, that job becomes scarce in an economic sense.

Had the nation's economists understood general equilibrium economics and economic planning then, as they now do, American capitalism might have been eliminated altogether in the vital centers of economic life. As it was, the search for stability, which had formerly produced controls in a narrow range of industries and over specific economic practices, now resulted in a proliferation of controls. Ideas, later called Keynesian, "propping up capitalism on its leaning side," came to the rescue. The intellectual descendants of Leon Walras, the nineteenth-century French economist who developed the basic theory of general equilibrium from which modern economic planners derive their inspiration, had to wait. Their time had not come.

Nor was there any real possibility that Americans would adopt the economics of socialism, Marxian or otherwise. From the day laborer to the hereditary millionaire, ownership of property, ultimately the land and its hereditaments, gave American life its economic rationale. As the great labor economist Selig Perlman wrote, this widespread property ownership made the American worker fundamentally a conservative.[5] Hence the New Deal, no revolution, was the engine of continuous electoral triumphs for its sponsors. Even American business leaders and social reformers like Gerard Swope of General Electric had been invited to make their contributions to the New Deal idea bank, and did.[6] It was traditional, it was familiar and basically congenial, and, so far as most property owners (although not, perhaps, the owners of most of the property) were concerned, fundamentally conservative.

Although Roosevelt and Keynes appear in history as saviors of the established order, institutionally the country in 1940 was more like it had been in 1914 than was the America of 1914 like it had been in 1870. In 1940 there was far more federal nonmarket social control than had existed in 1914, but in 1870 there had been only a trace. The New Deal fulfilled the Populists' dreams and undermined laissez-faire capitalism for good. In the 1930s the demands for a larger measure of social and economic stability at the expense of doctrinal purity could no longer be held in check.

INTERLUDE OF THE TWENTIES

In the twentieth century, the United States, beset by continuous crises, reacted to needs for rapid action by instituting a nearly ubiquitous network of direct federal control procedures, rules, and prohibitions governing economic life. From the First World War to the 1990s, nearly 40 percent of our existence as an independent nation, reliance upon the price mechanism greatly weakened. The decade of the 1920s was the single exception. Before the twenties, increasing federal control went back more than another five decades. Essentially half of our history as a nation thus has witnessed a rising structure of federal government control. Indeed, it is somewhat surprising that belief in the virtues of laissez-faire economics has survived at all, an oddity noted by Lord Bryce as early as the 1890s.

The twentieth century has been a time of war and economic crises that seem to have sapped the ability of Americans to solve their economic problems by reliance upon private decision making. Yet to some extent the belief in the laissez-faire doctrine remains. The decade of the 1920s accounts for some of the surviving power of the laissez-faire doctrine. The twenties were a fabled interlude. Most of the World War I controls and government-sponsored economic creations had passed, temporarily, into history. Nonmarket control was nearly back to traditional levels, which by then included the host of *Munn*-doctrine state laws the courts busily suppressed. Efforts to pass labor and welfare legislation had tough going in the 1920s, and new farm support programs failed or were vetoed. The nation experienced rising per capita incomes controlled primarily by the price mechanism, the Antitrust Division, a few regulated industries, and some progress toward labor-favorable legislation in such areas as the railroads.

But in the 1920s one already could see the new style of federal government on the horizon: every area of economic endeavor would have its governmental controller. The Federal Power Commission was established in 1920 to control hydroelectric development. The Air Commerce Act of 1926 marked the beginning of federal control over aviation—subsidies had begun a year earlier. The Federal Radio Commission was set up in 1927 to allocate wave lengths for broadcasting. Even Herbert Hoover believed in the necessity of regulation, but had some odd notions about how it worked: "Distinction must be made between (a) the regulation of business activities, which has been part of the American system of individualism, (b) dictation of business activities, which is fascism, and (c) government operation of competitive business, which is socialism."[7] He believed that technological progress made regulation an absolute necessity: "We may dismiss any system of unregulated business. . . . We can no more have economic power without checks and balances than we can have political power without checks and balances. . . . We have too many people and too many devices to allow them to riot all over the streets of commerce. . . . The only system which will preserve liberty and hold open the doors of opportunity is government-regulated business."[8]

He was not even very firm about socialism. Congress made its first attempt to run Muscle Shoals in 1928, but Coolidge refused to sign the bill. Hoover vetoed a similar bill in 1931, and the TVA did not surface until 1933. Hoover agreed to continue with Boulder Dam, honoring a bill signed by Coolidge. But Hoover was a Californian. In his head, what was bad for the Tennessee Valley was good for the arid west.

Federal expenditures, $18.5 billion in 1919, had fallen to $3.3 billion by 1929. From 1920 onward a steady federal budget surplus, a decline in the number of federal employees, and a steady level of federal revenues at about $4 billion had accompanied a rise in real income (1929 prices) from $74.2 billion in 1919 ($71.6 billion in the 1921 recession) to $104.4 billion in 1929. Between 1919 and 1929 annual per capita real income rose from $710 ($660 in 1921) to $857. The strict curtailment of immigration following the restrictive acts of 1921 and 1924, together with the shrinkage of the wartime participation rate in the labor force, meant that the number of workers seeking jobs had not expanded rapidly. Unemployment reached nearly 12 percent of the labor force in the 1921 recession, but from 1922 to 1929 was at relatively low levels, 5.5 percent in 1924, 1.9 in 1926, 3.2 in 1929. Average weekly earnings throughout the 1920s were more than double those of the immediate prewar period, and by 1929 were about even with those of the 1920 boom year, but prices at the time were more than 10 percent lower. A housing construction boom in the 1920s had generated construction expenditures of nearly $24 billion in 1926–27, more than double the best prewar year, and a figure not seen again until the inflated late 1940s. In addition, there was the fabled stock market boom, with industrial share prices rising by a factor of four between 1921 and 1929.[9]

In these circumstances only limited movement was made toward further imposition of federal intervention beyond the new industries of radio and air transport, and agriculture and the labor movement. The market mechanism seemed to be working. Until 1929 the administrations of Harding, Coolidge, and Hoover maintained a selective laissez-faire stance.[10] They opposed unions and farm-support proposals, and the Supreme Court fought doggedly against social reform legislation. After the wartime experience, the nation underwent a period of relative quiescence too, and even of reaction against, government regulation. Not that the 1920s brought utopian conditions. It was simply that a sufficient increase in general well-being blunted criticism of the market economy, and those who agitated for extensive new incursions of nonmarket controls failed to find the necessary mass support. In the 1930s all this changed.

Memory of the twenties made the depression of the 1930s all the more perplexing. What one must comprehend about the 1930s is the extremity of the reversal of form. For those who were not adults in the 1930s the depression is difficult to comprehend, and the amount of New Deal expenditures seems unimpressive now; today federal outlays alone equal ten times the gross national product of 1929. Even though the New Deal produced few fundamentally new kinds of nonmarket control, a prodigious accretion of familiar control mechanisms came into existence in a matter of five years or so. Imposition of that much control in a political democracy measured Americans' disillusionment with their own creature, free-market capitalism as it existed by 1933. In the Hoover administration's fading months businessmen were praising the masterly economic foresight of Mussolini, and, as Herman Krooss reported, "Some of the glossier magazines were openly urging someone to 'appoint a dictator.' "[11] John F. Kennedy's father wrote of that time when men "would have given half of all they possessed to save the rest."[12]

The country had been through depressions before and had experienced the characteristic political phenomena associated with extensions of nonmarket controls, most recently in the Progressive Movement and Wilson's election in 1912. There were breadlines in the 1890s, real privation even in 1921. There had been dramatic financial crises before. The business cycle had played a prominent part in national life since the panic of 1837 and contributed to federal creation of nonmarket social controls after the Civil War. But the apparent suddenness and economic devastation of the 1929 crash and its aftermath made the contrast between the 1920s and the 1930s terribly vivid.

There were other elements whose psychological effects are difficult to weigh. Potential alternative economic systems, in the USSR, and to some extent in Sweden, and in the socialist literature of the 1930s, aided the cause of those who wanted direct government solutions to private economic problems. It seemed that superior alternatives to laissez-faire existed. The worldwide depression of the 1930s could not fail to produce the most severe criticism of contemporary capitalism. But the severity of the collapse, the indifference, folly, cynicism, hypocrisy, and morbid pessimism of the Hoover government, and the much-publicized disclosures of corruption in business combined to support arguments that the system was all wrong. The heady experience of the Wilson reforms and the bold achievements of the World War I government organizations were fresh in memory and made planners and activists more audacious. The men and women who, like Rexford Tugwell, were going to roll up their sleeves and make America over again believed from prior experience that something really could be done by government action. But there was also abundant resistance to radical innovations by businessmen, political leaders, and the justices of the Supreme Court of the United States.

The 1929 Crash and Its Aftermath

The unfortunate President Hoover, devoted as he was to the public virtues of individualism, as he saw it, and to a restricted notion of constitutional limitations upon the federal power, was the wrong man at the wrong time. Apart from some conservative ventures like the Reconstruction Finance Corporation, created to rescue giant firms faltering at the very heights of the economy, Hoover's administration offered little indeed. The "no business meetings" policy pilloried by John Kenneth Galbraith mirrored the paucity of ideas among Hoover's advisers.[13] It is not the case that his economic advisers knew better, or that his attitudes represented a negation of accepted economic wisdom.

"We will not surrender ourselves into prosperity; the budget must balance."[14] These words, spoken in 1932, implied a blueprint for further stagnation in Hoover's mind. Yet the statement represented the apex of orthodox economic thought. Keynes's discoveries still lay in the future. Those who anticipated Keynes, who advocated the later Keynesian economic nostrums, had mostly gained their wisdom from economic writers like the English economist John Hobson or the Americans, William T. Foster and Waddill Catchings, who were beyond the pale of intellectual respectability. Experience in government finance, apart from wartime spending, had not encompassed thinking about aggregative effects.[15] The major exception among public figures, Eccles, had discovered the elements of macroeconomics on his own, and his New Deal blueprint of Febuary 1933 was characterized by *The New York Times* as "bombastic" and "inflamed."[16]

The entire experience of government intervention, from colonial times through the antitrust and developing federal regulatory traditions, was one of restraint and prohibitions. The basic vision in this tradition was that of a dynamic private economy, straining at the leash, constrained within the established rules of society by nonmarket controls. There had been no doubting American capitalism's ability to produce the goods, however inequitably they were distributed. A stagnating economy that had to be motivated into life by government action was something strange, conceived of by visionaries, socialists, and cranks. Hence the New Deal program, expansionary as it was meant to be, was laced through with rule making, prohibitions, and new restraints upon private enterprise. The tradition held, and the tradition overwhelmed most radical departures from the conventions of the American system, then, and to the present day.

Despite the depression's severity, the initial policy paralysis is understandable. After all, later in the 1970s, public policy was equally stymied by another massive and novel economic phenomenon, major peacetime inflation; the Nixon, Ford and Carter governments, with clouds of post-Keynesian economic advisers hovering about, proved as helpless to cope as had Hoover when he faced the economic abyss of the 1930s. Economists have probably made too much fun of the Great Engineer.

Every sector of the economy was stricken in 1933. Agriculture had already suffered, following the collapse of farm prices in 1921. Within that year prices of staples had fallen 50 percent and aggregate farm income had fallen a third. The great housing boom of the 1920s peaked in 1925. Then in 1929, in the midst of apparent general prosperity, the stock market crash wiped out billions of dollars in investment values. The nation's wealth structure received a stunning blow from which it did not recover for decades. The psychological effects would haunt the nation literally for generations. By 1932 industrial production was a mere 52 percent of the 1929 level. In current prices, the GNP had fallen 44 percent in just three years. As Krooss put it, the precipitate contraction ". . . in three and a half years would wipe out all the economic growth achieved in the previous quarter century."[17] Federal revenues fell by 48 percent in the same period, ensuring that Washington functionaries comprehended the drift of events. By then, known unemployment had jumped from 1.6 million in 1929 to a vast army of 12.1 million, or nearly a quarter of the labor force.

In housing and heavy industry the reductions in activity were disastrous. Housing starts totaled 937,000 in nonfarm areas in 1925; by 1929 the number was 509,000; by 1932 it was 134,000; and by 1933 a mere 93,000 units. Income in the construction industry fell from $3.8 billion in 1929 to a mere $800 million in 1933. The housing industry, so often the mainspring of economic activity, had been nearly extinguished. Steel output, 56.4 million long tons in 1929, was a mere 13.7 million in 1932, a three-year decline of more than 75 percent; 1,161 locomotives were produced in 1929, 123 in 1932, and 63 in 1933; 85,000 freight cars were produced in 1929, 3,300 in 1932, and 2,200 in 1933; 1,481 passenger cars were made in 1929, 71 in 1932, and only 7 in 1933. The new automobile industry was also staggered. Factory sales of motor vehicles, 2,790,000 in 1929, were down more than 75 percent to 617,000 in 1932. Bituminous coal output, which accounted for over half of the mechanical energy produced in the country, declined 43 percent in just three years. Days worked per man per year fell a third in that industry. Reflecting such changes in activity, the wholesale price index fell by a third from 1929 to 1932, and prices of farm products, already far below their postwar peak in 1919, fell so sharply that in 1932 farm prices were less than a third of those realized by farmers in their last period of farm prosperity. Agricultural income, $8.3 billion in 1929, was only $3.3 billion in 1932. Agriculture was a disaster area. The *New York Times* composite stock index fell more than 90 percent, from 312 in September 1929 to only 13.7 in 1932. New issues of corporate securities were $9.4 billion in 1929 and a mere $380 million in 1933, a reduction of some 96 percent. American capitalism seemed simply to be canceling itself out.[18]

The human misery produced by this malfunctioning of American capitalism is beyond all calculation. The deepest in our history (in terms of the decline in the indicators of economic activity), the depression lasted throughout the 1930s, and in 1940 unemployment was still 14 percent. Only the massive defense expenditures and armed forces buildup of World War II ended unemployment, as the economy began a secular expansion that was to continue, fueled by continuous military expenditure, until now. From the 1974 recession into the 1990s American economic growth was fueled by inflationary Cold War money infusions resulting from massive federal deficits.

If the New Deal failed to end unemployment, it was for lack of muscle, not lack of movement. Government action in the 1930s was multifaceted. Some of it was unorthodox and far removed from tradition; for example, the attempt to cartelize industry in the NRA codes, the explicit advocacy of deficit spending to expand national income, and obligatory collective bargaining imposed by the Wagner Act. Much government action, however, was patchwork and reformist, based upon experience built up since 1887. Apart from mandatory collective bargaining the direct consequences of the unorthodox policies were ephemeral. The Supreme Court outlawed the cartels of the NRA in the "Sick Chicken" case in 1935. Expansionary deficit finance, however radical in conception, was exercised too feebly to produce decisive results. The wartime and full employment deficit of 1943, $57.4 billion, was more than double all of the New Deal deficits of 1933–40 combined, which was $25.2 billion, a figure almost equaled by the first wartime deficit alone, $21.5 billion in 1942. Hence fiscal policy did not end the depression. In his 1951 autobiography, *Beckoning Frontiers*, Eccles wrote: "We were never able to take up the . . . slack. . . . We did not spend enough."[19] It was an assessment subsequently verified by econometric analysis.[20]

But indeed a great deal of the New Deal's traditional nonmarket social controls, prohibitions, restraints, and regulations became permanent fixtures in the American economy. It is here that one best understands Roosevelt and the New Deal. They did not try what would work; they tried what would be accepted. Rexford Tugwell, who went to Washington in 1933 so full of hope as a member of the original Roosevelt "brains trust," wrote acidly in 1968 of the country's basic vision of itself in 1932. To Tugwell the proposals of Roosevelt's conservative advisers were utterly unrealistic. They still wanted reforms suited to an economy of rugged individualists, of small businesses that could be "forced to compete by enforced antitrust laws," and in which "prohibition would be the only duty of government."[21] Tugwell wanted to accept and encourage the concentration and oligopoly that had become characteristic of modern business in order to put it to work, by semicompulsion, in the interests of stability and full employment.

Roosevelt was conservative enough to want to be elected and practical enough to accept the hopelessly contradictory 1932 Democratic platform, which promised both relief to the stricken economy *and* a balanced budget. For Roosevelt in 1933, the only fear was fear itself;

for Tugwell, the real fear was that the tradition would rule in the end, as it did. Americans thought, in fact, in terms of tradition. When the first sign of a real recovery of prices came in 1937 the government panicked, cut expenditures, and the Federal Reserve Board and the Treasury took steps to restrain the boom (with 14 percent still unemployed) as if the 1920s might recur.[22] Keynes, noting this pathetic instinctive reaction after all that had been done since 1933 to try to make prices rise, made the withering remark: "They profess to fear that for which they dare not hope." Experiment was over in Washington. The major New Deal legislation of 1938, the Fair Labor Standards Act, was as conceptually new as the Elizabethan *Statute of Artificers and Apprentices*; the new Agricultural Adjustment Act, designed to raise prices by restricting output, had its remote American ancestor in the Virginia scheme of 1639;[23] and the Natural Gas Act and the Civil Aeronautics Act not only developed out of recent and similar legislation but, employing the nonmarket control devices of the regulatory agency, were children of the Interstate Commerce Act of 1887, itself a descendant of colonial practices. The stage was set for a massive infusion of specific federal control, but along traditional lines. Enthusiasm for the social control of the price mechanism—free markets—had about dried up. The aggregate fiscal responsibility implicit in the Keynesian revelation had to wait for the Employment Act of 1946.

The New Deal and Financial Control

The New Deal began with the banking crisis of 1933. Despite a long history of jiggering with the monetary standard, of controlling the business habits of commercial bankers by state and federal laws and agencies, and of experimenting with central banking off and on since 1791, the nation's financial system was again at an impasse in 1933. The money cranks, reformers, moralists, theorists, vested interests, politicians, and bureaucrats were going to get another round of fun and games with the country's money. In his inaugural address Franklin Roosevelt exploited the national frustration: "The money changers have fled from their high seats in the temple of our civilization. We may now restore that temple to the ancient truths. . . . There will be an end to speculation with other people's money."

These phrases were apparently wonderfully effective on that occasion, but in fact it is not apparent now what it was he meant to say, if anything. The financial system was spectacularly prostrate, but the economy's other sectors were hardly in rude good health. Speculation could hardly be eliminated so long as capitalism survived at all. So far as ancient truths were concerned, Roosevelt was about to take the country's money off the gold standard, by devaluation and by forbidding American citizens to own monetary gold. Gold coins in circulation were a thing of the past. The Federal Reserve System, having failed to control bank failures, was to be supplemented by deposit insurance, the securities industry was to get nonmarket control, and the Securities and Exchange Commission was to encourage virtue in Wall Street. Moreover, Hoover's Reconstruction Finance Corporation would purchase bank stocks so that the banks could subscribe to deposit insurance. The government entered directly into housing and agriculture. Investment banking was separated from commercial banking. The nineteenth-century Populist demands were met, and the halfway reforms of the Progressives would be extended. These changes in financial practice left the unit banking system intact, the state banks without federal charters, and the money supply freed from a strict gold limit. (There was also another silver purchase act.) Private ownership of the banking system remained fundamental. So the celebrated New Deal financial revolution was something less than that.

Why such reforms were necessary is easily seen: the decision of the market had become intolerable and nonmarket controls were introduced accordingly. Despite the Federal Reserve System and experience gained in the 1920s, the American financial system had continued to be as unstable as it had been before. The gold standard could not be maintained. The remains of the free-banking ethos suffered a blow; but, considering the antibanker propaganda of the New Deal,[24] the nonmarket controls left a remarkable portion of the old structure intact. In any case, the money changers had almost driven themselves from the temple.

Formation of commercial banks was a growth sector in the early twentieth century. Although banks had always been subject to more regulation than had ordinary businesses (for example, banks had to be chartered), the regulation was irregular. State charters contained easier conditions than those granted under the National Bank Act. From 1900 to 1921 a net of 4,419 new national banks came into existence, and 13,604 new state-chartered banks contributed to a total of 31,076 separate commercial banks in 1921. From that year to 1928, 5,055 of these went out of business. In 1929, 659 banks closed their doors. Then the failure rate accelerated: 1,352 in 1930; 2,294 in 1931; 1,456 in 1932; and in 1933 4,004 failed to reopen after the bank holiday. There were 16,305 fewer commercial banks by 1934 than there had been in 1921, of which 14,820 were failures. Such a financial holocaust was unprecedented. The new administration clearly had to act now that the nation was living by private script, tokens, and promises to pay whenever the banks reopened. Before Roosevelt was inaugurated, state governors were declaring bank holidays (closing all the banks) to stop deposit runs, and by inauguration day, March 4, 1933, the banks in thirty-eight states had been closed, along with the New York Stock Exchange, the Chicago Board of Trade, and other major financial and commodity exchanges around the country.[25]

Considering the circumstances the government's actions were remarkably effective. The day after his inauguration FDR called a national bank holiday by executive order and suspended gold payments, using war powers remaining from 1917. What followed was not universally acclaimed, but it set up new conditions for banking and finance in the United States that survived into the early 1990s (a longer life by nearly two decades than that of the Gold Standard Act of 1900, which only lasted until 1933).

The purely financial crisis centered upon price deflation, bank failures, and the stock market collapse. Whereas efforts to stabilize prices were concentrated in the NRA measures, concern with deflation produced part of the New Deal's solution to the banking crisis: disconnection from the gold standard. The action was so rapid-fire that daily dates are needed to follow the action. When Roosevelt made his famous inaugural address on Saturday, March 4, 1933, he said: "We must act, and act quickly." On Monday, March 6, he declared a national bank holiday under the Trading With the Enemy Act of 1917. Three days later, March 9, Congress passed the Emergency Banking Act of 1933, granting the government direct control over foreign exchange transactions and prohibiting specie exports. The next day an executive order empowered the Comptroller of the Currency to reopen the national banks with temporary federal deposit insurance. Deposit insurance had been tried unsuccessfully in eight states after the panic of 1907 (the funds were wiped out in the recession of 1920–21). Further in the past was New York's experience with its Safety Fund system in the 1830s. Despite failures of state deposit insurance schemes, federal insurance, combined with extensive controls over the insured banks, was seen as a partial solution to deposit runs. In 1935 the temporary arrangements of the 1933 Bank Act were institutionalized by a new control agency, the Federal Deposit Insurance Corporation. The FDIC was empowered to borrow from the Treasury if need be. Because the public believed that the federal government now backed their deposits, there were, and have been in the subsequent sixty years, relatively few bank-deposit runs, even though the savings and loans disasters of the 1980s would have justified mass financial panic under the old pre-FDIC regime.[26]

The country had been officially on the gold standard since 1900 and had maintained (sometimes barely) specie payments at the U.S. Treasury since the post-Civil War resumption of payments in 1879. The gold standard, it was felt, would prove a barrier to reflation. Hoarding of specie was declared illegal by executive order on April 5, 1933 and arrangements were made to call in the nation's gold through the Federal Reserve banks. Two weeks later, on April 20, Roosevelt, again by executive order, halted automatic Treasury gold sales for export. The gold standard had ended in the U.S. Secretary of State Cordell Hull was dispatched to London, where on June 12 an international monetary conference convened to salvage the remaining international system. But a month earlier, on May 12, populism had intervened in the person of Senator Elmer Thomas of Oklahoma and his all-purpose inflation amendment to the new Agricultural Adjustment Act. Through that measure (described by Roosevelt adviser Lewis Douglas as "the end of Western civilization") the Treasury was authorized to borrow directly from the Federal Reserve System and to issue greenbacks to retire the federal debt obligations. The President was empowered to reestablish bimetalism, and to devalue the dollar by raising the gold price as much as 50 percent.[27] There were more "funny money" provisions. In the face of the Thomas Amendment, Roosevelt reserved freedom of action in matters of currency, and the London Monetary Conference collapsed. Thus the hard-won central bank cooperation of the 1920s had led to no new era in monetary affairs.[28]

By September the dollar had fallen by 35 percent on foreign exchanges. There was no sign of recovery in prices or economic activity, and in an October 22 radio broadcast Roosevelt committed himself to price inflation: "If we cannot do it one way, we will do it another." Following the whimsical reasoning of Cornell's Professor Warren that commodity prices and gold prices were automatically linked,[29] the RFC had begun buying gold at rising prices under an executive order of August 29. The necessary legal warrant was an unrepealed Civil War act. Commodities prices did not rise, but the price of gold did, and by January of 1934 was nearing $35 per standard ounce.

At that point, partly to abandon a futile course of action and partly to placate impatient inflationists and silver enthusiasts (who objected to such increases in gold prices alone), the Gold Reserve Act of January 30, 1934, was passed, vesting sole legal ownership of monetary gold in the Treasury, amending the Federal Reserve Act to make Federal Reserve notes redeemable in "lawful money" (not in gold), changing the Federal Reserve note cover from gold to gold certificates, and amending the Thomas Amendment, thereby *ordering* the President to devalue the dollar not less than 40 percent. By presidential proclamation the next day, the Treasury's $35 gold price was set (compared to the old par price of $20.67 per fine ounce). The dollar was thus "devalued" 40.94 percent. Something was also done for silver, the old Populist panacea. The sixteen senators from the silver states and their inflationist allies had already received a subsidy in the President's order of December 1933 authorizing Treasury purchases of newly mined silver at 64.5 cents an ounce (the market price was 43 cents). In June a new silver purchase act was passed ordering the Treasury to buy silver until its holdings were equal to 25 percent of the gold stock, or until the price reached $1.29 per ounce. An additional silver purchase act was passed in 1939 when, after the purchase of more than a billion ounces of silver, the price was still 43 cents. The entire world had been drained of its silver.

Those whose contracts contained gold clauses (like the Massachusetts law of 1654, which stated that all contracts "for money, corn, cattle, or fish shall be satisfied in kind according to Covenant") were thwarted in their attempts to collect debts, including federal bonds, at the old gold values. Such actions were voided by a Joint Resolution of Congress of June 5, 1933, a Supreme Court decision of February 18, 1935, and a further Joint Resolution of August 27, 1935. Creditors who had given $1 in gold value before 1933 received 59.06 cents in return. This state of affairs reminds one of Gouverneur Morris's dire prediction at the Constitutional Convention in 1787, which seems worth quoting again: "Emissions of paper money, largesses to the people—a remission of debts and similar measures, will at some time be popular and will be pushed."[30] Morris, like Alexander Hamilton, did not trust popular assemblies.

In tandem with these purely monetary nostrums came fundamental banking reform in the bank acts of 1933 and 1935. The 1933 act removed securities affiliates from the commercial banks, prohibited payment of interest on demand deposits, gave the Federal Reserve Board power to control margin requirements for loans against securities collateral, and allowed savings banks to join the Federal Reserve System, among other reforms. When FDR offered Marriner Eccles the chairmanship of the Federal Reserve System Eccles agreed only on condition that he be empowered to rewrite the Federal Reserve act; the 1935 legislation was the result. The Bank Act of 1935 further strengthened central control of the financial system by setting up the present-day seven-man Board of Governors of the Federal Reserve System. The Secretary of the Treasury and the Comptroller of the Currency were removed from the board, and the monetary base was redefined to include "sound assets" as collateral for Federal Reserve credit. They eliminated a constraint, "real bills," that was embodied in the Fed's rules for collateral, (and incidentally opened the way for federalization of commercial bank assets when World War II came and the government stuffed the banks with war bonds). Fourteen-year appointments were established to assure independence from given administrations and to make all seven governors permanent members of the new Federal Open Market Committee. The Federal Reserve Board thus controlled Benjamin Strong's creation, the system account, which was the combined sales and purchases of securities by the Federal Reserve District banks. The most powerful instrument of modern monetary control was thus created.

The Board of Governors also was empowered to set and change the legal reserve requirements of the member banks and the interest paid by them for time deposits, among other less fundamental provisions. The Bank Act of 1935 was an omnibus reform measure the like of which had not been seen since the Federal Reserve Act was signed by President Wilson in December 1913.[31]

In the act also was contained new control of the securities industry—the other money changers. The usual appalling revelations of abuse of power and insider information had led already to the Securities Act of 1933, setting out information disclosure rules to be administered by the Federal Trade Commission. A new law, the Securities and Exchange Act of 1934, established the Securities and Exchange Commission, another independent regulatory agency given wide police powers (augmented by the Public Utilities Holding Company Act of 1935) over the industry's exchanges, the conditions of issue and sale of securities, and, it was hoped, the business ethics of the industry's members—an eternal quest. The 1934 act gave the Federal Reserve Board power to regulate margin requirements for securities transactions using bank credit.

Thus in two years the role of the free market in the nation's financial heart was greatly reduced even though private ownership of financial institutions was left intact. These were reforms which events seemed to justify. Abandonment of the strict gold standard with a fractional gold backing for Federal Reserve notes (reduced in 1941, abandoned in 1968) gave sufficient flexibility to sustain the enormous increase of Federal Reserve notes in circulation, plus demand deposits, from $40.8 billion in 1933 to $228 billion in 1971. In that year fiscal excesses required abandonment of the last tie to gold, the Treasury's commitment to buy and sell gold in foreign transactions at a fixed price (still $35 an ounce). By then the automatic adjustment to market conditions postulated in the classical gold standard system, once considered the free market's most stringent disciplinary device, was scarcely understood beyond the world of a few academic specialists in such arcane matters. The Federal Deposit Insurance Corporation, with wide powers of control over its members, had eliminated deposit runs, and even bank failures had become rarities. The Federal Open Market Committee continues as an independent control, despite efforts by succeeding administrations to influence the System's policies. It was generally believed that the SEC had made financial markets far more stable, until the 1987 stock market meltdown and the spectacular insider trading and fraud scandals of the 1980s that occurred despite all the rules and regulations. In the junk bond mania of the late 1980s the financial sector's ever-inventive entrepreneurs found new avenues of financial leverage not anticipated by the reformers of the 1930s. In the world of financial legerdemain time never stands still.

More radical solutions, including the suggestion that the banks be nationalized, had been ignored by the New Deal reformers, and private ownership with mixed private and government nonmarket controls gave the financial sector a certain air of unreality; it was no longer strictly free enterprise, but it was not socialism either. It was a distinctly American example of nonmarket social control. On the whole, Tugwell's fears were well founded, and in finance the reforming tradition had ruled.

Conservation of Land and Labor

Whereas regulation by agency, the police power, and by antitrust enforcement were traditional, and thus could be expanded without tampering with the fundamentals, some other New Deal actions were strong modifications of tradition. Possibly the strongest, conceptually, were in the areas of conservation and labor. Inducements to private conservation measures had been contained in the nineteenth-century public land disposal laws. The gradual closing of the public domain to homesteading and the establishment of national parks, forests, and grazing lands were also conservation measures. But how could government control the uses to which a man put his own private property?

This became a problem because our fee simple real property tenure descended from that English tenure in which payment of "rents and services certain" extinguished the feudal chain of property right and the full right of "waste" went to the property owner. In the United States that tenure was bestowed after the Revolution by payment of the purchase price and continued payment of the quitrent, now transformed into real property taxes by those successors to crown and proprietor, the state and local governments. The landowner in fee simple could do pretty much as he pleased with his property. One important long-term consequence was in many areas a wasted land; trees were cut down, and the land eroded. The system lay at the root of historian Christopher Lasch's quip that American capitalism's concept of long-term economic development was to leave the continent a "smoking ruin." The invisible hand of laissez-faire had created an ocean of stumps and eroded gullies where once the nation's virgin forests had stood guard over the treasure house of natural resources that the colonists had struggled to exploit. In addition, and despite successful wartime experience with direct government production, the tradition of minimal government competition with the works of private property ownership—recall that Monroe, Madison, and Jackson thought the federal government had no power to build internal improvements—raised powerful philosophical and legal barriers to direct government conservation efforts outside the public domain, or even on government lands. All of this had to be overcome before the TVA, or the Atomic Energy Commission (now the Nuclear Regulatory Commission), or the Space Agency (now the National Aeronautics and Space Administration), or even elementary environmental regulations could see the light of day.

The dam at Muscle Shoals on the Tennessee River had been built under war powers, the Defense Act of 1916. Senator George Norris of Nebraska introduced legislation in 1922 to create a government corporation to operate the project. This legislation, kept alive by Norris year after year, eventually would become the Tennessee Valley Authority. Henry Ford made an offer, too, as a representative of the private sector, although the offer was withdrawn in 1924. The Tennessee Valley project immediately was confronted by opposing private interests—state-chartered utility combines. Hence Coolidge refused in 1928 to sign the Norris bill. Where there was no opposition, as in the case of Boulder Dam, not only did Coolidge sign the bill, but Herbert Hoover, who had participated in planning the project, undertook the financing of the dam, which now bears his name, with federal funds. On TVA, though, Hoover's position was the purest of free-enterprise constructions, as he said in his veto of the Muscle Shoals bill in 1931: "I am firmly opposed to the government entering into any business the major purpose of which is competition with our citizens."[32] Hoover was from California.

"Our citizens" were in fact private parties operating state-estab-lished monopolies. As the Court said later, upholding TVA under the commerce clause and war powers, in *Tennessee Power Company v. TVA* (1939), the local power monopolies had "no right to be free from competition." Hoover had been unable to see that, just as his political myopia caused him to see no conflict of interest where the western deserts would be made to blossom by Hoover Dam.

TVA, created in 1933 by Congress, was part of an effort by which the federal government, under the commerce clause, gained the ex-tensive powers that made modern-day water use and conservation laws possible.[33] Our water laws are a curious mixture of English and American common law and variations upon the Code Napoleon.[34] In England the king had a right of highway in navigable water. Navi-gation was commerce, so the right and highway in American law could be established by evidence of navigation, no matter how slight. TVA's legitimacy was partly based upon commerce derived from navigability. The doctrine was now enormously expanded. Obvi-ously, real control of navigation involved the whole watershed, and flood control as well. In 1941, in *Oklahoma v. Atkinson Co.*, the Court ruled that "Congress may exercise its control over the nonnavigable stretches of a river in order to preserve and promote commerce on the navigable portions." But it went further and, with TVA in the background, included flood control as well. There was "no constitu-tional reason" why Congress "should be blind to the engineering prospects . . . why Congress cannot under the commerce power, treat the watersheds as a key to flood control on navigable streams and tributaries."[35] By such reasoning was the king's right to a high-way expanded through the maze of American riparian law to the level of modern control, which can, and probably must, dictate the nature of wastes placed into waterways, if we are not to choke on our own offal.

Human labor, even if by the 1930s it had come to be thought a natural resource, would still not have been an easy candidate for gov-ernment assistance, protection, and development. But there were far more than property rights standing in the way of such things as es-tablished labor unions, minimum wage laws, safety regulations, or the fair-employment laws of our own day. American labor, as previ-ously shown, had the Elizabethan statute as its remote legal ancestor, and progress had to begin from a quasi-servile status. In fact, in com-mon law a labor organization had been, *ipso facto*, a criminal conspir-acy.[36] After *Commonwealth v. Hunt* (1842), labor organizations in the United States were no longer considered to be criminal conspiracies per se, but the road to legal establishment, to acceptance inside the general social fabric, would prove a long and bloody one leading finally to New Deal legislation and to federal establishment by the Court in *NLRB v. Jones and Laughlin* (1937).

Escape from legal constraints in the instances of conservation in the broadest sense, together with the legal establishment of labor unions by the Wagner Act, were great social and political achievements that gave the Roosevelt era much of its color: the great multipurpose dams on the rivers, the power projects, and the employment of men and women on terms protected by their government. But these changes meant that if the market would no longer freely decide whether a tree would be cut or a man would work overtime at a given wage, something else would. The result was proliferation of more nonmarket control devices. Such was inevitable.

Another legal shift was required to erase the constraints of history upon the property rights of a person in his own labor. After the long battle for the right to organize, in the end it was government authority in the Wagner Act of 1935, and only that, which gave organized labor a secure place in American society. Moreover, it was again the commerce clause that enabled the federal government to succeed where the unions had failed in their long struggle.[37] The Sherman Act of 1890 had been applied against organized labor in famous and sweeping decisions. The Sherman Act said that *every* combination in restraint of trade—and a union and a strike are that at least—was illegal. The prosecution of Eugene V. Debs in the Pullman strike (1894) started under the Sherman Act (Debs actually was convicted of contempt). During the First World War organized labor had generally found a friend in the Wilson administration: the War Labor Policies Board, the Mediation Commission, and the War Labor Board had all encouraged organized labor and union wages in defense work. Setbacks in the courts in the 1920s arising from union activities such as strikes and boycotts, despite the Clayton Act, motivated further use of strike-stopping injunctions to halt organizing drives. Congress acted in favor of organized labor, and Hoover reluctantly signed the Norris-LaGuardia anti-injunction legislation in 1932. A year later, with a new administration, Section 7a of the National Industrial Recovery Act stated flat-out that "employees shall have the right to organize and bargain collectively through representatives of their own choosing."

If there was any logic to the NIRA, legal collective bargaining and compulsory unionization were implied. If companies were to form price-fixing and output-limiting cartels in the industry codes of the NIRA, it was only logical that wages should also be subject to collective agreements. In 1934 Roosevelt established the National Labor

Relations Board to arbitrate such agreements, but the Supreme Court's *Schechter* decision in 1934 struck down the NIRA for excessive delegation of congressional power. To protect organized labor, new legislation, the Wagner Act, was written in the framework of the commerce clause. It was that power—together with Roosevelt's threat to pack the Court—that prevailed. The commerce clause became the blanket authority under which New Deal social reforms passed the courts. The established legal doctrine that manufacturing was not commerce (buttressed by the language of the Clayton Antitrust Act), and hence could not be regulated by Congress, was at last overthrown by a five-to-four decision. The majority opinion held in *NLRB v. Jones and Laughlin* (1937): "When industries organize themselves on a national scale, making their relation to interstate commerce the dominant factor in their activities, how can it be maintained that their industrial labor relations constitute a forbidden field into which Congress cannot enter. . . ."[38]

Such a complete reversal also implied the demise of the doctrine that manufacturing was not commerce, providing the entrée for new federal legislation governing child labor, wages, hours, and working conditions. *Jones and Laughlin* did far more than just validate the Wagner Act; it further reduced the extent of belief in laissez-faire as a philosophy of universal validity.

The federal government's own employees had been beneficiaries of hours legislation since Van Buren's executive order in 1840 that limited the work day in the navy yards to ten hours a day. By 1892 all federal employees had the eight-hour day, while it was still twelve (and six days a week) in industries like steel. In the Hours of Service Act of 1907 and the Adamson Act of 1916 Congress had extended regulation of hours to railroad employees, under the commerce power. The stage seemed to be set for further advance along these lines by the New Freedom social reformers. But in 1920 the Republicans were back in office, and in 1921 Harding appointed William Howard Taft Chief Justice of the U.S. Supreme Court. Accordingly, conservatism had another chance to stem the liberal tide of nonmarket controls.

Abuses such as employment of small children and women at low wages and long hours in private industry had long been objects of attempted legal restraint at the state level. By the end of the First World War the time had seemed ripe for such reforms by federal legislation. But evolution of social philosophy and legal doctrine were now out of step, and in the 1920s the U.S. Supreme Court, in three famous cases, tried to restrain nonmarket control of the wage contract. Congress had passed a law in 1916 forbidding the interstate shipment of the products of child labor. This social reform proved premature: the Court held in *Hammer v. Dagenhart* (1918) that manufacturing was not interstate commerce, but rather "a matter of local regulation." Congress responded with its taxing power, and a discriminatory federal tax was placed upon such products by the Child Labor Tax Law. In *Bailey v. Drexel Furniture* (1922) that action was overthrown. On that occasion Chief Justice Taft wrote that child labor was "a matter completely the business of state government under the Federal Constitution."[39] States could, and did, legislate such matters, but Congress could not. An effort to circumvent the courts with a child-labor amendment to the Constitution finally failed when New York's legislature refused to ratify it in 1937.

But even state laws governing the wage bargain were subject to court interpretation, and the courts did not favor them. In 1923 the Court overturned the District of Columbia's 1918 minimum wage law covering employment of women and children in *Adkins v. Children's Hospital*. To the Court the issue was the wage bargain as a contract— substantive due process. Justice Sutherland, writing for the majority, argued in terms that stated the time-honored position of conservative thought:

> The right to contract about one's affairs is a part of the liberty of the individual protected by [the due process clause of the Fifth Amendment]. . . . There is, of course, no such thing as absolute freedom of contract. . . . But freedom of contract . . . is the general rule and restraint the exception; and the exercise of legislative authority to abridge it can be justified only by the existence of exceptional circumstances.[40]

Sutherland went on to argue that the minimum wage law was nothing more than vague and generalized price fixing. The idea that a minimum wage was progress or social justice Sutherland thought absurd. The important thing was the "liberty of the individual to do as he pleases. . . . To sustain the individual freedom of action contemplated by the Constitution is not to strike down the common good but to exalt it; for surely the good of society as a whole cannot be better served than by the preservation against arbitrary restraint of the liberties of its constituent members."[41]

Sutherland's argument clearly mapped out one side of the battles to come. The liberty of contract Sutherland celebrated was in fact a statement of laissez-faire economic philosophy that favored elevation of real property holders over labor property holders in the wage bargain. Such was the English and colonial legal tradition in which government wage and price fixing, successful or not, was common practice. What distressed Sutherland and his conservative colleagues was the imposition of government power on behalf of labor in the wage bargain, a change that had been coming since the last third of the nineteenth century and which the Court had only barely constrained in its battle against the spread of *Munn* legislation. The labor contract before *Commonwealth v. Hunt* was achieved when organized labor was still a criminal conspiracy in law. From 1842 to the First World War organized labor struggled against great odds, and after 1890 the favored weapons of strike and boycott were suppressed under the Sherman Act, while the injunction, the blacklist, and the yellow-dog contract, the weapons of employers, were supported by the courts. The idea that an employer, especially a corporate employer, was in a position of bargaining equality with individual workers—men, women, and children—was increasingly questioned. Oliver Wendell Holmes, dissenting from the pious incantations of *Lochner v. New York* (1905), wherein the Court overturned a New York law regulating wages in the bakery industry, attributed the Court's opinion to utilitarianism: "The Fourteenth Amendment does not enact Mr. Herbert Spencer's *Social Statics*."[42]

But government support of labor undermined fundamental freedoms of real property owners. That view was, and is, legitimate from the employer's view, and still obtains widely. Sutherland thus posed a crucial issue in *Children's Hospital*, and it would have been difficult to imagine how federal legislation could overcome these three fundamentally conservative rulings by the 1930s. Who could be employed and on what conditions, except where jobs were specifically dangerous to general welfare or were in industries in the *Munn* categories, "affected with a public interest," seemed safely excluded from federal power. But overwhelming political change came, and the Court would be forced to reverse itself completely in the face of that change.

Support for Sutherland's conservative identification of the free wage bargain with the general welfare withered as the depression spread. New Deal theorists held the opposite view, as had Wilson's bureaucrats who were sympathetic to organized labor in the First World War. The belief that wages were buying power appealed to those who held that capitalism's periodic business-cycle failures and specifically the market collapse of 1929–33 were caused by underconsumption.[43] The free wage contract was seen as an income-destroying evil as unemployment created an army of jobless men and women whose competition forced wages and buying power relentlessly downward. Indeed, wages and hours agreements had been worked into 557 of the NRA's industrial codes. Hence, when organized labor's victory came under the commerce clause through the

Wagner Act and *Jones and Laughlin*, the gates were opened for a multi-faceted victory over the conservative position.

The Fair Labor Standards Act of 1938, the last great piece of New Deal social legislation, was framed in terms of "employments in and affecting interstate commerce." So the New Deal's greatest weapon of social change, the commerce clause, was used again. There were many exempt classes (section 13a), including agricultural laborers, executives, seamen, strictly local businesses, and persons whose employment were covered by other legislation. A Wage and Hours Division was established in the Labor Department. Minimum wages were set with a fixed schedule to raise them in seven years by more than 60 percent while reducing hours. The workweek was set at forty-four hours, to be reduced to forty-two and then to forty. Time-and-a-half pay for overtime was set, and penalties were provided for "oppressive child labor," with exceptions for apprentices, learners, and child-actor persons on the order of a Shirley Temple.[44] Stiff penalties for violators of the act were provided. In the test case, *United States v. Darby* (1941), the Court ruled against a small-time Georgia lumberer who was forcing his workers to rebate wages to him. Justice Stone refused to distinguish between small and large producers in words that portended the fundamentally important test a year later of the new Agricultural Adjustment Act, *Wickard v. Filburn*. In *Darby*, Stone wrote: "Competition by a small part may affect the whole . . . and the total effect of the competition of many small producers may be great."[45] Control would be ubiquitous in the employments covered. The end had come for the doctrine that the free wage bargain was sacrosanct. *Hammer v. Dagenhart* was finally and explicitly reversed by *Darby*: "It should be and now is overruled." This was the end of a long road, not so much a revolution as the turning of the worm. The state power had changed sides in the wage bargain, and nonmarket control now supported the rights of labor against those of real property.

PREMEDITATED LIFE

Direct confrontation between New Deal activism and tradition came in work relief, in implementation of the National Industrial Recovery Act, and in the first Agricultural Adjustment Act. Income and jobs had become scarce during the 1929–32 economic contraction, and the consequent introduction of nonmarket devices produced a philosophical, legal, and constitutional clash of great bitterness and fundamental depth. Although by the 1930s the introduction of federal nonmarket controls to cope with basic economic problems might now seem to us to have been no occasion for surprise, the nature of the conflict between the New Deal and its opponents shows that faith in the traditional system had been merely shaken, not destroyed. Hence, the direct approach to depression problems embodied in federal work relief programs, the farm program, and the industry codes of the National Recovery Administration met a kind of opposition that differed from extension of traditional controls such as financial reform and augmented agency control.

Unlike the extension of traditional controls there were few real precedents for direct federal income-creating action. In fact the federal government in 1933 had to hire an outside consultant, Russell Black, to advise the existing departments how they might *expand* their expenditures.[46] Had the nineteenth-century canals and railways been explicitly employment-creating devices, or had the subsidy features of the long-established tariff system been widely understood, the New Deal direct-action programs might have seemed less novel. After all, Hoover had willingly signed the Smoot-Hawley Tariff Act of 1930, despite its massive subsidies to import-competing industries paid by the consumer. Had the control devices of World War I not been erected under war powers, or had private cartels and industry price-fixing not been theoretically illegal under the antitrust laws, the NRA's work might have received a friendlier reception from business and the courts. But in terms of the tradition these programs still would have been major departures. The failure of the Haugen-McNary bills in the 1920s indicated no great sympathy for explicit direct federal solutions to aggregate economic problems.

Narrowly viewed, the federal work relief programs were doubtlessly among the most successful programs of the New Deal. Their object was to put federal money into the hands of the unemployed with minimal expenditures on administration or equipment. A feeble effort at federal relief payments had been made under Hoover in the form of funds lent by the Reconstruction Finance Corporation to the states at 3 percent interest. The objection to even that much federal relief effort was based upon the tradition, descended directly from the Tudor poor laws, that work relief was a local matter; a problem, in the Republican context, for state and local government control. But Hoover had been willing to compromise, and some emergency relief money went to the nation's poor in the form of a loan. He also seemed convinced that work relief would destroy what he ambiguously termed "soul." Hence the federal government's venture into work relief was considered a usurpation by many and, even if necessary, distasteful. Despite the New Deal our subsequent history still reflects this tradition; for example, the financing of welfare payments and Aid to Families with Dependent Children (AFDC), and by federal grants-in-aid to the states. It should be remembered by those who criticize the New Deal for its failures in the delivery of emergency relief to the destitute that but for the robust energy and reckless humanism of people like Harry Hopkins and Rexford Tugwell, who were willing to ignore the tradition,[47] the human suffering of unemployment would have been far worse, and by rights, according to the tradition, should have been.[48]

As it was, every fifth federal dollar spent from 1933 to 1941 was for work programs and emergency public assistance.[49] The sums seem almost trivial now. Total federal expenditures from 1933 to 1941 were just over $72 billion, of which $14.1 billion were in direct income support to the unemployed, farmers, and students. But for a peacetime budget, where a full 37 cents of every dollar of expenditures went for war, past and future (defense, interest on the national debt, and veterans benefits), the federal income-support effort in the 1930s was impressive.

The millions of unemployed and poverty-stricken thus supported were the human consequences of market procedures and decisions. It paid no one to employ them. The idea expressed by Schumpeter at the 1930 American Economic Association meetings, that unemployment was due to excessively high wages, was consistent with extant economic theory, but further wage reductions hardly seemed a practical solution to the collapse of consumption expenditures.[50] Employment itself had become too scarce to rely solely upon the market mechanism to supply it. Again, as in other areas of the economy, if the market's decision was unacceptable, formal organization would have to replace it.

Mostly accomplished by grants-in-aid to the states, direct income-supporting expenditures were made by the following vehicles: the Federal Emergency Relief Administration ($3 billion, 1933–37), the Civil Works Administration ($807 million, 1933–34), the Works Progress Administration ($6.8 billion, 1935–41), the Civilian Conservation Corps ($2.6 billion, 1933–41), and the National Youth Administration ($465 million, 1935–41). There were many other smaller organizations, like the Farm Security Administration, which spent $273 million in emergency assistance in 1935–41. The Public Works Administration spent more than $3 billion in 1935–41, but its emphasis was on materials, architects, and skilled labor.[51] The direct-income support in PWA was for established businesses rather than the unemployed. In 1938 federal expenditures specifically designed to create jobs employed about 4 million, a formidable figure, but still less than

10 percent of the labor force. At that time unemployment was 19 percent of the civilian labor force.[52]

When the Second World War came these income supports were allowed to lapse. While they no doubt inspired many of the agencies of the Kennedy-Johnson-Nixon era, there has been no further effort on such a scale. There has never been another depression like that of the 1930s either. But the sustained high levels of unemployment of 1974–76 and 1982–83 make one unwilling to assign such things as the WPA and the CCC to the realms of pure history. They now constitute a precedent, and one hears on occasion the call to create their bureaucratic successors. They were massive programs, proving crucial stopgaps for millions of families; moreover, they created—in dams, roads, forests, and public edifices of all sorts—lasting contributions to the national welfare and culture. They never were meant to be efficient, so perhaps existence itself was their main virtue. As solutions to mass unemployment they were failures, as was the entire New Deal itself. But they did provide work and income for millions when the free market did not.

These spending mechanisms were part of that tangle of government agencies we call the New Deal, and indeed, few parts of its history are as confusing as the sequence: FERA, CWA, PWA, WPA, CCC, NYA, and FSA, the agencies that spent most of the explicit income-creating and income-supporting government outlays. On May 12, 1933, following the Eccles proposals to the dollar, Congress authorized $500 million for direct federal relief, the Federal Emergency Relief Act, to be administered in cooperation with state agencies—partly, let it be noted, in accord with tradition. The head of the Federal Emergency Relief Administration, Harry Hopkins, gladly spent the money—fast—but he also had something else in mind. During the 1932 campaign John R. Commons, the great University of Wisconsin economist, had supplied Hopkins (via Aubrey Williams) a description of a program for public works labor favored in 1898 by Samuel Gompers.[53] It was our version of the ancient English practice of "outdoor relief," but the Gompers posthumous sponsorship would help allay the opposition of organized labor. As head of FERA Hopkins sold the idea to Roosevelt. In November 1933, the Civil Works Administration was established. In three months Hopkins had employed more than 4 million people to build roads, schools, airports and spent nearly a billion dollars. Roosevelt panicked at the cost. CWA was abolished and FERA took over the unfinished projects.[54]

Meanwhile, the Public Works Administration, established as Title II of the National Industrial Recovery Act, June 16, 1933, and run by

Harold Ickes, plodded along, spending money too slowly to satisfy its critics. FERA was insufficient, and Roosevelt, showing his traditionalist nature, was anxious to remove the federal government from direct relief altogether. The solution was a return to work relief, this time the Works Progress Administration (changed in 1939 to Works Projects Administration), established under the Emergency Relief Appropriation Act of 1935. The WPA, run by Harry Hopkins, was the CWA revived. Both the PWA and WPA lasted until the Second World War provided a really adequate manpower and expenditure program to wipe out the depression of the 1930s.

The Civilian Conservation Corps was one of Roosevelt's favorites. He had toyed with such a program as governor of New York.[55] Perhaps following the Roosevelt family tradition, he was an enthusiast for conservation and the moral benefits of the outdoor life. The creation of the CCC was an early piece of New Deal legislation, beginning March 31, 1933. The National Youth Administration was part of the WPA and represented the social-reform ideas of Harry Hopkins.[56] The Farm Security Administration was established in 1937 under the Bankhead-Jones Farm Tenancy Act; its complex history included the Resettlement Administration of 1935 run by Tugwell, and earlier, the Interior Department's Subsistence Homestead Division and FERA's Rural Rehabilitation Division. The ideas of relieving rural poverty by grants, loans, and the resettlement of tenants and sharecroppers, were among the New Deal's most dramatic and apparently least effective measures; Eleanor Roosevelt was their enthusiastic supporter. But these measures were investments in human capital and, as such, deserve not to be harshly judged. Certainly the ideas basic to NYA continued through the GI Bill of Rights of World War II and in the many federal aids to education in our own era. FSA seems to have left few traces. It would be rash to say that we have seen the last of the CCC idea. The environmental movement continues to engender visions of young men and women from our urban slums wholesomely employed restoring our woods and water. These schemes, like the WPA, had put money into circulation by investment in people. It would be idle to advance any final judgment regarding their ultimate success or failure. When, in 1990, President George Bush asked that we plant a billion new trees, was he calling up spirits from the New Deal deep?

The National Recovery Administration, established June 16, 1933, under Title I of the NIRA, was both traditional and radical. Its main feature was the organization and administration of industrial self government, suspending the antitrust acts and allowing government-sponsored cartelization of industry. It was another throwback to World War I. Elaborate codes of business behavior regarding employment, investment, output, wages, and prices were to be established by mutual agreement. It was traditional in that a great deal of such collusion had already been (and is now) practiced by American businessmen. J. P. Morgan's "community of interest," intraindustry collaboration between firms, in stable and mutually profitable business conditions, together with Baruch's War Industry Board, were precursors of the NRA. What was radical about the NRA was that government would sponsor and encourage such activity, suspend the antitrust laws to do it, and whip up mass support through the Blue Eagle campaign.

The tendency to consider the NRA experiment ancient history is probably premature. Section 7a of the NIRA (giving the federal government's warrant to organized labor) is still with us in the amended National Labor Relations Act. Moreover, direct business and government collaboration to schedule and stabilize national income could be no temporary aberration in this century of military and economic crises. In many respects NRA, including its fire-eating director, General Hugh Johnson, represented knowledge gained about such matters in World War I; he was a liaison officer between the War Industries Board and the army. Men like Donald Nelson and Leon Henderson went from their NRA and New Deal experience into the federal bureaucracy of World War II—Nelson ran the War Production Board and Henderson headed the Office of Price Administration. During the Korean War the Defense Production Act (1950) revived government-business planning, using the techniques of World War II. This experience was lodged in the vast industrial and continuing procurement programs of the modern Pentagon.[57] Moreover, under the Defense Production Act of 1950, the President was granted authority to suspend antitrust regulation in cases involving national defense—a feature strongly reminiscent of NRA, with the words *national defense* substituted for *economic emergency*. In fact the oil companies had been given certain immunities under the 1950 act, and agitation for the act's abolition followed in 1974 when this information became public. By 1990 *national security* had become a substitute for *national defense*, and, considering Watergate, the Iran-Contra Affair, and use of the military establishment in the war on drugs presents us with a fairly chilling prospect. Rulers like Saddam Hussein of Iraq might motivate our military industrial complex into perpetuity, with Uncle Sam in the role of the world's chief cop—a never-ending chore.

The NRA linked a learning chain whereby an enormous piece of the American economy merged with the military machine, beyond the reach even of the traditional regulatory agencies and the Anti-trust Division. In the 1990s the military-industrial complex, now firmly embedded in the U.S. economy via Pentagon procurement practices, seemed to be immune even from the consequences of its own ineptitude: cost overrruns, failed weapons systems, bribery, and more. The whole idea of American capitalism as an economic system of private ownership and private decision making has been confounded by these developments. Until the implosion of the Soviet military-economic system in 1989–90 the military budget, larger in peace than in war, was considered sacrosanct. War and economic crises spawned this new economic system within the shell of American capitalism, and for that reason only a future of peace and prosperity would ensure the NRA its place as a mere historical curiosity; it was formed of too much that was congenial to American business and government, inefficient or not.

The NRA was the most comprehensive effort in modern American history to control the free market by government subversion of its basic processes. By 1933 belief in the power of free enterprise to end the depression was hard to find. The idea of self-government by in-dustry was widespread. Businessmen could agree among themselves on mutually profitable activities, but to do that, not only would the free enterprise system have to collaborate with government, but the antitrust laws and the whole tradition would have to be abandoned. In his book *Executive Opinion*, Herman Krooss quotes Bernard Baruch on the supposed problems of overproduction. Drawing upon his wartime experience with the War Industries Board, Baruch said that what was needed was a "tribunal which should have power to sug-gest and to sanction or license such common-sense cooperation among industrial units as will prevent our economic blessings from becoming unbearable burdens."[58] Tugwell had come to similar con-clusions from research into the mechanisms of industrial change. He conceived of the economic system as an "operating organism" that could only function properly if all its parts worked together. But the accepted view denied that, and held that the system functioned best by perfect competition between its members. Hence, as Tugwell put it, "the progressive formula for reform since the 1880s had been the breaking up of big businesses and the protection of small ones."[59] This was inappropriate under the circumstances, Tugwell believed, and he thought a new conception was needed. Competition would only breed more depression—too many goods pushing prices and wages lower. Not only must industrial activity be coordinated, but agriculture must be controlled and its output determined by overall economic needs. To Tugwell, the way out was "controls of production and prices, and supports for the unemployed and the farmers." The NRA and the AAA, as it turned out.

In the business sector the crucial vehicle was the trade association. Hundreds of trade associations existed, large and small, some dating back to the Civil War and earlier. Economists had traditionally viewed such associations with a reptilian eye, partly because of Adam Smith's famous axiom: "People of the same trade seldom meet together even for merriment and diversion, but the conversation ends in a conspiracy against the public, or in some contrivance to raise prices. . . . Though the law cannot hinder people of the same trade from sometimes assembling together, it ought to do nothing to facilitate such assemblies; much less to render them necessary."[60]

The NRA was thus to be everything Adam Smith deplored. A contrivance to raise prices was what the NRA was. Moreover, the NRA encouraged industries to form trade associations that could cooperate with each other and the government in the formation of the industry codes of business behavior. When the Temporary National Economic Committee investigated 1,311 trade associations extant in the late 1930s, it found that a full 23 percent of them had been organized between 1933 and 1935 in response to NRA programs, and negotiation with the federal government was by far the most important activity of all trade associations.[61] By 1935 the NRA had approved 874 industry codes, of which 560 provided for some form of intraindustry price fixing and 422 provided for the direct exchange of price information; many of the codes also arranged for divisions of markets and restriction of output to force prices up. By such means, of course, entry into industry was restricted. Clair Wilcox's famous TNEC monograph, *Competition and Monopoly in American Industry*, listed the sorts of things the NRA codes allowed businessmen to arrange among themselves: "All of these codes contained provisions which governed the terms and conditions of sale . . . detailed regulation [of] such matters as quotation, bid, order, contract, and invoice forms, bidding and awarding procedures, customer classifications, trade, quantity, and cash discounts, bill datings, credit practices, installment sales, deferred payments."[62]

The list was a long one, a catalog of activities forbidden under the antitrust acts. When Henry Ford was approached by General Hugh Johnson to support an automobile industry code, the tyrant of Dearborn refused, saying he thought the whole thing was "not legal."[63] In *A.L.A. Schechter Poultry Corp. et al v. United States*, the famous "sick chicken" case, handed down May 27, 1935, the Supreme Court agreed with Ford. It was not the Justice Department's first choice to test the NIRA, and it killed the whole business. The Court ruled that

Congress had delegated too much power to the President. If the Schechter brothers sold diseased chickens and violated the wages and hours provisions of the Poultry Code, it was not illegal. Not only was the code an example of "delegation running riot," Justice Benjamin Cardozo wrote, but the business of the Schechter brothers was not interstate commerce but local manufacturing, since chickens received from New Jersey were not resold outside New York (*Hammer* had not yet been overturned). Hence Congress was powerless to intervene. By 1935 the tendency for Adam Smith's axiom to hold was only too apparent in price fixing and other exercises of monopoly power, and even a segment within New Deal officialdom was happy enough to see the experiment end.

Early in 1936 the Court also rejected the agricultural part of the first New Deal in *United States v. Butler* on the ground that the tax levied on processors to support farmers was improper use of the taxing power; it was "the expropriation of money from one group for the benefit of another." But this is, after all, a simple definition of *any* tax system, and the Court was not ruling against taxes per se. By 1936 it was clear that the old Court was determined to stop the economic side of the New Deal. The President recognized this attitude for what it was and proposed to pack the Court by appointing extra and friendlier justices in response. Nor should this have been altogether surprising. The Court that was trying to block the expansion of direct government control over business enterprise in 1935 and 1936 was still largely the Court of *Hammer v. Dagenhart*, *Truax v. Corrigan*, and *Children's Hospital*. It was also the Court that had battled valiantly against the flood of *Munn*-doctrine state laws such as those adjudicated in *Wolff Packing Company v. Industrial Court of the State of Kansas* and *Tyson v. Banton*. While *Nebbia v. New York* in 1934 might seem to have closed the door upon the doctrine of "business affected with a public interest," it opened another door wide: "it is clear that there is no closed class or category affected with a public interest."[64]

It was the function of the courts, the ruling went, under the due process clauses of the Fifth and Fourteenth Amendments to determine in each case whether government regulation was "a reasonable exertion of governmental authority."[65] The Court seemed determined that the New Deal, as embodied in NRA and AAA, would not pass. The Court had stanched the surge of *Munn* legislation in the 1920s, and seemed to believe they had triumphed again in the 1930s with the federal government. After the session in which the *Schechter* decision was read, old Justice Louis Brandeis, whose favorite advice to his law clerks had been, they complained, to "go back to Montana," called in New Dealer Thomas Corcoran to the robing room and told him to tell Roosevelt that the Court was not going to let the government "centralize everything." A. M. Schlesinger Jr., in *The Age of Roosevelt*, quotes him: "As for your young men, you call them together and tell them to get out of Washington—tell them to go home, back to the states."[66]

In the first Agricultural Adjustment Act, passed May 12, 1933, a lot of historical chickens came home to roost. The Greenbacker movement, the dried-up prairies of the Populist Revolt, the failures of the Haugen-McNary campaigns, the unpaid mortgages, the burgeoning surpluses, the misery of rural poverty—all the years of frustration for the farmer, from the Civil War to the New Deal, were to find ultimate justification in the AAA. Moreover, so strong was farm sentiment (and so desperate the crisis) by the 1930s that the fundamental provisions of the 1933 AAA, acreage control and loans against stored crops, were rewritten into the new AAA of 1938. The 1938 AAA not only was upheld by the Court after its 1937 change of heart, but in a test case, *Wickard v. Filburn*, the Court's reversal of itself was as sweeping as its earlier reversal regarding organized labor had been.

Both the Agricultural Adjustment Act and the Emergency Farm Mortgage Act were early (May 1933) New Deal measures. They both involved direct federal payment to agriculture. The main Haugen-McNary nostrum had been disposal of America's farm surpluses by dumping them abroad. But the foreign food market was destroyed by rising quotas and tariffs, and negotiating them back down would take more time than the Roosevelt administration felt it had in 1933. In any case, there was no evidence that the problem could be solved that way. The New Deal's farm program was to be autarkic: domestic solutions mainly, achieved by dumping money on the problems.

The Emergency Farm Relief Act and the Farm Credit Act, passed in June, together with the reorganization of federal farm lending agencies, produced in 1934 the Farm Credit Administration, which refinanced 20 percent of the nation's farm mortgages. The Populists had demanded that legal tender be created to lend on farm mortgages. With the tradition of the Massachusetts land bank of 1740 and the pre-Civil War wildcat banks, the idea that land should be treated as a prime commercial asset, as security in financial dealings, was hardly new. That the government should *force* the nonagricultural part of society to lend to farmers—which is what legal-tender government loans would have been—had been the Populist demand. Such was achieved indirectly by the FCA. Relief money was paid to the rural sector by the predecessors of the FSA. The land could be financed and the poor cared for, at least minimally. Could loans now be made by the government against the security of stored harvested crops? This was another Populist demand (the Subtreasury plan). Crop loans were now to be made by the Commodity Credit Corporation: food supplies were to be controlled through crop acreage limitations.

Imposition of nonmarket controls over farming in the 1930s made fundamental social reform the consequence of free-market failure to produce results satisfactory to farmers. They still had political clout and, following Director's Law, they manipulated the federal government to redistribute wealth in their favor. This behavior follows strictly the basic model of American behavior outlined in chapter 1. But the farm program was more than mere manipulation of government to serve vested interests along the lines suggested by Douglass North and Lance Davis in their book *Institutional Change and American Economic Growth*. The broad national interest was held paramount in the legislation, and reform came from above in the service of that interest, or so the architects of the policy believed. A fairly close historical parallel was early railroad and canal construction, wherein it was argued that governments achieved their ends by manipulating congenial private interests. Farmers, after all, had suffered long without decisive government action. But the collapse of farm income in the early thirties was seen by economists like Tugwell and practical politicians like FDR to underlie diminishing market power. Cheap food was only good for the nonfarm sector if it did not destroy the agricultural sector's ability to buy nonfarm products and services. With basic farm prices down nearly 70 percent in 1933 from the highest 1920s levels and farm income down 60 percent from 1929, and with enormous supplies on hand, the prospect was for an even further and drastic price and income reduction. Wheat supplies in 1933 were three times their normal level; there was enough cotton on hand to meet a normal year's consumption.

The solution was seen to be loans to farmers against their crop holdings, together with supply control through compensated acreage reductions financed by a tax on processors of agricultural commodities—the tax that incensed the Supreme Court when it attempted to kill the scheme in 1935. To make loans against crops, an agency was needed that could raise funds in vast but irregular amounts (since crop fluctuations were irregular). Experience with earlier farm legislation also suggested that minimal congressional participation would be wise. Fast results were needed. The World War I experience now proved decisive. A government-owned, state-chartered corporation, such as the Emergency Fleet Corporation (chartered in Washington, D.C.) or, more directly, the United States Grain Corporation (chartered in Delaware), would be the answer. On October 16, 1933, the

Commodity Credit Corporation was chartered in Delaware; it got a federal charter in 1948, a good year for such things. Its capital stock was government-owned. It was run by a board of federal officials, and it had authority to borrow to make loans and manage inventories of stored crops. Its first creditor was Hoover's RFC, now run by New Dealer Jesse Jones. The RFC was itself a reincarnation of the 1918 War Finance Corporation. Tradition built upon itself.

The domestic allotment idea is usually credited to a Montana State College professor, Milburn L. Wilson.[67] Tugwell had met Wilson and his staunch ally, Henry Wallace, at the 1932 Democratic convention in Chicago. According to Tugwell, Wilson already had worked out the entire scheme, including the tax on processors to pay farmers for crops not grown (originally the idea of Henry I. Harriman, president of the U.S. Chamber of Commerce). As the scheme developed, it included the idea of parity prices and local referendum, so that there was a democratic input, and not just centrally planned compulsion. Output targets on basic crops were to be determined with an eye to consumption estimates and stocks on hand, and farmers were paid for not growing crops and were loaned money on their unsold inventories. If the loans were not retired by the farmers, the crops became the property of the CCC.

The allotment scheme survived *Schechter* in varying permutations, including a soil conservation measure, and remains today at the heart of the farm program, now greatly enlarged to include a soil bank, acreage diversion, and crop-land conversion schemes. Surpluses have been distributed to the poor, to schools, and to foreign assistance programs. When the new 1938 AAA was passed the extent of central control was greater than before. Wallace's notions about a controlled market supply, the "ever normal granary," were built in, but there were now not only acreage controls, conservation, crop loans, subsidies, but federal crop insurance as well, administered by the new Federal Crop Insurance Corporation. The ubiquitous power of the scheme was set in test cases, the *Mulford* case (1939) and later in *Wickard v. Filburn* (1942), in which the Court took a completely general-equilibrium point of view, and held that even wheat grown by a farmer (Filburn) for his own use was subject to the allotment:

> It can hardly be denied that a factor of such volume and variability as home-consumed wheat would have a substantial influence on prices and market conditions . . . such wheat overhangs the market, and, if induced by rising prices, tends to flow into the market. . . . If we assume that it is never marketed, it supplies a need of the man who grew it which would

otherwise be reflected by purchases on the open market. Home-grown wheat in this sense competes with wheat in commerce.[68]

Recall that in colonial Massachusetts bakers were forbidden to make undersized loaves for their own use, no loopholes. Recall that in *Darby* even the small-time one-man lumber operator was held to threaten the Fair Labor Standards Act by paying unlawfully low wages. The reference to interstate commerce in *Wickard v. Filburn* was crucial. As in so much of the New Deal's legally viable legislation, it was the commerce-clause revolution that saved the day. In the *Butler* decision some amendments (for example, the milk-shed controls), based upon the commerce power, were left intact by the Court. Other commerce-clause controlling legislation had been upheld, and the Agricultural Marketing Agreement Act of 1937 had been written in that light. Other changes were institutional. In 1935 the Rural Electrification Administration was created, and it set out, by organizing electrical cooperatives, to bring the American farmer fully into the twentieth century. By the 1930s private capitalism had failed to bring electrical power to 90 percent of the nation's farms. By the route of cooperatives REA succeeded where capitalism had failed.

Thus by the end of the 1930s the rudiments of a long-term agricultural program of nonmarket control were in place. The proliferation since then of federal government involvement in the lives of farm families (in dwindling numbers) flowed naturally from the New Deal experience and legislation. There is clearly no sense in which such a history could be judged a success or not, unless of course everyone was demonstrably better off with it than they would have been without it, or the happiness of those better off was measurably greater than the unhappiness of those made worse off. There are no such measures. By the end of the 1930s the surpluses were as big as ever, despite renewed dumping abroad. William Leuchtenberg concluded ruefully: "Only the war rescued the New Deal farm program from disaster."[69] In 1936 there were 6.7 million farm families; in 1957, 4.9 million; and in 1969, a mere 2.7 million. By 1990 only 2 million farm families existed, just over 1 percent of the population. The federal government was laying out more than $20 billion a year in farm subsidies, mostly paid to the wealthiest farmers, as I will discuss in the next chapter. The program did not solve the farm problem; the program changed it into something different—a premier part of the great American boondoggle, or getting the government to pay for something the free market could never even conceive of.

After all the revolutions in technology, the unimaginable rises in agricultural productivity, and the pandemic expansion of agricultural controls and subsidies, it turned out to be, as in medieval times, food shortages that raised farmers' incomes. In 1988 drought burned the Great Plains, and in 1986–87 the Agriculture Department paid farmers to destroy two million milk cows and take 78 million acres of farmland out of production. The waste in the program, beyond hyperbole, finally produced a rise in prices by 1989. Demand was still price inelastic; Engel's Law still ruled. The United States, with its unexampled gift of nature and its continent-wide agricultural endowment, still had found no equilibrium. No combination of laws, agencies, programs, Wallaces, Tugwells, or the fulfilled dreams of the Populists and Greenbackers had yet produced lasting farm prosperity. But one indubitable result of this disequilibrium has been a mass of federal nonmarket control fastened onto the American farmer that neither he nor his descendants is likely ever to see disappear, or even diminish. The unlooked-for consequence of the Populist dreams was the transformation of the American farmer, some have charged, into a ward of the state. What has bothered American traditionalists most about this is the absence of evidence that the remaining American farmers mind it a bit. The farmer no longer lives on Turner's frontier.

The Tradition and Social Insurance

Nowhere was the force of historical inertia more dramatic than in the opposition to the more explicit social-welfare measures of the New Deal, laws designed to help people presumed unable to help themselves. To establish minimum wages, hours legislation, and rules against the employment of child labor, the doctrine that manufacturing was not commerce first had to be overcome, along with the argument that women and children employed in factories and sweatshops had competently entered into valid freely-negotiated contractual relations. Organized labor not only had to overcome the common-law tradition of criminal conspiracy but, what was more difficult, the legacy of the *Statute of Artificers and Apprentices*, which haunted us for centuries with its implications that labor was "below the salt" and that working people were unworthy members of society and deserving of regulation by their betters. Such ideas are by no means unknown even today. Workmen's compensation laws, when they did finally come as state legislation, came only by prevailing against the antique, and English, legal doctrines of contributory negligence by a fellow servant and the idea of normal risk in the employment contract. Unemployment compensation, payment from public funds to those without jobs, was up against the science of economics, which then decreed that large-scale involuntary unemployment was impossible in the free market, combined with the legacy of the old English poor law: valiant and sturdy beggars (the able-bodied unemployed) were the undeserving poor. Any social insurance for the aged faced the American tradition, taken over from the English and unchanged through American history—believed fervently by Hoover, less so by Roosevelt—that such assistance, even for the blind, the insane, or the totally handicapped, was the unique responsibility of local government. Toward all such ideas for any improvement in the condition of the lower orders, the great English economist David Ricardo had cast his baleful eye.[70] Additionally, the belief that the responsible and prudent could provide for themselves without any interference by government officials prevailed. Those who were not responsible deserved to suffer. The parable of the talents was an article of faith to the descendants of the Puritan fathers.

It was, and is, this massive tradition, handed down generation after generation, that was partly overcome by the New Deal. Its social legislation was piecemeal, defective, and insufficient to achieve its ends, whether considered laudable or despicable. It remains, patched up and improved here and there, social insurance, as it is known in the United States. Even without the heavy hand of the past, the problem of introducing it would have been staggering. But a federal solution also meant a federal bureaucracy, and thus the possibility of heavy-handed abuse; the Social Security number became the American pigtail, to be attached to all personal documents, enabling, via data storage and retrieval techniques, the potential capture of all in a central data bank. There were those in the 1930s who could foresee the current situation—the Social Security number atop Form 1040—the transformation of the welfare state into the harasser state. But the need for social insurance seemed more immediate than the dangers of its abuse.

The traditional treatment of these social problems was based on the wisdom of a preindustrial society. The world of industrialization made many of the old assumptions obsolete, especially the consequences of industrial fluctuations, which had become a problem of international dimensions in the last half of the nineteenth century. Not only could no individual insure himself against periodic unemployment or, alternatively, inflation, but neither could individual nations. The homilies of President Hoover were simply the product of inept coping, a man of the old style explaining why airplanes could never fly.

Thus the American version of the welfare state was developed against a hostile intellectual environment but was the product of real economic change. In fact we were the most laggard of the advanced industrial countries, especially in regard to national social insurance. We were not an especially backward people in the realms of social thought, but the federal structure, together with tradition, militated against a unified federal welfare state; Ricardo would have approved.

Workmen's compensation laws led the way for social insurance. Since the battle had to be waged against the common law, suit by suit, legislation amending that procedure that required employers to insure themselves, began at the state level. At issue was the appalling injury rate of modern industry and the proposition that society collectively should insure its workers against such dangers. The object was to produce a no-fault system and free the worker from the need to prove negligence by his employers and to sue for damages. The Germans had enacted superior workmen's compensation laws in the 1880s, in which a fairly uniform system rested upon the Reich's obligation to protect its workers—Bismarck's "soldiers of industry." A decade later the English followed with employer-liability legislation, but it was not compulsory and was weak and ineffective compared to the German system. The American states copied the English, and after World War II the English copied the Germans. The result for us was, and is, an irregular and undependable coverage, some 60 percent of it by private carriers. Benefits for loss of work, medical payments, and rehabilitation are not uniform; each state has its own standards, and where litigation is required, variation within states exists. Maryland had an employer's liability law in 1902; Mississippi completed the coverage only in 1948.[71] These laws are meant to correct a gap in the social system that the free market could never cover.

Inferior as our workmen's compensation system is, it did play the role of icebreaker for federal social insurance. In 1934 Roosevelt appointed study committees to recommend a system to relieve the aged and to provide pensions and unemployment compensation. The resulting Social Security Act was signed in to play the role of icebreaker for federal social insurance. In 1934 Roosevelt appointed study committees to recommend a system to relieve the aged and to provide pensions and unemployment compensation. The resulting Social Security Act was signed into law August 14, 1935, making us, among other things, the twenty-first nation in the world (behind most other modern countries) to enact a national system of old-age pensions. The need for such action was the result of industry and urban growth. The aging worker and his wife had no place. There was no subsistence agriculture for the aged urban poor. In the 1930s any retirement they had provided for themselves likely had been impaired or wiped out by the depression. In addition, millions of the aged poor were on relief in their homes, or in county or township poorhouses and farms, with their personal property deeded to the state, living out the end of the old Tudor poor laws in America.[72]

The 1935 act provided for mandatory contributions by workers to their own retirement. It is not really insurance and there is no contract between the insured and the system. For those who could not come under the act, federal grants-in-aid to the states were available on a matching basis, making the standard of comfort supported by the federal government dependent upon the level provided by each state. Grants-in-aid to dependent children, the insane, and the disabled developed the same way, via the states, and state-based programs became the vehicle for health insurance for the aged and the poor as well. The federal government has gotten considerable advantage from their management of the Social Security payouts in modern times. Increased Social Security taxes makes it possible for the federal government to disclaim responsibility in its regular budget for increased taxes to improve welfare, while at the same time, inclusion of Social Security payments within the published budget expenditures of the Department of Health and Human Services makes the aggregate federal budget appear to be more humane—less proportionally military—than it in fact is. In a splashy display of wit and political dueling, in 1990 Senator Daniel Moynihan (D., N.Y.) used the news media to publicize this federal sleight-of-hand, pointing out that the Social Security surplus was making the hemmoraging federal deficit $65 billion a year smaller than it actually was. He proposed a cut in Social Security taxes to give the money back to the people. It was vintage stuff.

Our system of state-managed unemployment insurance was also instituted under the 1935 act. It is entirely financed by payroll taxes on employers, on the theory that a differential tax levied on the basis of performance would encourage employers to use the labor factor with less irregularity—as if the business cycle were not an independent cause of layoffs as far as the individual firm is concerned. Also, reliance upon state systems catered to the ancient tradition of local aid in relief of wages. The states were coerced into participating by a federal tax upon employers, 90 percent of which would be rescinded if employers belonged to an approved state system. The federal government also volunteered to absorb the administrative costs of state systems. Taxes and benefits differ among the states, so ours is a system only in the sense that all states are covered. It not only is far better than nothing, but has been shown to be useful as a business-cycle stabilizer. Just one nationwide uniform system is in operation, and that is for railroad employees.

Fortunately our social insurance system has never been static. It has changed many times since 1935 and has been improved and broadened. It laid the groundwork for the comprehensive European-style welfare state that is certain to be produced by the first, and overdue, general reform of our national system. We will be, as always, decades behind other advanced industrial countries. The legacy of Tudor England, the heavy dependence on local administration of poor relief, is administratively cumbersome and expensive and has contributed to antisocial phenomena, including public-housing abuses and migrations of the rural poor because of state welfare differentials. A national minimum income guarantee (suggested in the 1930s for the aged by Dr. Francis Townsend, the social reformer), obviously the next general move, would go far toward elimination of the Tudor and hence colonial legacy. But until then the multiplicity of jurisdictions will continue to work their uneven will. From an economist's viewpoint, what our social insurance methods have done to labor mobility, factor use and prices, and managerial practices is beyond imagination. Nonmarket social control inevitably has such consequences, for good or ill.

Controls and the New Technology

Technical change in transportation and communications produced new control agencies under the logic of common carriers and the ancient rules subjecting such businesses to regulation. The airplane as a commercial vehicle was put under federal control by the Air Commerce Act of 1926, which imposed safety regulations. In 1934 controls were strengthened and extended by establishment of a Federal Aviation Commission to study regulation of the industry. It had been subsidized since 1925; by the 1930s both the ICC and the U.S. Post Office had control powers as a result. The Civil Aeronautics Act of 1938 established the Civil Aeronautics Authority as an independent agency. The control was changed again in 1940, when the Civil Aeronautics Board was established with powers over rates. Subsequent laws of 1958 and 1966 effected a concentration of safety control in the new Department of Transportation, but left the CAB with independent rate-setting powers. Thus all four options for social control—number, entry, price, and quality (safety)—were determined by nonmarket control of air traffic. The industry grew enormously, but whether it was due more to CAB wisdom than to government subsidies and contracts is a question. What was not a question was the contribution of the competitive free market to this industry. That contribution was small indeed. The CAB in 1984 became one of the rarest of phenomena, a government agency dissolved. Since then the industry has restructured itself.

The CAB extended the line of control over common carriers that I have traced from medieval times through the colonies and the nineteenth-century railroads. Whereas the original object of control was protection of the public interest by restricting monopoly power, the power of regulation limits entry into the regulated industry, so industries controlled develop vested interests in nurturing and maintaining the control. It was often charged that the CAB had succeeded in raising and maintaining high air fares in this country more effectively than a private cartel could ever hope to do.[73] Since 1985 fares on main routes have fallen, at least in real terms (and on branch routes have risen), the industry has continued to grow; there is now a shortage of terminal and air space in the large cities. Since government built those airports in the first place, government is now called upon to solve the new problems. Is there another way? No one will ever know.

Control of entry by government was dramatized in 1962 by federal creation of a private monopoly, the Communications Satellite Corporation, to begin a system of satellite communications for the private sector with generous assistance from the government. The plan was reminiscent of the First and Second Banks of the United States, except that no stock was allocated to the federal government; instead, 50 percent was reserved, originally to AT&T, ITT, and other private companies in telecommunications.[74] The corporation was an example of government instigated, sponsored, and organized capitalism—a time-honored form of enterprise in this country from colonial times and the canals and railroads onward. Control over the Communications Satellite Corporation was vested in a New Deal creation, the Federal Communications Commission.

The FCC was organized in 1934 in response to rapid changes in the commercial exploitation of radio. The ICC had exercised control over radio communications under the Mann-Elkins Act of 1910. The radio was a common carrier by nature. In 1927 Congress established a Federal Radio Commission, which lasted until the FCC was organized. It is of interest thus to see a control power (over common carriers), developed in medieval England, extended by American institutional history and practices into the fringes of outer space half a millennium later. Originality is far more rare in institutional development than in technology, partly because of the genius of the courts. By the late 1980s the country was effectively interlinked by the new computer technology. In November 1988 an enterprising Cornell graduate student entered the national computer space with a "worm" that closed down, temporarily, thousands of computers across the country. The federal government prosecuted the young man, seeking $250,000 and a jail term. A federal statute did apply, but the logic was the law of trespass. The judge in the case, examining the arcane evidence, said ruefully: "For those of us educated in the '40s most of this is totally incomprehensible." The old system was still being stretched to encompass the new.

The New Deal faced the exploitation of petroleum energy sources, now maturing under the myriad uses of refined petroleum products. Economies of scale (and hence potential monopoly) had made the petroleum industry a target of nonmarket control from early in its history. It is the curiosity of this industry that, uncontrolled, it generates monopoly, but if monopoly is restrained the industry runs into a riot of small producers because of the ubiquitous "jackpot effects" of drilling and pumping. Andrew Carnegie had tried to corner the Pennsylvania petroleum market in the late 1850s by storing the raw oil in a small lake bed; there was more oil underground than he imagined. Later, John David Rockefeller, who understood how much underground oil there might be, achieved substantial monopoly powers by more sophisticated methods, only to be stopped by the Supreme Court when it ordered Standard Oil broken up. There had been more litigation in the 1920s concerning monopoly power, and in the Teapot Dome Scandal even the federal government had been besmirched by the temptations of this rich industry.

The petroleum codes of the NRA had been thrown out by the *Schechter* decision, so with monopolies partly suppressed and intra-industry cartelization broken, Congress intervened in 1935 with the Connelly "Hot Oil Act" to stop rampant development of oil fields by the free market. The law relating to underground oil was of ancient English origin, that pertaining to underground water. Water was, as Blackstone put it, "a movable, wandering thing"; it was like *feroe naturae*, game, that belonged to the hunter in hot pursuit. Man had a usufructuary right to the use of water—it belonged to the first possessor, but once back in the common supply it belonged again to all. The oil pools lay under the surface property of all in the area. If one Texas rancher pumped his oil, he could legally drain off his neighbor's while he was at it—hot pursuit. Without monopoly constraint, competition would produce an oil boom and exhaustion of reserves wherever oil was discovered. It was a strictly boom-and-bust industry under competition, but oil was also an exhaustible natural resource. Under the 1935 act the present system began whereby oil transported in interstate commerce could only be pumped according to quotas established by a chain of decision-making authorities, ranging from the Interior Department's Bureau of Mines to the Texas Railroad Commission (representing the largest state producer). This produced a quantitative control over some of the industry, a rare exception to the general pattern of American controls. The depletion allowance in the federal income tax code made this exception palatable. In 1938 Congress gave the Federal Power Commission control over natural gas pipelines.[75] The tax laws came to determine investment and exploration; the trade laws governed imports. The industry was largely government controlled, from exploration to consumer. In 1972, as the nation faced fuel shortages, it appeared that the control mechanism was incompetent. There was agitation to remove control of natural gas from the FPC, and it appeared that the country's oil supply would ultimately become the province of some agency more effective than those that had failed the nation. In 1989–90 the reforms failed and New England shivered when fuel oil rose 50 percent in a month during a December cold snap. The market distributed, in its way, and the bureaucracy dithered, in its way.

The antitrust controls under the Sherman and Clayton acts had been greatly weakened by the NRA episode. After *Schechter* had overturned the NIRA and the codes of fair competition, Congress attempted to maintain some nonmarket controls over the price system by two amendments to the antitrust laws. In the Robinson-Patman Act of 1936 an attempt was made to protect the small retail merchant from the price competition of chain stores by constraining volume discounts given by manufacturers. In 1937 the Miller-Tydings Act amended the Clayton Act by permitting enforced price setting in states that had passed fair trade laws. These laws lasted until 1976. Thus the antitrust tradition, which had begun as a movement against large-scale industry had, logically enough, proceeded to support small businesses by constraining competition. It was, and is (as seen in the 1973 IBM decision under the Sherman Act and the Xerox settlement of 1974 with the FTC), the curious outcome of our antitrust methods that, most often, the attack against monopoly is for large-scale production and low prices, not for restricted production and high prices, the classical monopoly model.

War Again: The Employment Promise

The war came in 1941 and ended the New Deal. Much of the New Deal control structure survived and became our legacy of those years. In addition, the wartime experience of 1941–45 created a whole new set of institutions that joined those of the Populists, the Progressives, the New Freedom men, and the creations of the depression years. These I will treat in the next chapter. First, however, two pieces of the 1930s experience that had enormous long-run consequences for the American economy must be considered.

To begin with, there is the intellectual matter of Keynesian economics. Economists and statesmen alike came to believe from the experience of the 1930s and the logic of Keynes's book, *The General Theory of Employment, Interest and Money*, that aggregate economic activity could be controlled by adroit use of the federal power, and that it ought to be. There was full employment and more until 1945. In 1946 Congress passed the Employment Act. This law can be categorized as revolutionary. It lies outside the tradition. Unlike the New Deal legislation, the Employment Act accepts direct federal responsibility for the level of employment and economic growth. The act had begun as a full-employment act, but Congress so filled it with verbiage about "free competitive enterprise" and other incantations of our national ideological voodoo that its meaning was obscured. By radical excision the object of the act can be rendered clearly enough: "The Congress hereby declares that it is the continuing policy and responsibility of the Federal Government to promote maximum employment, production and purchasing power." The 1946 act is the origin of the President's annual *Economic Report* and where the Council of Economic Advisers came from. It is the legislative line that divides the modern government of the United States from its past, from Herbert Hoover, and even from Henry VIII and his daughter, Elizabeth, who had charged the local parishes with the obligation of poor relief.

Second, the Executive Order 8248 of September 8, 1939 must be considered. It created the modern Executive Office of the President as part of Roosevelt's effort to free himself from congressional scrutiny.[76] This arrangement served well in World War II. It was to that organization that the Bureau of the Budget was moved. There came to be lodged there under successive presidents the Council of Economic Advisers, the CIA, the National Security Council, the Office of Economic Opportunity, Office of Policy Development, the Special Representative for Trade Negotiations, the Council on Environmental Policy, the Office of Science and Technology and much else. A time would come when the administrative assistants to this office would include Henry Kissinger, H. R. Haldeman, and John Ehrlichman, and when an attempt would be made to spread the doctrine of executive privilege over this entire apparatus of control. A decade later the Iran-Contra affair of the Reagan administration provided a further illustration of EOP infirmities. Executive orders and executive agreements are methods of lawmaking by the President beyond the easy control of Congress. In Executive Order 8248 Roosevelt set this country on a completely uncharted course. Other presidents were happy enough to follow his charismatic lead, and from 1939 to the present, great and infamous events alike have stemmed from this power, including fundamental contributions to our burgeoning apparatus of nonmarket control over economic life.

Chapter 6

THE GUARANTEED ECONOMY AND ITS FUTURE

> Let us insist that Government can and must solve
> problems, that it can and must eliminate poverty and
> reduce inflation, that it can and must set goals and define
> a vision for the nation.
> —*George McGovern, 1978*[1]

> Ronald Reagan was a two-term governor of California,
> and whatever his accomplishments, the restoration of
> "free enterprise" was not one of them. Had he become a
> two-term President, he (and we) would have found that,
> after the ideological smoke had cleared, not all that much
> had changed.
> —*Irving Kristol, 1978*[2]

> All means of production in the United States—people,
> land, buildings . . . produce our national income.
> Spending by government currently amounts to about 45
> percent of national income. By that test, government
> owns 45 percent of the means of production that produce
> the national income. The U.S. is now 45 percent socialist.
> —*Milton Friedman, 1989*[3]

GETTING FROM THERE TO HERE

Consider the three quotations that festoon this page. Liberal George McGovern was addressing Americans for Democratic Action, hard-core "L word" types. On that occasion in June 1978 he further stated (according to the *New York Times* account) that government was the only "humane" institution in this country. Irving Kristol assumed in 1978 that the last had been heard of Ronald Reagan's presidential ambitions, and that his whole campaign had in any case been of the usual hot-air variety: this country would not have changed much even if the Great Communicator had been elected president. But then he was elected, twice, and regaled the country on his Saturday radio show with exciting stories of balanced budgets and imaginary feats of fiscal prudence. When he finally rode off into the sunset Kristol was only wrong in one respect, the change had been (from his vantage point) for the worse. The extent of achieved deregulation was ambiguous, and the fiscal condition of the federal government was beyond any known imagining when Reagan and the neoconservatives hit Washington in 1981. There was more government, bigger government, more expensive government, than there was when the Democratic big spenders were excused from the executive office in 1980.

Friedman's complaint was hardly news, except that he called our spending machine socialism, which it hardly is by conventional measures: only the means of production *both* owned and operated by the government would really classify as socialism under the old definitions. But why quibble? There is no doubt that he is right about the control part: what government buys is not bought by others. Government spending *is* control. Friedman went on to say that the extent of regulations, nonmarket control, meant that the 45 percent figure was an understatement, but admitted being baffled by "how to express the importance of such controls as a percentage of national income." The problem is indeed baffling, the ideal measure would be to know what the national income would have been without the controls, and that we do not know.

A study written before 1976 (and published in 1977, as was the first edition of this book) on the history of nonmarket controls could justifiably have a generally depressing flavor—if one were opposed to the unchecked proliferation of nonmarket controls. It was clear enough that regulations diverted economic growth and development away from paths that technological and market-warranted structural changes would have induced on their own. Such consequences could be justified in a democracy if the changes produced by the controls were somehow in the public interest. But just saying it does not make it so. There is no acceptable definition of *the public interest*. The controls always serve *some* interest, or else there would be no controls. But the circumstances in which the public interest alone would be served must be fairly exotic.

On the other hand, we do not let the free market run riot either. We do not allow the free market—yet—to determine who will live and die, or what drugs may be ingested unsupervised by our citizens. We do assume, moreover, that there are higher laws and sources of wisdom superior to individual free bargaining. We do not agree what those higher sources are, but they are constantly appealed to in order to justify our laws and customs. Marriage obligations are still enforced in the courts, politicians are legally restricted in their fund-raising efforts, and automobile operators must be licensed because we believe the state should determine who is on the public roads.

The problem with our methods has been lack of focus and that the regulations can be applied for a universe of reasons, from licensing barbers to nuclear power stations. We can allow or prohibit access to abortions for women employing reasons only a court of law or theology would accept. In this case, as is often so with morals legislation, there is no logic—only emotions. Not surprisingly, the mass of controls that had come to exist by the end of World War II had no overall logic, but each separate control had its own reasons.

As the mass of controls metastasized by the 1970s it seemed to be heading for gridlock. Murray Weidenbaum, a careful student of regulation, states it bluntly: "From the establishment of the Interstate Commerce Commission . . . to the passage of the Toxic Substances Act in 1976, government regulation of economic activity in the United States steadily expanded."[4]

By the mid-1970s, however, the resistance to geometric expansion of the number and variety of nonmarket controls had gained sufficient strength that a backlash began, which yielded the much-heralded decontrol efforts of the Carter and Reagan presidencies. I will briefly survey the post New Deal expansionary spasm of federal nonmarket controls, and then turn my attention to decontrol efforts, and a final survey of the prospects that lie ahead.

There are two parts of our modern history to comprehend: first we need to see, in outline at least, the way war and its needs expanded the control mass. Second is the matter of uses of government to achieve social ends. First I consider the wars, beginning in 1939, and then the uses of government to achieve social reforms after the New Deal era.

WARS AGAIN

Federal government controls greatly expanded in World War II. Mobilization for war began long before the Japanese attack on Pearl Harbor. Using powers existing from World War I legislation, Roosevelt set up the National Defense Advisory Commission in May 1940. In so doing he avoided confrontation with a Congress already hostile because of the Selective Service Act. The NDAC was the umbrella organization from which the main apparatus of the economic war effort was developed. The commission was placed within the Executive Office in the Office of Emergency Management, safely away from congressional scrutiny. Similarly, using Civil War legislation, the National Defense Research Council was set up in June 1940 at the urging of Dr. Vannevar Bush to mobilize scientists.

This organization inherited defense research done under the leadership of the Bureau of Standards, and then, from the day before Pearl Harbor, another subsidiary, the Office of Scientific Research and Development, took over the research that led to the development of the atomic bomb project.

From the NDAC came, ultimately, the Office of War Mobilization (1943), the War Production Board (1942), and the Office of Price Administration (1942). The Controlled Materials Plan began in 1942, and in that year the War Powers Act authorized the President to allocate vital materials by priorities. This was done primarily by the WPB. In the Stabilization Act of 1942 price control powers were provided, administered by the OPA. With the rationing of some consumer goods (for example, gasoline), price controls, priorities established for vital materials, and exemptions from Selective Service to move personnel to essential employments, the vast enterprise of economic mobilization was carried through. The World War I experience had supplied the New Deal with men and ideas. Now the New Deal provided essential managerial and organizational talents for a new war effort. Prominent New Dealers held the crucial posts at the top: Donald Nelson heading the WPB, Leon Henderson in charge of OPA, James Byrnes at the Office of War Mobilization.[5]

The reformed banking system was used to help absorb the deficits. The Federal Reserve System piloted into the banking system a vast increase in the national debt as the federal deficits mounted. The figure for gross federal debt, about $49 billion in 1941, stood at nearly $259 billion in 1945: a more than five-fold expansion in four years. The private banking system absorbed about $70 billion of this increase, the Federal Reserve Banks increased their own holdings by $22 billion, the various fund-holding government departments and agencies invested in another $40 billion or so, and bond sales, payroll savings, and other smaller investments accounted for the rest. The long-term consequences of this effort hung over the financial sector for years. Management of these vast sums led the nominally independent Federal Reserve System into an unhappy collaboration with the Treasury that ended only in the spectacular confrontation between Marriner Eccles and the administration, a confrontation that led to the Accord of 1951 and the exit of Marriner Eccles from government service. Eccles said that the absorption of federal debt by the banking system had turned the Federal Reserve System into an "engine of inflation."

During the inflation of the late 1940s there was little scope for offsetting monetary policies by the Federal Reserve. Federal Reserve authorities agreed to support government bond prices while the private sector liquidated its federal debt to acquire funds for rebuilding private securities portfolios.

The war expenditures were covered in part by increased taxes. Total government receipts, $7.1 billion in 1941, rose to $44.5 billion in 1945 but, with expenditures of $98.4 billion that year and a deficit of nearly $54 billion, the role that debt finance had to play is fairly obvious. The individual income tax yielded $1.4 billion in 1941 and $19 billion in 1945. These taxes were increased by raising the rates, imposing surtaxes, and lowering exemptions; then, in 1943, the Current Tax Payment Act created the pay-as-you-earn system. Here was a crucial turning point. This wartime measure, which became permanent, was a profound change. For the first time in American history, the federal government had an automatic and easily collectible cut of the income of every working person. The majority of the national income was earned by America's millions of wage earners. Now this source could be readily tapped by the federal government. Not surprisingly, American history did not repeat itself. Unlike the periods following the Civil War and the First World War, the aftermath of World War II did not include a major decrease in government taxation.

There followed a shift in incidence of taxation away from business firms and onto individual wage and salary earners—a long-term increase in regressivity which has not yet ended. Corporate income taxes, including the excess profits tax, rose from about $2.6 billion in 1941 to $16 billion in 1945. For the future of the federal government's command over resources, the pay-as-you-earn tax was now crucial. By 1950 corporate income taxes had fallen to $10.8 billion, but individual income taxes were $17 billion. By then the Cold War was intensifying, with the outbreak of hostilities in Korea. In 1953 corporate taxes were $21.6 billion and individual income taxes were $31.6 billion. Increasingly, the burden of higher government expenditures fell upon the individual income-tax payer. By 1960 those taxes were $40.7 billion, while corporation income taxes were only $21.5 billion.

At that point the Social Security taxes came into play as a device to finance those government expenditures that could be classified as social reform. Those taxes, $11.2 billion in 1960, grew to $46.4 billion in 1972. The Social Security tax is one of the most regressive in our system. Individual income taxes were $86.5 billion in 1972, but in that year corporation income taxes were merely $30.1 billion, even though corporate profits were the highest in history, and the stock market, not surprisingly, reached unprecedented heights. Thus a social reform measure of the 1930s became an invaluable source of increased tax revenues to meet the country's social needs while defense budgets mounted. This episode, hardly one of the more celebrated progressive breakthroughs of the era, might be labeled: "Soak the Poor." Social Security taxes, combined with the pay-as-you-earn income tax, became the basis of a fiscal transformation. In 1960 individual income taxes were 44 percent of total federal tax receipts; corporation income taxes, 23 percent; and Social Security taxes, 16 percent. In 1974 individual income taxes yielded 45 percent of the total, corporate income taxes a mere 16 percent, and Social Security taxes had increased to 26 percent. By 1987 corporate incomes taxes yielded a mere 12.4 of the total, personal income taxes 43 percent, and social insurance taxes 35.8 percent.[6] Bad enough from a fiscal viewpoint, by the end of the Reagan years most people were paying higher Social Security taxes than they were personal income taxes.

Given the progressivity of the income taxes and the regressivity of the social insurance taxes, and given that the majority of those in lower income classes were stuck with both payments, the United States became a curious kind of welfare state by the end of the 1980s, in which the poor were taxed for the benefit of the relatively rich. This was especially obvious, since most federal expenditures were not to support the poor, but were transfers to providers of goods and services to the government.

For the most part, the World War II system established lasting precedents, despite the postwar efforts of both the President and the Congress to dismantle different parts of it. But just as the New Deal revived and gave extended life to institutional innovations of World War I, so the Korean War emergency, which came only five years after V-E Day, produced reincarnations of World War II control practices.

The exigencies of continuous Cold-War pressures enfolded many of these wartime practices into the regular federal control structure. Also, the legitimacy of federal controls became an accepted part of economic life. What was once considered an extraordinary imposition of federal power, say, automatic payroll deduction of the income tax, became normal. Even the extraordinary tax rates of wartime came to be accepted as reasonable.

The Korean War occasioned the re-creation of a skeletal version of the World War II control system. The crucial elements of the Korean War institutions of physical control were then absorbed into the permanent federal establishment. The basic legislation, the Defense Production Act of September 8, 1950, was still law, as amended in 1974. Congress then began motions to abolish the DPA after it was discovered that the act had been used to shelter the oil companies from antitrust laws.[7] This legislation empowered the President to shield businesses from the antitrust laws in the interests of national defense. The explicit power to control wages and prices granted in the act ended in 1953, but similar powers were granted again by Congress in 1970. Since this power is one of the oldest government powers, no real question of its legitimacy has arisen.

The Office of Defense Mobilization, established in 1950, was merged in 1959 with the Federal Civil Defense Administration to form a new Office of Civil Defense and Mobilization. In 1961 the Kennedy administration changed the OCDM to the Office of Emergency Planning, lodged in the Executive Office of the President, where it remained until 1973.[8] When the oil crisis struck, the OEP turned in a laughable performance, its head having left office with no plans and with no certainty as to the disposition even of its records.

A controlled materials plan, like that of World War II, was established in 1950, and the Department of the Interior established a Defense Materials Administration in the same year. The system had among its chores not only defense materials acquisition, but also materials for the Atomic Energy Commission. In the same year a National Production Authority was established in the Commerce Department to create a system of defense priorities. When the NPA was abolished in 1953 its functions were transferred to the Commerce Department's Business and Defense Services Administration, which then had the power to determine priorities and allocate vital materials.[9]

In an age of recurring crises and priority needs, a modern nation clearly had to secure its vital material supplies, and the necessary control could hardly depend upon the price mechanism to assure supplies for extraordinary or emergency government needs. The defense controls served the ill-fated Vietnam War effort: men and materials were delivered to Vietnam in a vast supply effort. The war's failure was not due to insufficient commitment of troops and supplies, but to its misbegotten moral bankruptcy. Finally even the Nixon administration wanted no more of it. Gerald Ford was left on watch to see the last Americans taken by helicopter from the roof of the Saigon embassy. More nonmarket controls had been required, and they partly represented experience learned from our earlier war emergencies.

The Korean War had produced an emergency, but mobilization was only partial, and the emergency was over by 1954, fiscally by 1953. The experience after World War I, however, was repeated after the Korean War, as it had been after World War II. Once expanded by the fiscal force of war expenditures, the size of government, measured by spending outlays, did not then contract to prewar levels. Another zero was added to the federal numbers. This phenomenon occurred after each of our major wars from the Civil War onward.

The calculations are simple enough and show in the more expensive wars a permanent change in order of magnitude of government expenditures. In the five peacetime years from 1856 to 1860, mean federal budget expenditures were $69 million per year; in the five postwar years from 1866 to 1870, mean expenditures were $378 million per year. Federal expenditures never fell back to prewar levels again. In the five years from 1912 to 1916, mean annual expenditures were $712.8 million; 1919 marked the high point of World War I expenditure, $18.4 billion. Starting peacetime calculations in 1920, the mean annual rate of expenditure from 1920 to 1924 was $4.2 billion. Again, prewar levels of expenditures, below a billion dollars a year, were never seen again. In the five New Deal years from 1937 to 1941, mean budgeted federal expenditures (excluding social insurance payouts from 1936 throughout these calculations) were $9.2 billion. From 1947 to 1950 (excluding 1946 as a year of war, $60.4 billion, in a fiscal sense), mean expenditures were $37.8 billion. The New Deal levels, now considered small, were never seen again. Mean expenditures in the Eisenhower years after the Korean War were $71 billion, nearly double the previous peacetime levels from 1947 to 1950.[10] The forty-year Cold War added two zeros, and by 1990 the nation faced a package of federal expenditures that exceeded a trillion dollars.

Each war inflated the economy and gave the federal spending mechanism a scope it did not previously have. The historical expansion of the federal sector, before the Cold War, had been mainly achieved by a few short bursts of wartime spending, not by a steady rise related to the country's population growth, or the GNP it produced. After each war there were expanded interest payments and new veterans benefits, as well as the actual growth of government costs. Once a new plateau of expenditures was achieved the gains were held. For this reason alone, those who proposed some abatement of federal expenditures in the post-Vietnam War period had little reason to hope. The tax system ensured self-financing of government expansion. In 1990 the cry was again heard that there should be a peace dividend. But feeding time at the federal trough is always crowded, and the peace dividend had been claimed several times over before the corpse of international communism was cold.

The enlarged government share occurred automatically when the government began to inflate the economy by deficit finance. These expenditures inflated personal incomes, automatically enlarging the federal cut of GNP because the fixed progressive income tax rates shaved off increasingly more as incomes rose. Automatic deductions from wage and salary earners thus supported the modern federal establishment on a scale unimaginable to the New Dealers. Inflation made federal deficit spending largely self-financing via progressive income tax schedules. Government does not fear inflation; in fact, as a general proposition, inflation tends to ease the problems of government finance.[11]

Because of debt monetization and inflation, the expansion of government was almost self-financing, as discussed earlier in this chapter. Consider table 6.1.

The period begins with wartime finance. From 1965 to 1973 debt and money-supply increases yielded strong increases in nominal GNP and hence in federal tax revenues. This relationship held roughly until 1980, although it took higher deficits (debt increases) to maintain the rate of increase in federal revenues. Then in the Reagan years the economy required huge debt increases to keep the mechanism pumped up and tax money flowing into the Treasury.

The Treasury maintained itself but the economy weakened. Output per man hour increases had fallen to dismal rates by the 1980s, but federal revenues were again rising more rapidly than GNP. So continued inflation paid dividends to the Treasury. Inflation paid others too, but not those who worked for wages. Their position collapsed in the later 1970s and improved only a little in the 1980s, and by 1990 they were worse off in real terms than they had been in 1973. Nearly twenty years had passed without an increase in real wages; that was extraordinary, and may not have happened since economic upheavals following the Civil War.

The period since the Vietnam War has been one of relentless deficit financing by the federal government. The national debt in 1989 stood

TABLE 6.1
Federal Finance and the National Economy [Percentage Rates of Increase per Annum]

	Gross Federal Debt	Consumer Prices	M2	Federal Revenues	Nominal GNP	Output per Man Hour	Real Wages (Nonfarm)
1965–73	5.4	7.3	11.0	10.0	13.1	8.5	+4.6
1973–80	14.3	11.2	12.8	13.3	16.1	6.2	−1.3
1980–89	21.1	6.0	10.3	13.9	11.1	1.3	+0.5

Sources: Statistical Abstract of the United States (various issues): *Economic Indicators,* December 1989. All data are end-of-period comparisons.

at $2,658 billion compared to $321 billion in 1965; the $2,337 billion difference is roughly the net sum of the federal deficits since 1965. (In dealing with such numbers it is useful to recall that there are one thousand billions in a trillion.) The Federal Reserve System has been forced to purchase debt constantly to hold down interest rates. The result has been a relentless increase in the supply of money. This measure, M2, was $459 billion at the end of 1965 and stood at $3,145 billion at the end of 1989.[12] Since money supply has constantly increased faster than productivity (output per man hour) the consequences have been inevitably inflationary.

It is thus no wonder that federal government expenditures have grown far more rapidly than has the GNP since 1940,[13] and it is no wonder that among the federal programs proposed each year the one no one seriously advocates is a big reduction of the federal sector. The big revenues encourage new spending, and this spending, placed adroitly, is politically advantageous to office holders. What has been lacking until 1990 has been any politically viable major alternative to military procurement to sop up the flood of tax money that automatically pours into the Treasury each year. Continued budgetary expansions are necessary to avoid surpluses and deflation. The military-industrial complex may thus be seen as partially the consequence of the pay-as-you-earn income tax of 1943 made permanent. The economy has responded to these changes, now close to fifty years in existence, with the sad result by the 1990s that whole sectors of American life—industries, cities, settled populations— have no way to live except as steady recipients of federal expenditures. Of direct government employment alone, it is estimated that a full 10 percent of our entire population experiences a federal paycheck for its living expenses.[14]

There has never been anything like this in our history. This had become the real welfare problem in the American economy, and it had nothing to do with the poor, with black welfare mothers, or with unemployment-compensation chiselers. With automatic taxation paid in upon the very processes of creative economic life and an unrestrained ability to create debt and then to monetize it through the financial system, with guaranteed fiscal fulfillment from the ensuing inflationary consequences, the federal government's own outlays have become the greatest growth sector, by far, in the American economy. Those who could share in this ever-growing treasure trove gained accordingly. By 1990 nearly a fourth of GNP was directly absorbed by the federal government alone on a nonmarket basis: taxation and spending programs are politically determined. So one consequence was a nightmare: our economy had become the largest arms-producing machine in history. Much of the product could not be absorbed by our own forces and was openly for sale to an unstable world, making it all the more unstable. Terrorists, revolutionaries, and dictators alike had the advantages of (subsidized) U.S. military technology. The globe was littered with corpses killed daily by American weapons. It was considered unpatriotic to criticize this development even though the American democracy had been changed out of all recognition by it.

This has been our version of Sir John Hicks's "administrative revolution."[15] Government expenditure is no longer based upon established need; instead, the size of GNP establishes the need for government expenditure to funnel the river of taxes back into the private economy via the continuous government spending stream. Like so many of the control devices established since 1887 the taxing mechanism continues without question and obviously is not going to magically disappear, or reduce itself, of its own accord. As can be seen from the 1986 income tax revision, even reform is extremely difficult. Like the regulatory agencies, the federal tax system has become established with a life of its own, kept going by automatic inclusion of all, with taxpayers "voluntarily" assisting in the preparation of the necessary paperwork, Form 1040.

Such were the bases of the federal fiscal system as the steady expansion was peaking in the mid-1970s. Yet in the many-sided crises of 1973–74 centering on food, fuel, and materials, the federal bureaucracy was woefully inadequate. Inflation, not the bureaucracy, rationed the goods. The poor simply went without. Despite all the nonmarket controls, the price mechanism solved the problems for the most part with the highest peacetime inflation in American history, distorting the flow of expenditures and income distribution and contributing in 1974–76 to the worst recession since the 1930s. To stem the inflationary mentality that grew out of the late 1970s another recession was induced by the Federal Reserve System in 1982, led by its hard-nosed chairman, Paul Volker.

The economic impact of World War II was, like its 1917–18 predecessor, both an acceleration of recent historical trends and a glimpse of the future. Anyone familiar with our institutions of nonmarket control will recognize that major New Deal innovations remained, some of them—like the Commodity Credit Corporation and the Agriculture Department's bureaucracy—still stuck in the ruts of the 1930s. The laws of the 1930s could be dangerous in the 1970s, but institutional inertia is powerful. Thus, in 1973, as the first food shortage since colonial times gathered momentum, the federal government was still paying farmers to restrict acreage and was still subsidizing exports (the Haugen-McNary nostrum). It thus subsidized the Soviet government into the largest wheat purchase in history, stripping the grain elevators.

Other traditions remained. Nixon's comprehensively inept control system came with such ease because of the institutional changes of the Second World War, the Korean War, and the Cold-War aftermath.[16] By 1971 few pockets of resistance to federal direct controls remained. Public Law 91–379, the Economic Stabilization Act of 1970, passed by Congress as a challenge to Nixon on responsibility for inflation said: "The President is authorized to issue such orders and regulations as he may deem appropriate to stabilize prices, rents, wages, and salaries." That, he proceeded to do. But, as the reader of this book will readily comprehend, far more than Vietnam and previous wartime experiences had combined to produce this sad denouement of American capitalism. From butter to steel, available supply was the product of one or another government policy, agency, or bureau. Transportation, by water, land, or air, communications, by satellite, post, telephone, television, or radio, the price of money, the use of land—there was little left of the pure form of free enterprise that was not now subject to federal nonmarket controls. Ten percent of the goods and services output was controlled by federal regulatory agencies; an estimated 80 percent of all economic activity in the private sector was subject to antitrust control. Even by the early 1970s government expenditure had removed some 35 percent of economic activity from private uses; in 1973, 20 percent of the GNP was used directly by the federal government, and 15 percent by state and local governments through processes that involved little free-market allocation. Those figures in 1929 had been about 12 percent in total, with budgeted expenditures of the federal sector (*smaller* than those of state and local sectors) just over $3 billion, which was only 2.9 percent of the GNP. By 1973 the GNP was ten times the 1929 figure (current prices), but the federal sector had grown by a factor of 86. All of these developments had reduced capitalism in its pure form, the private ownership and *control* of productive resources, to a mere shadow of its former self. One way or another, government had become the silent partner of most enterprises.

By the early 1970s the economy was a cornucopia for most Americans. In 1940, GNP was $100.5 billion, or $770 per capita. In 1971, GNP was $1,140 billion, or $5,420 per capita. In constant dollars (1958 prices) from 1941 to 1972 real GNP grew just over 208 percent ($263.7 billion to $812.4 billion) while the population increased only about 61 percent. Also, of course, per capita income is higher in the United States than in most other advanced countries, save Norway, Sweden, and Switzerland, and, apart from the industrial countries and Arab oil sheikdoms, incomparably higher than that enjoyed by two thirds of mankind. If it is argued that the steady imposition of nonmarket controls over economic life made the American economy less efficient than it otherwise would be, it could hardly be argued in these sorts of crude aggregate terms that many other major economies supplied their citizens with more goods and services. Perhaps such considerations also entered into the profound lack of serious objection in August 1971 to Nixon's famous anti-inflation speech (which was, in fact, a blueprint for planned inflation) and the ensuing controls. The system worked, whatever you wanted to call it.

But there is something else to consider. The growing national security state was probably weakening ideological support for capitalism in its vital form. We had been warned of this danger in another context. In 1942, the great economist Joseph Schumpeter published a brilliant, gloomy, provocative, and much underrated book about capitalism and its future.[17] *Capitalism, Socialism and Democracy* is generally a gloomy book, because Schumpeter was an admirer of classical capitalism for its economic achievements and the resulting life-style, especially the individual freedom associated with capitalism. He believed, however, that capitalism would fade away, not for Marxian reasons, but for the opposite reasons—its inexorable successes as a system of production.

The system would reach its greatest productiveness, he wrote, under the leadership of giant firms exploiting scale economies, mainly using the late nineteenth-century organizational innovation, the generalized corporate form. These great firms would reduce to impotence the private entrepreneur, the small-scale capitalist. In so doing, the corporation would undermine the social and political *raison d'etre* of the middle class, that group whose values created the commercial milieu of industrial capitalism. The giant firm would rob the bourgeoisie of its leadership and vanguard function in the capitalist economy. Hence: "The true pacemakers of socialism were not the intellectuals who preached it but the Vanderbilts, Carnegies and Rockefellers."[18] The separation of ownership from control via the sale of stocks fatally weakened the capitalist enterprise as a social organism:

> The capitalist process, by substituting a mere parcel of shares for the walls of and the machines in a factory, takes the life out of the idea of property. It loosens the grip that once was so strong. Dematerialized, defunctionalized and absentee ownership does not impress and call forth moral allegiance as the vital form of property did. Eventually there will be nobody

left who really cares to stand for it—nobody within and nobody without the precincts of the big concerns.[19]

Moreover, the intellectual defenses of capitalism were doomed, again by success. A far larger proportion of the population would achieve higher education and thus a sharpened critical understanding of capitalism's shortcomings and inequities. With no practical experience of any other system to temper their remarks, the intellectuals' withering criticism would pick away at the moral supports of capitalism: "Capitalism inevitably and by virtue of the very logic of its civilization creates, educates and subsidizes a vested interest in social unrest."[20]

By the late 1960s corporate concentration in the American economy was astonishing. By 1967, of the 200,000 active corporations in the manufacturing sector, a mere 200, or 0.1 percent, shipped 42 percent of all manufacturing production, delivered 40 percent of the manufacturing payroll, and employed more than a third of all employees. Other sectors were even more concentrated. By 1971, there were 13,687 commercial banks. The fifty largest, a mere 0.36 percent of the total, held roughly 48 percent of total bank assets in the nation. There were 1,805 life insurance companies, and the ten largest owned 57 percent of the industry's assets; the top fifty, only 2.8 percent of the total, held 82 percent of the whole industry's assets.[21] Recall that fear of the rising corporations motivated the late nineteenth-century reforms that had introduced and multiplied federal controls.

As for the intellectual props of capitalism—the work ethic of Richard Nixon, or, as usually expressed, the free enterprise and rugged individualism of the Elks Club and Chamber of Commerce luncheons, the stock-in-trade of hopeful conservative politicians—they had been rocked seriously by the events of 1929–33. But the assumption of federal responsibility for aggregate output and employment, together with constant surveillance under the regulatory commissions and the Antitrust Division, had cast a further pall over private capitalism. Faith in *caveat emptor* was a fading belief—a fadeout accelerated by the production of inferior, dangerous, and defective products by the nation's largest and most profitable firms, and their sensational exposure by Ralph Nader and other consumer militants. The scholarly purist might think of the ancient doctrine of *assumpsit* and weep; but not if you are modern enough to believe that free-riding is rational behavior for the free rider. In that case, the apparent decline of morality is a minor matter; you have merely nonfeasance. Moreover, the long Cold-War years had intertwined the interests of the Pentagon with those of politicians needing the votes that came from defense spending in their districts, universities needing research funds, and industrial enterprises whose profits depended upon the federal defense largess. All of these had, in fact, undermined motives for independence from government. In the military-industrial complex, a wide open stomping ground was produced for advocates of a realignment of the nation's priorities, such as J. K. Galbraith and Seymour Melman.[22] Their work exposed the way defense expenditures, channeled through the upper reaches of the industrial and intellectual system, had seduced thousands of firms and millions of workers into dependence upon government for their daily bread. The national security state, by pouring funds into the great defense-contracting firms (noncompetitively, and thus creating economic rents) was adding financial muscle to Schumpeter's arguments. Who cared *what* might happen to a firm like General Dynamics?

The Vietnam War added to all these troubles. The American business community had routinely supported the President, as it always had in the nation's wars. But this time patriotism compromised it severely, and what might be called "Schumpeter's army"—the millions of young people in colleges and universities who opposed the Vietnam adventure—linked their righteous indignation over the war with the alleged war-profiteering of a hawkish business community. The system's total involvement in an aggressive Asian war was made the more insupportable because the war drained off vital government financial resources from the Civil Rights movement. As Martin Luther King had said of it: "The bombs we drop in Vietnam will explode in America's cities." There followed a unique alienation of millions from both the American political system and American capitalism that staggered the nation, drove a president from office, and left American capitalism with the weakest popular commitment it had experienced since the depths of 1932.

With a government ruthlessly pursuing a foreign military adventure, paid for largely by mounting deficits, inflation continued; the Nixon government, unwilling to pay the price of the war by increased taxation, fell back upon direct controls, the third such policy commitment by the federal government since 1941. The results in 1972–73 were farcical, and such was no surprise, since so much of the Nixon program was economic nonsense, or else, like the price freeze of the summer of 1973, a simple blueprint for disaster. What saddened the student of American economic history was the supine acceptance of the Nixon programs by American business leaders. Here the dark accuracy of Schumpeter's vision was demonstrated. There seemed to be no one left who cared. In his speech of August 15, 1971, the President spoke of "a new prosperity without war," of "greatness in a great people," of the plan to "break the back of inflation—without the mandatory price and wage controls that crush economic and personal freedom." He went on to speak of that "inner drive called the competitive spirit," the need to be "number one." But who he imagined was his audience for such effusions is a mystery. By 1971, wars and crises for three decades had pushed nonmarket controls far beyond the legacy of Roosevelt and the New Deal. Not people but government made things happen, caused inflations, or stopped them. People went to work and paid taxes. Businessmen watched the government regulations that affected them and they worked with their partner, the IRS, sharing in the revenues.

THE WELFARE STATE EXPANDS

Beginning with the election of John Kennedy, peaking with the presidency of Lyndon Johnson, and expanding slowly in the regime of Richard Nixon, this country experienced a huge spasm of social welfare legislation and programs at the same time it tried to launch an aggressive war in Southeast Asia. It is not certain which program was meant to subvert the other, but in the event, they both failed. Table 6.2 contains a summary of this new legislation, divided by regimes, Kennedy-Johnson, Nixon, and after.

Professor Weidenbaum lists here only the major laws that impinge upon human behavior in business practice. Assessing this amazing list, in the light of the discussion in chapter 1 regarding modern thought about the causes of regulation, one scarcely knows where to turn. It is obvious that many special interests have been paid off by this mass of legislation. The 1990 Clean Air bill, a loophole-riddled freak laden with government-expenditure boondoggles was passed in a Congressional "special-interest feeding frenzy."[23] In 1990 a bill was signed to protect the rights of the disabled in the workplace, and a new civil rights bill was en route. Clearly no single theory could explain it except on the levels of highest generality. You could quote the ancient cliché: Every nation deserves its politicians.

If we were Germans or Russians some deep-thinking scholar might pontificate about our love of *ordnung* or of a national yearning to feel the weight of authority across our backs. But this mass of control legislation has come from the freedom-loving United States Congress, most of it *since* the Great Society epoch, in the regimes of successive presidents who promised, if elected, to get the government off the people's backs. One is inexorably driven back to the colonial law codes and their design to govern all by authority. But those laws

TABLE 6.2
The Great Society and After

Date	Title	Date	Title
1962	Food and Drug Amendments	1965	Water Quality Act
1962	Air Pollution Control Act	1965	Cigarette Labeling and
1963	Equal Pay Act		Advertising Act
1964	Civil Rights Act		
1966	Fair Packaging and	1967	Flammable Fabrics Act
	Labeling Act	1967	Age Discrimination in
1966	Child Protection Act		Employment Act
1966	Traffic Safety Act	1968	Truth-in-Lending Act
1966	Coal Mine Safety Act	1968	Interstate Land Sales Full Disclosure Act
1969	National Environmental Policy Act	1973	Vocational Rehabilitation Aid
1970	FDIC Amendments Act	1973	Highway Speed Limit
1970	Poison Prevention Packaging Act	1973	Reduction Act Safe Drinking Water Act
1972	Consumer Product Safety Act	1974	Campaign Finance Amendments
1972	Federal Water Pollution Control Act	1974	Employee Retirement Income Security Act
1972	Noise Pollution and Control Act	1974	Hazardous Materials Transportation Act
1972	Equal Employment Opportunity Act	1974	Magnuson-Ross Warranty Improvement Act
1975	Energy Policy and Conservation Act	1978	Fair Debt Collection Practices Act
1976	Antitrust Amendments	1978	Age Discrimination in Employment Amendments
1977	Department of Energy Organization Act	1980	Federal Trade Commission Improvements Act
1977	Surface Mining Control and Reclamation Act	1980	Comprehensive Environmental Response, Compensation, and Liability Act
1977	FLSA Amendments		
1977	Export Administration Act		
1977	Business Payments Abroad Act		
1977	Saccharin Study and Labeling Act		
1981	Cash Discount Act	1986	Superfund Amendments and Reauthorization Act

TABLE 6.2 (*cont.*)
The Great Society and After

Date	Title	Date	Title
1984	Drug Competition and Patent Term Restoration	1986	Asbestos Hazard Emergency Response Act
1984	Cigarette Safety Act	1986	Age Discrimination in Employment Act
1984	Insider Trading Sanctions		
1988	Employee Polygraph Protection Act		
1984	Insider Trading Sanctions Act	1990	Clean Air Act

Source: Derived from Murray Weidenbaum, *Business Government and the Public*, 4th ed. (Englewood Cliffs, N.J.: Prentice Hall, 1990), pp. 39-44.

were written by stern Puritans who meant to cleanse the earth and humble its inhabitants. Our new version of such control statutes came from a society that shows no particular religious or moral motivations. The large numbers of environmental regulations show an intention to cleanse the earth, but not in anticipation of the Second Coming.

In fact we simply continue along the familiar paths of group interests, always wrapped in the flag. None of the laws in table 6.2 existed when John Kennedy was elected in 1960 a mere three decades ago. *So who needs them?* After all, not any of the country's most pressing social ills—street crime, drugs, illegitimacy, homelessness, the health-care crisis—are dealt with by them. What one does find is quality of life enhancement for the affluent majority. Attempts to control environmental destruction by polluters, and to enhance the life-styles of top three fourths of our population seem to be the main concerns. We see Director's Law in action, with the economy manipulated in favor of a group, the broad middle class, whose votes control the state. In the 1960s it was said that the Sierra Club consisted of millionaires and hippies. The taste became contagious. If table 6.2 be considered as a welfare state, it is mainly of the American variety: Socialism for the Rich.

Yet if the environment is not protected from the ubiquitous toxicity of our modern industrial economy the whole point of American economic progress—to achieve and propagate the good (consumer) life—will simply move out of reach. Life on top of a carcinogenic garbage dump cannot really be made very good.

There are two general questions to consider here: Are there any limits to the scope of acceptable regulation? What happens when the limits, if there are such, are approached? Bertrand de Jouvenal said of power that there is enough of it in the world to control the lives of all persons: if the individual persons do not have it, then *someone else does*. In 1989 the East Europeans broke out of their socialist prisons, showing dramatically that bureaucratic control of humanity does finally surpass tolerable limits, even in police states.

In *Brave New World* Aldous Huxley allowed the disaffected to flee to Indian country in the American West. In our modern reality the disaffected may find their havens to be radioactive nuclear waste dumps when they arrive. One really cannot flee from the mess we have made. In 1990 an expedition climbed Mt. Everest to clean up the trash. The coastal research bases in Antarctica are littered with trash; the very oceans are fouled. We fear the Greenhouse Effect because of our output of fluorohydrocarbons; our fluorohydrocarbons may have eaten a hole in the ozone layer. We are regulating because, overall, we believe we need these regulations to hold back the destructive consequences of our material economy. Although there are numerous examples of foolish, harassing, trivial, and abusive federal regulations, those are usually aberrant malfunctions. The laws were passed to improve life, not just to harass citizens. But if we could learn anything from experience, it is that regulatory outcomes are only rarely the ones foreseen in the regulations.

Again, we can learn from American history. There are basically two modes of regulation in this country, the ICC kind, industry-agency, and the Sherman Antitrust Act kind, rules that apply to all. In the industry-agency case the regulator is charged with the welfare of the regulated, but in the Sherman Act kind, the enforcing agency (the Justice Department) has no responsibility for the fate of the governed. Whereas the ICC kind of regulator might be captured, there is no way a target of the new *intrusive* regulation is likely to capture the courts. The two models were always there. In colonial times ferries and draymen were regulated, but so were morals; that regulation cut across all classes. When the colonial forefathers laid down regulations about the clothes that could be worn, or the sizes of horses that might be allowed to roam freely, or who could buy a drink in a tavern on Sunday, the rules applied to all. That is why I referred to the Sherman Act as a behavioral sumptuary law for business; it applies to rules and structures without regard to industries. OHSA and EPA are the same—they intrude into every part.

Until the Great Society era most of our nonmarket control was of the ICC kind, industry-agency. But the 1962 Air Pollution Act, the 1964 Equal Pay Act, and the 1964 Civil Rights Act applied to all. They were novel laws compared to industry-agency laws like the Securities Exchange Act, but novel only if you have forgotten about the Sherman Antritrust Act and the colonial statutes. We had been there before. Professor Weidenbaum calls these "traditional" and "new model" regulatory techniques,[24] but I would call them just *industry-agency* and *intrusive*. Going back into the mists of history it is hard to say which is the more traditional. Professor Weidenbaum traces intrusive controls, or "social regulation," back to the Animal and Health Inspection Act of 1874.[25] But what about the Americans of pre-Revolutionary times? Those who began a law in 1662 governing clothing worn with the words "the Rising Generation are in danger to be corrupted and Effeminated"[26] meant to cover most people. If you do not want them effeminated, then legislate accordingly. We did it then, and we do it now.

These notions about the general uses of government regulation remained in our famous Puritan tradition, and we never hesitated to try to regulate morals or social improvement. State legislatures pass laws to govern the sexual conduct of citizens in their own bedrooms, and we think nothing of it. We have just passed a time of ideological hysteria when we legislated against *belief*: penalties followed if one believed the version of history propagated by the intellectual descendants of Marx and Engels. One characteristic of the mass of intrusive laws that followed the Great Society is that they tend to be (apart from a few lapses like the unfortunate Federal Trade Commission Improvements Act of 1980) efforts to improve society in ways the society would not go unless so pressed. They thus represent George McGovern's paradigm quoted at the beginning of this chapter—government should take an active role in our country.

BUREAUCRATIC PARTHENOGENESIS: POSSIBILITIES

A further dimension to the growth of intragovernmental nonmarket controls is the legislative one. The idea of governmental legislation *without Congress* is an oddity, given our Constitution. Yet it is common enough; rule making by regulatory agencies and special offices in the executive branch is precisely that. But there are still constraints.[27] The day has not yet come when mere presidential edict is considered sufficient legislative activity to be considered law. For example, in *Youngstown Sheet and Tube Company v. Sawyer*, when the Supreme Court overruled President Truman's order authorizing the federal government to take over the steel mills during a crippling strike, Justice Hugo Black wrote: "The Constitution does not subject lawmaking power of Congress to Presidential or military supervision or control."[28] Yet agency rule making is an everyday occurrence, as it must be, in a governmental apparatus of such proportions as ours. The citizen still has access to the courts, as, for example, when he runs afoul of the mercurial rules of the IRS, or when a firm contests a ruling of a regulatory agency such as the FTC. Also, most of the control agencies have internal appeals procedures. However, the rules and procedures of so many different control agencies are a mass of confusion, and the amount of nonmarket control is now so extensive that some coordination of rule making would doubtless be of advantage. But coordinated rule making by the control agencies would be potentially far more powerful than the noncongressional legislative activity that we have seen thus far in our history.

We have such a generalized rule-making body. In the Census Bureau's list of independent establishments and government corporations, along with such august organizations as the Federal Reserve System, the Farm Credit Administration and the Tennessee Valley Authority, a little-known title appears: the Administrative Conference of the United States. What is this? The Administrative Conference of the United States is an assembly that attempts to coordinate the rule-making activities of the regulatory bodies, and as such, looks like the beginning of our version of France's *conseil d'etat*. The agencies of nonmarket control each represent *a specific solution to a specific problem*. As such, they hardly represent a coherent system of planning and control, but rather a congeries. They are becoming a real system under Public Law 88–499 of 1964, the Administrative Conference Act. This organization's growth is worth watching.

The structure of our independent agency establishment would be, for the reader of this book, a shorthand history of perceived or imagined failures of the price mechanism as a social control system since the Wabash case in 1886. The ICC, the FTC, and the Federal Reserve System represent the beginnings. The Federal Maritime Commission is the legatee of the Shipping Act of 1916; the Federal Power Commission and the Veterans Administration (1930) come from the relatively quiet twenties. The New Deal flurry is represented by such control bodies as the TVA, FCC, NLRB, SEC, and FDIC. The Nuclear Regulatory Commission, the Environmental Protection Agency, the National Aeronautics and Space Administration, and the National Foundation on the Arts and the Humanities reflect more modern experiences. These are but a selection from many with a similar historical provenance.

These organizations are indeed little historical monuments. But they still function, and the questions must be, how well, and what continuing functions do they serve, if any. It should be borne in mind that an economic cost is involved: configurations of productive activity that differ from those the free market alone would have produced. If this were not true, then there would be no justification whatever for the controls. But since the free-market mechanism would produce a different balance of consumers' and producers' preferences in terms of economics alone, the costs and benefits of the nonmarket controls deserve to be constantly scrutinized. For example, clearly the Environmental Protection Agency has an ongoing function. The environmental movement is of recent origin, and the job of restructuring what is left of the natural ecology and managing the country's life-style to preserve and protect the land, air, and water is one that now commands the support and enthusiasm of millions. But the Environmental Protection Agency was created by Richard Nixon by executive order, and has since grown to great economic consequence. Is it to last forever? And if not, why not? At this moment in time the answer might well seem to be yes. We would be wise, though, to keep some options open, but this has not really been done. Likewise, we still have all of the original major independent agencies, or their direct successors, as if the problems they were introduced to solve had never changed or been solved. In October 1973 it was proposed by the natural gas producers that the FPC control of pipeline transmission should be suspended. The initial reaction was that a return to the allocation of the price mechanism was unthinkable. It should have been thinkable, or else the slow accretion of nonmarket control in this country would eliminate the elements of efficiency in the price system even more than was then the case. In 1978 new legislation, The Natural Gas Policy Act, gave a new agency, The Federal Energy Regulatory Commission (FERC) power to exercise remaining controls over natural gas with the complete deregulation of new gas production in 1985.[29]

A good argument could clearly be made that the lives of the control agencies should be made renewable, or not, on a regular basis. How many, given our present railroad system, would now renew the ICC if some other options were regularly available? The economy would gain if nonmarket control bureaucracies were constrained in order to periodically prove their superiority to the price mechanism.

In the Executive Office of the President, the options for renewal and change exist more readily. Roosevelt reorganized this part of our government by executive order in 1940, and then proceeded to use it during World War II without the necessity of normal congressional scrutiny. By this power, for example, he illegally placed in camps some 115,000 Japanese-Americans in 1942 to show how sternly he was resisting the Empire of Japan. President Truman continued the technique. For example, when the Senate refused to cooperate in the establishment of the International Trade Organization, following the Havana Conference in 1947–48, the President fell back upon the General Agreement on Tariffs and Trade, which he had endorsed by executive agreement and which the Office of the Special Representative for Trade Negotiations in the Executive Office was established to implement.[30] We got international cooperation on trade and tariffs despite Congress. The Executive Office is used to provide freedom and flexibility to the President that would be difficult to achieve with the older apparatus of government represented by the classic government departments.

Like the independent agencies of the federal government, the offices and councils of the Executive Office of the President partly embody bureaucratic artifacts of modern American history. The Office of Management and Budget represents not only the Roosevelt era, but efforts to reform the federal budgetary processes dating back to President Taft and beyond. Only in 1974 did Congress, in response to the budgetary crisis, make a serious effort to provide its own equivalent to the OMB.[31] The Council of Economic Advisors is an artifact of the depression and wartime experiences that resulted in the Employment Act of 1946. The National Security Council is the product of the Cold War, and so was the Office of Emergency Preparedness—its historical trailers going back as far as World War I.

The advances in technology of our age and the government's need to keep abreast of them have produced a sequence of offices, councils, managements, and administrations that glide like mercury through the government's organization tables over the years. These control devices can come and go mainly by executive initiative, and the associated apparatus has not the permanence of the established agencies, foundations, boards, commissions, corporations, and services whose line of descent in modern times begins with the ICC. Officials of the Executive Office, like the foreign-affairs specialists W. W. Rostow and Henry Kissinger, or domestic specialists like those of Watergate and Iran-Contra fame, do not hold office with the same long-term tenure as do those in the independent regulatory establishments.

In all parts of the federal control apparatus our history has bequeathed us the physical reality of government outside the tripartite divisions of the federal Constitution. The regulatory government is as real as is the regular government of the legislative, judicial, and executive branches. The small beginnings of the Populist era yielded a fulsome harvest of bureaucracy blessed by the older traditions of colonial America and its mercantilist and Britannic parent.

The agitation for decontrol in the 1970s bore some fruit, but ambiguously, in the 1980s. Most successful, it would seem, were the deregulatory efforts in ground and air transport. ICC rule in the trucking industry had seemed the height of absurdity in the 1970s when truckers were forced to travel empty after off-loading their cargoes, in order to keep freight rates high and spread the work around. The number of trucks had been limited, and rents were created for those fortunate enough to have the ICC permit. Freight rates were too high. The Motor Carrier Act of 1980 (following minor reforms in 1975 and 1979) gave extensive decontrol to trucking; freight rates fell, the number of carriers rose sharply (as did bankruptcies), and so did the quality of service.[32] Railroads gained significant decontrol in the Staggers Act of 1980 (after years of fierce struggles *against* deregulation led by some shippers and all the rail unions—those who stood to lose rents).

The CAB passed into history in 1984; the Airline Deregulation Act of October 1978 had begun the process. No new trunk carriers had been created by the CAB since 1938, so the Airline Deregulation Act, phasing out control of routes and rates was new ground, even for existing carriers. They had never known a competitive market. Most airline executives opposed deregulation at first.[33] In the 1980s real air fare rates fell. There was upheaval in the industry, including major carrier bankruptcies as the ways of the free market had to be learned. Small cities lost previously subsidized jet service, and the new hub-and-spoke route system developed. Marginally more competition resulted from the shakeout of airline companies. But no new major airports were built after the 1970s so the growth of demand for air service was producing major delays throughout the system by the 1980s. Delays in Chicago could (and did) leave loaded airplanes waiting on the ground for clearance from Los Angles to Boston. Nevertheless, most economists seemed to consider airline deregulation a success.

The same could be said for the breakup of AT&T. An antitrust suit under the Sherman Act had been filed by the Justice Department in 1949 against AT&T in an attempt to force divestiture of Western Electric, the manufacturing subsidiary. By a consent decree in 1956 AT&T undertook to freely license its patents. Nevertheless, by 1974 thirty-five private antitrust suits had been filed against AT&T over equipment. Then, in 1974, the Justice Department filed a "massive" suit,[34] charging monopolization in equipment, long-distance service, and local service. The end had come for Ma Bell on January 1, 1984. The company kept Bell Labs, Western Electric, and the terminal equipment business. The company was allowed to enter any other business free from regulatory control. AT&T gave up local phone services, but retained long-distance service. Competitors entered the equipment and long-distance businesses, and the local telephone companies spun off from AT&T remained regulated monopolies. Despite early complaints, the AT&T breakup was counted as a success for deregulation, since the company had in fact been a vast regulated monopoly for many years.

The results of other deregulation attempts went from ambiguity to the threat of unprecedented disaster. Amid much hoopla the Reagan administration took regulatory powers away from the independent agencies and distributed them among the regulatory units of the Executive Office. These actions were a source of some wonderment to students of deregulation: "The shift from congressional and agency power to presidential power in regulation cannot properly be termed deregulation."[35] Even the bureaucracy was unimpressed.

> Reagan succeeded in reducing the number of regulations promulgated each year, slowing the growth of agency budgets, institutionalizing the role of [the Office of Management and Budget] in the regulatory process, imposing cost-benefit analysis on executive branch rule making, and appointing regulatory and economic advisers who shared his pro-market, anti-regulatory views. Nevertheless, Reagan failed to bring about major legislative change.[36]

To make regulation even more political than it was in 1980, in the next eight years the Reagan regime managed to appoint all 63 members of the 15 key independent regulatory agencies, something Congress had always wanted to avoid; takeover of the agencies by a single administration. But regarding the possibilities of major deregulatory legislation, a commission to make recommendations under the fescue of Vice President George Bush, after much initial fanfare vanished without trace in 1983. A paper dragon.

Deregulation in gas and oil was opaque. I previously noted the partial decontrol of natural gas production and distribution. In the latter 1970s, the Carter administration had begun storing crude oil in the Strategic Petroleum Reserve. In 1980 came the Crude Oil Windfall Profit Tax Act (an excise tax, not a profits tax, actually).[37] The complex regulation of oil prices of the 1970s (reactions to various oil shocks of the period) was ended by President Reagan in 1981. The strategic reserve remains (presumably constantly growing), along with the excise tax and U.S. participation in various international oil industry agreements. The industry is thus partly free market, and partly not.

Financial deregulation has been only partial, with blurring of distinctions between various kinds of deposits and a tightening and rationalization of reserve requirements for depository institutions. The Depository Institutions and Monetary Control Act of 1980 was the major instrument of decontrol and reform, and it was followed by financial disasters of all sorts. The great bank failures (and federal bailouts, such as Continental Illinois) were topped by the savings and loan bankruptcies, and the organization of the Resolution Trust Corporation to bail them out at a projected cost to the Treasury of $350 billion. If that figure in fact is reached, the cost will be about the same as the nominal cost of World War II,[38] and about ten times President Mikhail Gorbachov's initial asking price for all Soviet installations in Lithuania. The bailout may cost more. The figure $500 billion has been bandied about. What caused the S&L imbroglio? By 1990 incompetence and outright fraud were running neck-and-neck in published accounts. Together with the gamey financial scandals associated with insider trading and leveraged buyouts, and the great stock market meltdown of October 1987, it can hardly be said that we have managed to find the optimal level of financial regulation. The issue is therefore left to those who already *know* what to do: they tend to advocate either no regulation at all or a return to close regulation of the kind imposed upon the financial system by Marriner Eccles back in the 1930s. Eccles was a man who knew bankers well and distrusted them altogether.

In any case, considering the avalanche of new regulation of the kind listed in table 6.2, the triumphs of the deregulators discussed are fairly minor. We live in a time when even the urine of professional athletes is a concern of regulatory power, and is inspected accordingly. One can welcome a bit of deregulation, if one is so inclined, but the amount we have experienced is hardly a return to the robust free enterprise economy one used to hear about at election time.

STAGFLATION AS A LIFE-STYLE

The marvelous neologism, stagflation, became current in the 1970s to describe a world of inflation and stagnant real growth. When Lyndon Johnson went to war in 1965, federal budget expenditures were at an annual rate of $118 billion. In 1973 the annual federal expenditure rate was $260 billion, an increase since 1965 greater than all the previous increases of federal expenditures in our entire history. But that was only the beginning of modern federal finance. By 1976 the federal government was struggling to hold expenditures at the level of $400 billion. Ten years later federal expenditures were $990 billion and by 1990 nearly $1.2 trillion.

Such considerations bring us back to the Employment Act of 1946, its consequences, and its problems. Let it be said that such expenditures did not, and do not, produce full employment, but have produced the highest rates of peacetime inflation in our history. What these expenditures do to "promote free enterprise and the general welfare," as the act puts it, is ambiguous at best. At least one Nobel laureate, as shown at the beginning of this chapter, believed that by 1989 the country had become 45 percent socialist.

The administrative device of the 1946 Employment Act was the Council of Economic Advisers, economists appointed by the President and supported by an appropriate research apparatus. For the most part the members and chairmen of the CEA have been academic and financial establishment figures. Since the tools available to the council and government in our circumstances are insufficient to achieve almost any policy aims, it is pointless, even unkind, to criticize the council for anything, except possibly missteps like the sophomoric blunders of the 1973 price freeze, which could not help but produce automatic shortages. The council only makes recommendations, one source of information input into a governmental taxing and spending machine that receives an infinity of other inputs regarding how much money should be spent, by whom, paid to whom, and where. For whom the council's statements are prepared is something of a mystery, since it is clear that the President rarely follows their advice, and the public merely has its intelligence insulted by such predictions as those in the 1972 Economic Report of the President, prepared by the council, which, among other things, confidently predicted that inflation was about over.[39] The real novelty of the council is not what Professor Galbraith called the "feckless incompetence" of the 1973 council, but the implications of its very existence. In 1976 the council was still predicting the end of the inflation, and in 1982 President Reagan placed the council into deep background after disagreeing with its views of the consequences of forthcoming federal deficits in the range of $200 billion a year. By 1990 the council still existed, but it was no longer the oracle of economic wisdom it had been in its glory days of yore, for example, in the fine tuning days along the New Frontier.

In terms of ideological history the federal government's direct assumption of responsibility for employment and welfare was as nearly a total reversal as one could imagine. The reversal has two parts. The first part, the legal turnabout with acceptance of such responsibility in Washington, was previously discussed. The second part assumes that the federal government can in fact work such control over economic life as to guarantee the future level of full, or nearly full, employment. By 1990 doubts have deepened about this assumption. Against the wisdom and possibility of such control was our understanding of the country's past economic development and of what could possibly be achieved by free enterprise if it were to continue to exist. In the first instance one had the idea of capitalist development, expressed best by Professor Schumpeter. Depressions, deflations, and unemployment were necessary aspects of capitalist development. These were the periods of forced realignment of productive factors necessary to achieve the efficient combinations which would enable the next period of expansion to succeed. In the 1974 and 1982 recessions the forced realignments were held to show the wisdom of Schumpeter's view. But the financial disasters of the late 1980s were of such magnitude that the federal bailout became the policy tool of choice. The S&L disaster alone was still unresolved when the defense industry, after decades at the federal trough, faced shutdown and the terrifying prospect of finding productive employment in the civilian world. Saddam Hussein's aggression in the summer of 1990 seemed to give our defense establishment—Stealth bombers and all—at least a temporary respite.

The second consideration is the sheer physical problem of control over such a vast thing as a consumer-oriented capitalism with its billions of annual decisions independently and simultaneously made. Many economists believe that the prospect of really effective non-market control in such a world is about as likely to succeed as King Canute's orders to the ocean waves. This popular wisdom was expressed in 1931 by Senator Albert Gore of Oklahoma when he said that passing laws would no more improve the economy "than you can pass a resolution to prevent disease. This is an economic disease. You might just as well try to prevent the human race from having a disease as to prevent economic grief of this sort."[40]

The abandonment of such pessimism was partly the result of the World War II mobilization, during which full employment, with massive armed forces, was finally achieved, and partly the result of the policy implications of Keynes's *General Theory*. With cyclically balanced budgets and the right fiscal and monetary policies, a guaranteed full employment economy seemed a real possibility. But one facet came to be forgotten by the CEA's practitioners of the "dismal science," and that was *price stability*, a part of the original promise of

the managed economy. In the first flush of post-World War II enthusiasm for the managed economy, the strategic principles of fiscal and
monetary management were thought generally to be the following:
"Government tax revenues should be higher relative to government
expenditure in periods of high employment than in periods of substantial unemployment;" and, "Money and credit should be relatively tight in periods of high employment and relatively easy in periods of substantial unemployment."[41]

Those statements were written in 1950, and the eminent economists who penned them were diverse spirits—Emile Despres, Milton
Friedman, Albert Hart, Paul Samuelson, and Donald Wallace. Behind
their statements lay a set of axiomatic beliefs about both economic
theory and historical reality relating to the American experience with
the peacetime business cycle. A federal budget balanced only over
the course of the whole business cycle, if at all, together with adroit
monetary management that stimulated expenditures in slumps and
constrained them in booms would do the trick. Prices might fluctuate
relative to each other, but a faithful execution of policy relative to
agreed-upon theory and facts would avoid any marked trend in
prices.

In any event, those forces that made price stability in the American
economy unattainable proved to be the rock upon which the original
fiscal policy ideals were broken. The dream could not be realized,
given the facts.

Whether full employment with price stability could actually have
been achieved in a peacetime economy remained unknown, because
in 1950 began an era of ceaseless increases in government expenditures, the great "Keynesian updraft," related to the Cold War and the
growth of welfare-state expenditures. Real shortages in 1973–74,
combined with Federal Reserve efforts to offset the mounting federal
deficit with a resolute tight-money policy, produced *both* the highest
peacetime interest rates and highest price increases we had ever
known. Throughout the 1980s the combination of inflation and high
real interest rates continued under the relentless increase in expenditures and continuing federal deficits.

Such possibilities were foreseen by economists. In 1951, when Korean War expenditures were mounting, Professor Arthur Smithies
foresaw not only the war's destabilizing consequences regarding pol-
icy-making, but glimpsed things to come in the structural sense: "It
is likely that the long period of military preparation on which we are
now embarking will bring permanent changes in the relation of government to business, and control measures that are inconsistent with

private enterprise today may be permanent and compatible features of the economy tomorrow.''[42]

Since reality cannot be deduced from general principles, Smithies could not foresee precisely how the new perpetual military establishment would exist in a private economy like ours. But less than a decade later, President Eisenhower had a more vivid premonition of the future, recognizing the changes that had taken place during his administration:

> We annually spend on military security more than the net income of all United States corporations.
>
> This conjunction of an immense Military Establishment and a large arms industry is new in the American experience. The total influence—economic, political, even spiritual—is felt in every city, every statehouse, every office of the Federal Government. We recognize the imperative need for this development. Yet we must not fail to comprehend its grave implications. Our toil, resources, and livelihood are all involved; so is the very structure of our society.
>
> In the councils of government we must guard against the acquisition of unwarranted influence whether sought or unsought, by the military-industrial complex. The potential for the disastrous rise of misplaced power exists and will persist.[43]

By now, of course, there are scarcely words of sufficient drama to describe the consequences: *trillions* spent on military demand since 1950; an international situation in which such a condition came to be considered normal, perhaps even desirable; a constant need for new, more sophisticated weaponry (and more expensive on each round). It came to pass that military waste no longer counted. Politicians competed with each other in denouncing welfare chiselers, education, and school lunches, but military waste, the vastly expensive toilet seats and ash trays became the subject of talk-show humor, and little else. Who could control it? Star Wars would cost, for openers, $40 billion; we had to have it. The Stealth bombers were to be more than $500 million each; we had to have them. Hauling out and refitting the old World War II battlewagons cost further billions; we had to have them too.

A decade after Eisenhower's speech Professor Seymour Melman ended his definitive study of the consequences, *Pentagon Capitalism*, with another such warning, beyond the eleventh hour:

> Rarely does a single social force have a controlling influence in changing, swiftly, the character of life in a large and complex society. The expansion of the Pentagon and its state-management is such a force. Failing decisive

action to reverse the economic and other growth of these institutions, then the parent state, if it is saved from nuclear war, will surely become the guardian of a garrison-like society dominated by the Pentagon and its state management.[44]

Instead of that the military expenditures became an accepted farce, hardly justified by the invasions of Grenada and Panama, but certainly justified by macroeconomic theory. After all, if the federal government did not spend the money, who would? The idea of giving it back to the taxpayers, the great promise of the new Reagan administration in 1981, proved to be unacceptable. The Pentagon's expenditures have been another vast imposition of nonmarket control upon American capitalism, a direct removal from the GNP of a large portion, perhaps 10 percent a year (counting all the quasi, or hidden, military expenditures in the federal budget), for straight military needs. Until 1989 Congress showed little enough willingness to constrain seriously the gross military demand. Then as the Soviet military enemy began to fade from view the queuing began to spend the "peace dividend" even as the military still claimed to need more weapons to face the melting Cold War. The U.S. government was becoming a major support of the Soviet dictatorship to keep the USSR from falling apart as its captive nations sought their independence from the Leninist nightmare.

The military expenditure has been triply inflationary: first, because the financing of its aggregate size usually requires deficit spending; second, because military expenditures generate income in the civilian economy in the form of money demand, but return no product to the civilian economy to help soak up that demand; third, because military expenditures notoriously allow leeway for seller-induced price increases, and for cost overruns.

What can be said of military expenditure can be said also, perhaps to a lesser degree, of most other federal outlays, and one is reminded of Adam Smith's commentary in 1776 on such matters—words that might well be engraved in stone at the Pentagon:

> Great nations are never impoverished by private, though they sometimes are by public prodigality and misconduct. The whole, or almost the whole public revenue, is in most countries employed in maintaining unproductive hands. Such are the people who compose a numerous and splendid court, a great ecclesiastical establishment, great fleets and armies, who in time of peace produce nothing, and in time of war acquire nothing which can compensate the expense of maintaining them, even while the war lasts. Such people, as they themselves produce nothing, are all maintained by the produce of other men's labour. Those unproductive hands, who

should be maintained by a part only of the spare revenue of the people, may consume so great a share of their whole revenue, and therefore oblige so great a number to encroach upon their capitals, upon the funds destined for the maintenance of productive labour, that all the frugality arid good conduct of individuals may not be able to compensate the waste and degradation of produce occasioned by this violent and forced encroachment.[45]

We need not go all the way with Adam Smith to understand his meaning: resources used by the government are not available to the private sector. The larger, relatively, the government sector, the more to the point is Smith's view of the great powers of the late eighteenth century. We have maintained for four decades the largest and most expensive military power in history, but seem to have escaped with the basic economy still intact: 55 percent of GNP still disposed of by the private sector. But we face a dilapidated infrastructure, decades of social problems unresolved, and the banana-republic budgetary techniques outlined in table 6.1.

The remorseless increase of federal spending in 1950–90 was partly achieved by visible taxation, and partly by a defter method—inflation. In either case the consequence, the removal of goods and services from private use, was the same; in the first instance because money demand was directly expropriated and transferred in the form of taxes; in the second instance because government bought whatever it wanted at whatever was the necessary price, and consumers paid for it by nonconsumption, finding their own money incomes insufficient to compete with government purchasing. In the first case, the expropriation has been achieved by democratic means: Congress authorized the expenditures openly. In the second case the method of expropriation was less obvious: Congress raised the debt limit (an action the average citizen cannot comprehend), deficit spending occurred, and the price mechanism, together with timely actions of the Federal Reserve System, was used to remove goods and services from the nongovernment economy. The result was an increase in the national debt and, in due course, the money supply. Because of income multiplier effects, prices, the money supply, GNP, and the federal government's progressively structured tax haul increased proportionately more than did the initial increase in the national debt. As can be seen in table 6.1 these relationships generally held until the 1980s when the weakening economy required more and more debt to produce the next round of federal revenues. The euphemism for this form of expropriation in the jargon of economics was an "income-adjusting economy," and the people were told they were better off thereby. The hoax was transparent, but was infinitely more acceptable politically than would have been direct expropriation of goods and services to foot the federal bills.

The modern economy, suppressed by nonmarket controls of all sorts, topped by a total government absorption of more than 40 percent of everything legally produced, and a government structure that, at all levels, employs every sixth person in the labor force— these are major components of the economic world we have produced and must live with. The world of full employment and price *stability*, envisaged by the economists of 1950, now seems utterly utopian.

As shown in the long journey through this book, our situation is not the unique product of recent events. We have long had the seeds of it growing in the institutions of American economic life. A slowly growing, slowly inflating economy may be our foreseeable future, since neither a movement into a planned economy nor a return to significantly greater reliance on the price mechanism has been among the options produced by our leaders.

It is in this light that we can look back to President Nixon's "economy of phases" as a pathetic institutional reaction, borrowing ideas from the past, the Wage Board, the Price Commission, the Cost of Living Council, the price freeze, and other emergency reflexes. In the early months of the Ford administration there was no apparent agreement on anything that might be done. President Ford's ideas were not well received, especially his call for higher income taxes as an anti-inflationary device—a sour joke since the government could be expected to spend all it could, and tax and borrow as well. After failing to get from Congress just a few hundred million dollars more to extend the Vietnam agony, Ford then reversed himself and became an advocate of tax cutting. It was WIN time: Whip Inflation Now. Those days were bathos. There seemed nowhere to go but up.

Combined with inflation at home, the policies of 1950–90 had succeeded in reversing a balance-of-payments position, the current-account surplus financed by net foreign lending, which had been solidly based since the 1890s, and most of the time since the 1870s. The nation's foreign exchange position was turned into a shambles by the Vietnam War presidents, and the international monetary system, the achievement of Keynes and White and Bretton Woods, painfully constructed for twenty-five years, was shattered. We then developed a gigantic current-account deficit and became the world's largest net capital importer—debtor nation—to the dismay of modern Populists who view foreign investment in the United States with alarm. In recent years industrial policy has been advocated as the road out of our troubles. This idea involves an interleafing of bureaucracy in both the public and private sectors: promising new technological departures would be identified and encouraged by governmental favoritism in the targeted areas. Why not have the ICC do it? One can hardly become enthusiastic about government solving problems the government largely created.

Chapter 7

EPILOGUE: THE LONG VIEW

The Tripartite Economy

In the afterglow of the Reagan Revolution, which blossomed and wilted against the backdrop of this country's long history of government intervention in economic life, it will be useful to appraise the prospects. What we have evolved is an economic world conceptually divided into three parts: (1) the government fiscal sector, (2) the uncontrolled private sector, and (3) the regulated private sector.

The question is: What is the object of American economic life, and can it be achieved by our present methods? "Life, liberty and the pursuit of happiness" are the goals Jefferson originally set out, and they have long been held to be acceptable goals by us (and lately by reformers from Berlin to Beijing). Economists, who deal only in a narrow range of human motivation, have tended to interpret "the pursuit of happiness" as the pursuit of private wealth, and widespread wealthholding is most equitably and abundantly achieved by economic growth. Moreover, because of the Employment Act of 1946 economic growth is an *official* target for policy in this country. Economic growth is measured as an increase in output (GNP) per head of population. This can be achieved in many ways, but in the long run it has been just technological improvement that has made such growth possible.[1] There are simple rules of the road for our tripartite economy, if economic growth is to be sustained, or improved upon.

The Government Fiscal Sector

The government fiscal sector is the world of taxing and spending. To achieve maximum contributions to long-term growth this sector requires both inflationary and anti-inflationary options: the power to induce and the power to constrain the growth of the economy periodically. To have these options, government revenues must sometimes be greater than expenditures. The logical target here is not a balanced budget per se, but a budget that can sometimes be in deficit, and sometimes be in surplus according to the best estimates of the economy's needs at any point in time. This is, or was when it existed, called discretionary fiscal policy. The object of policy should be to achieve this power if the fiscal sector is not to be just a permanent deadweight on society. Government *can* contribute to economic growth in its fiscal affairs. All other policies, including monetary policy, can be adjusted to the fiscal targets, once they become more than merely attempts to reduce the current federal deficit, an activity that is likely to occupy most of the 1990s. In the four decades of the Cold War we have lost the ability to have a meaningful fiscal policy. But it could be achieved again, with any luck.

THE PRIVATE UNREGULATED ECONOMY

Economists generally agree about optimal policy regarding privately-negotiated economic transactions: enforce private contracts and maximize the extent of competition in the system. Using the antitrust laws, we have tried to protect competition for a century. In a bargain reached freely by private parties, both come away satisfied, an outcome that is thought by economists to be desirable.

But these actions do not eliminate all perceived needs for government action. Even private contracting can sometimes be deemed socially destructive and motivate intervention. Private drug buyers and dealers reach mutually satisfactory agreements every day, and we object. The bargain is held to be bad for our society, but it certainly is good for the raw-materials producers in countries like Peru and Columbia. Similarly, bargains reached between American cotton growers and British users of that fiber before 1861 were mutually satisfactory; good for the manufacturers of cotton textiles, good for the plantation owners, but not so good for American slaves. War ended slavery, and we now are in the midst of a war on drugs by military and semimilitary means.

But obnoxious private bargains also can be subject to court action without overt force or constant regulation, and the extent of the private economy not subject to agency regulation maintained. In other words, it is possible that not all private sector activity end up controlled by government agencies.

THE REGULATED PRIVATE ECONOMY

The evidence would seem to indicate that the regulated private sector is not likely to shrink. Indeed, it could continue its growth almost without limit, since controls can be set over controls, agencies over agencies. There being no overall logic to this sector, apart from the realization of self-interest through the capture and use of government regulatory muscle, the object of policy ought to be to maintain growth of regulation under close scrutiny, and to keep its operating costs as low as is practicable, thus reducing its contribution to fiscal drag. The public interest cannot be known, but private interests can. The beneficiaries of private interests may be counted upon to make their wishes known to legislators and regulators. The thousands of PAC employees in Washington are not there to lobby for better government. Since regulatory outcomes have been, historically, full of surprises,[2] the ability to reform and restructure this sector should not be lost. Perhaps creation of a regulatory inspector general would be a good idea, so that an adversary procedure would be available to protect the public, as in our courts of law.

It is legitimate to study history for its own sake. We want to know why we have the sorts of nonmarket controls we do, and how and when they came into existence. That much this book has shown. What are the lessons to be learned from this history? Here one leaves certainty and enters a shadowy realm. But history informs the present, so, it is argued, we should seek the answers. There are several answers, and they do not yield the kind of robust message that can readily be turned into campaign slogans at election time. Anyone seeking a thousand points of light in the world of government regulation faces a daunting task.

Two sets of facts stand out. First, the nonmarket controls are, and always were meant to be, guides and restraints upon a growing private economy. They are not in themselves a production system, and it would take considerable ingenuity to transform them into growth-promoting forces on even a modest scale. Moreover, many of the most powerful control devices were designed either to support or to raise prices, mainly by reducing supply. So these devices are not, as they stand, going to aid us in any long-term fight against inflation, itself the inevitable consequence of our banana-republic fiscal policy. Second, in the private sector the motivating force for growth (income- and employment-creating production) is profit, directed by the price mechanism, and that is now widely distrusted if it is not subject to nonmarket control. So we are at an impasse, and continue to have moderate stagflation (a little bit of real growth, a little bit of inflation and a core of long-term unemployment). The end of the Cold War does present new possibilities for technological modernization, but one cannot know in advance how much we will benefit from the opportunity.

Sufficient growth does not occur, as the economy is, to sustain full employment, largely because of the deadweight of taxation and controls. The proportion of our population living below the poverty line has been increasing since the 1970s.[3] Strong social and political forces constantly press against any reduction of that deadweight. Indeed, the first reaction to the idea of a "peace dividend" in 1990 was where to direct the expenditures. Senator Moynihan's scheme to cut Social Security taxes and return the money to the taxpayers, was not well-received. Nor would we expect it so to be.

Given the history, structure, and functioning of the federal control agencies, it is difficult to take seriously the remaining political agitation to reduce the size of big government. The control bureaucracy is part of our modern social fabric, carefully woven in over many decades. It will not just go away, and the people would not tolerate its abolition since they believe that it at least serves them. As shown in chapter 2, in the 150-odd years of colonial America institutions that no longer served either changed or vanished. Then as now the desire to control market outcomes by nonmarket control devices flourished. Whatever the objections one may have to the regulated way of economic life we now enjoy, one cannot say, on the evidence, that the controls have somehow become obsolete. They continue to flourish robustly.

The planned economy also is an unlikely alternative, more unlikely now then it was when Tugwell went to Washington in 1933, because of the stench Soviet-style totalitarianism has given to the very word socialism. It no doubt will rise again, but not until the smell of 1917–89 goes away. In any case, planning requires quantitative controls to be effective. Where we have had such, in the oil industry and, to some extent, in agriculture, the results have hardly been in the public interest by almost any definition. And in any case, those quantitative controls have nearly always been used to constrict output and employment. Such results are not solutions to problems of stagflation and do not contribute to economic growth—more output, more employment.

What should be done then? Are we to experience more of the same, year after year? The answer is most surely yes if we do not change our ways.

Indeed, creation of control agencies has become almost biological. It is almost as if we believe that every new technology *must* require its own government controller. No economic activity should be free of control. In the October 1987 market crisis it was immediately put forth that program trading had caused the great meltdown in stock values. The accusation was floated by brokers and traders as a defense against an angry public that believed that the traders themselves, by failing to make orderly markets on that fatal Monday the 19th were guilty of mis-, non-, or malfeasance at least. Sell orders totaling about 350 million shares had piled up in open-line computers over the weekend and it was the disorderly and delayed execution of those orders that finally reduced the Dow Jones Industrial Average by more than 500 points in a single day.[4]

The twentieth century world of computers and the nineteenth century system of open outcry had proved in such circumstances to be incompatible, and, predictably, it was proposed to control or even to outlaw the new technology to protect the old, along with the rents accruing to those who operated it, the traders. Despite any convincing evidence that the meltdown had been caused by program trading Congress was considering in March 1990 a bill to place such trading under direct government regulation.

The question was, *what* government? The Securities and Exchange Commission and the Commodity Futures Trading Commission were involved in an unseemly jurisdictional brawl over this new line of regulatory business, and the proposals included creating an entirely new agency to regulate securities that had "characteristics of securities and futures."[5] This is close to agency reproduction. The fact that computerized trading, a result of technological advance, was adopted by some because it was more efficient (that is, growth producing) than open outcry was apparently lost. The idea that an advance in technology might be left *unregulated* was not even considered.[6] The two agencies were fighting over their proprietary rights. It was like the IRS view of life: The government *owns* the national income; if it decides not to tax a certain part of it, that is called a *tax expenditure*. In this, the IRS conception is that the income rightly belongs to the people in Washington, D.C., and not to those who earned it. If it is not taxed, then that is generosity on the part of the federal authorities. The desire to impose controls is very powerful, and is a generalized force in this country.

Despite the power of rent-seeking activity, productive change must still originate in the private sector, wherein lies the only real possibility of cost-reducing innovations that could raise real output enough to offset the inflationary tendencies of the spending and control policies of the federal government. But beneficial changes need not be draconian. If the private sector could grow more rapidly than the public sector for just a few years—a reversal of history since the Eisenhower administration—then labor could be increasingly employed in noninflationary economic activity. If this occurred the tax load might be reduced; this alone would be an incentive to further expansion of the private sector.

There are two important general points to emphasize about our galaxy of control bureaucracy: (1) the total number of nonmarket control devices in the present American economy is simply vast; and (2) whereas they comprise a control congeries, they are not a system, in the sense of a unified or coherent planning system. Let me highlight these two points once more.

This book has traced the origins and development of nonmarket controls through property rights in land, chattel goods, labor contracts, public callings, monetary history, tariffs, and more. I have explored the ancient provenance of all of these back into colonial times and English history. I have recalled the myriad devices by which English, then colonial, then American society set the ground rules for economic life; the rule of *caveat emptor* was shown developing in connection with this framework. I have shown further how at the federal government level a structure of similar, related agencies of nonmarket control developed piece by piece. In each case local and then a national justification was advanced for the control. This has meant a multiplicity of nonmarket controls over economic life from the local hack license, or beer parlor, to the Satellite Communications Corporation. It is not that there are just a few well-known and well-understood cases of nonmarket control in this country, but that there are unnumbered thousands of separate nodes of control. From the viewpoint of economics, our nonmarket system is not coordinated within itself according to any general principles. It is simply an outcome of history. The rationale for much of this control is by now ancient history, some of it unknown except to a few experts. Yet the control continues unquestioned.

Secondly, economic life is constrained by these controls; that is, without them, economic life would have, or would acquire, a different configuration. For example, without the National Labor Relations Act, wage-push inflation might never have been heard of. Industry-wide strikes could not occur without the legal establishment of collective bargaining. Our nonmarket controls constitute piecemeal planning in a crude sense because they delimit what may or may not be done, from the ICC to the local Good Humor man. But do the methods we have represent the best or even the most congenial methods of control? In the roll call of the federally organized independent agencies, for example, are many living (and, some say, half-living) historical artifacts. Do we want them all to exist in perpetuity? Because it was held that the railroads failed to serve the national interest by reliance upon the price mechanism in the 1880s and the ICC was established to correct that situation, have we in this information an argument that the ICC should exist forever? What are the reasons that, more than a century later, the ICC should not join the CAB in history's dustbin?

All of the nonmarket control mechanisms we have might well be scrutinized from the viewpoint of economic efficiency and social desirability in the light of modern conditions and knowledge. The larger issue of individual freedom is also involved. Freedom to do what one wants, as Justice Sutherland stated in his great argument (in an unhappy cause), is the most prized possession of Americans. That is what the world wants, and hopes to adopt, from our ideological and institutional structure. Such freedom is constrained, by definition, by the nonmarket control apparatus we have developed. To say this is not to argue that there should be no social control at all beyond the price mechanism. Americans clearly do not want that. But surely a timely review of this structure, much of it ancient, is in order. And indeed, sunset, or "regulatory agency self-destruct," laws were under consideration back in the years of the Carter administration. They might be considered again. Agencies, if only for budgetary reasons, ought to need some justification beyond mere existence to continue their lives.

It often is argued that the idea of individual freedom from control has been rendered obsolete by economic development. A giant interdependent economy, such as ours has become, makes the federal government's expansion inevitable, the theory holds. But it was not only in the narrow world of economics that the ideals of rugged individualism became obsolete. Our whole conception of the individual's place in the social order has changed, with increasing emphasis upon individual sacrifice to the collectivity: "Ask not what your country," etc. Continuous wars in this century and other crises contributed mightily to this development. As the great legal scholar Roscoe Pound wrote in *Social Control Through Law*, in 1942, the traditional ideal had been the individual person and his economic, political, and moral rights. Only in a fully competitive world could fulfillment come to the individual, and the process itself was nothing less than the capture, by the individual units, of their natural rights. The object of the law had been "to secure those natural rights, to give the fullest and freest rein to the competitive acquisitory activities of these units, to order the competition with a minimum of interference."[7] To Dean Pound this antique view lasted longer in the United States than in other advanced countries "because it did portray reasonably well a pioneer, rural, agricultural society in a land with a great unsettled public domain and natural resources awaiting exploitation."[8]

The change to a society less tolerant of the individual's rights when society's overall needs seem more pressing was the natural result of a society of growing complexity whose organizations were too large to be viewed as depositories of old-time individualism. Dean Pound thought that individualism must ultimately be replaced by cooperation and even by "regimented activity."[9] Such glum conclusions must have seemed bizarre in 1942, but in modern times they have become commonplace—the harassed taxpayer's Social Security number festoons the top of Form 1040 and by its ubiquitous presence on documents of all sorts has become the American pigtail.[10] The Internal Revenue Service Form W-4, which appeared in 1971, even coopted the taxpayer himself to inform upon his fellow taxpayer: "Employee—If you had no tax liability last year and anticipate none for this year, you may be exempt from income tax withholding by filing Form W-4F with your employer. . . . Employer—If you believe the employee claimed too many exemptions advise your District Director."

This kind of group compulsion is an ancient and obnoxious method of government control. One can imagine how an American historian would write this up if the tax form had been produced by the French government in the spring of 1789 or by the late President Ceaucescu of Romania. Still wrestling with form W-4, the IRS produced a version in 1987 whose complete incoherence elicited a huge public outcry, and forced its abandonment—a rare event.

It could be argued that rugged individualism still exists in the taxpayer's effort to retain some of his own earnings for his own use, but the collective demand for his income is now very large and is constantly growing. Pound was not too far off about the regimentation, not only in terms of expropriation of private income and wealth by government, but in terms of the amount of economic life now governed by federal, state, and local regulatory agencies; within the entire matrix of choices such agencies leave little enough freedom in economic decision making. It was no wonder that, while foreign investors sought safe haven here in the 1980s, many American manufacturers transferred their investments to foreign countries.

Our historical behavior has a further interesting characteristic, and that has been the irreversibility of the social control option. The nonmarket controls, especially at the federal level, represent the consequences of particular crises and particular problems, many of which existed long ago. The agencies of control are a form of government. But they are not democratic in the sense of representing anyone, or anything, except procedure for its own sake. As Max Weber said of appointed officialdom: "Bureaucratic authority is carried out in its purest form where it is most clearly dominated by the principle of appointment. There is no such thing as a hierarchy of elected officials in the same sense as there is a hierarchical organization of appointed officials."[11] Such criteria fit the major judicial offices and the independent agencies like a glove. And, as J. C. Northcote Parkinson said, this form of government tends to expand regardless of the amount of work done. How well does this form of government, extensive as it has now become, accord with our own notions of representative government?[12] Does an ordinary businessman have easier access to the Board of Governors of the Federal Reserve System, or the commissioners of the FTC, than did a colonial businessman to the Board of Trade? The connection is in neither case a direct or a representative one. How extensive in fact is the public input into the regulatory agencies? Even if one could assume—and one certainly cannot—that municipal licensing systems are subject to constant scrutiny and evaluation in the public interest at the local level, how true is this of the great national agencies? Should they not, at least, be as responsive as are the elected portions of government to changes in the national political spectrum? And if not, why not? How did the scandals at the Department of Housing and Urban Development, the savings and loan catastrophe, or the bribery at the FDA develop if oversight was operating?[13] The answer must be that the overseers were asleep at the switch. Can this sort of thing be avoided in future? Why not?

Appointment and tenure of commissioners in the federally established regulatory bodies is a functional combination of New England's colonial selectmen and the federal judiciary, and thus, theoretically, the source of even-handed and nonpolitical execution of the laws. In many cases, its seems, this has not been the case.

Moreover, the idea of real independence in the control agencies has greatly weakened. Under the Nixon regime the placement of partisan political appointees in the control agencies reached a new high. On the six primary regulatory agencies sat thirty-eight members; by mid-1973 Nixon had appointed twenty-eight of them. The chairmen of each of the agencies, the FCC, FPC, FTC, ICC, and CAB, were appointees of a single president—a situation that the staggered terms of those offices were designed to avoid. The practice of politicizing the regulatory agencies by appointments and control of their budgets did not begin with or end with Nixon though. As already noted, Ronald Reagan managed to appoint all sixty-three heads of the fifteen largest federal regulatory bodies. A bill was proposed in 1989 to put the Secretary of the Treasury back on the Federal Reserve Board,[14] thus undoing the work of Marriner Eccles in 1935 when he removed the Secretary of the Treasury and the Comptroller of the

Currency from their ex officio roles at the Fed. Eccles the banker believed that the loan officers and the borrowers should be different people.

The agencies have become notorious havens for politicians ousted from public life by the electoral process. But it should be remembered that the justification of regulation supposedly was that government regulation would be better for the people than the decisions of the marketplace. Few persons ever argued (although the historian Gabriel Kolko did, in the case of the ICC) that this form of nonmarket control was supposed to be a government-sponsored industry cartel.[15] It is a sad commentary that by now many experts believe that political abuse of the agencies has worked to infuse the economy with more monopoly and cartelization than the private sector ever could have achieved by its own devices had no controls existed at all.[16]

Such need not be the case. It was not so in the beginning. Have the regulatory bodies in fact operated impartially in the broad public interest, or is it true, as many change, that the regulatory bodies are typically mastered by those industries they are supposed to regulate? There is much to be said for facing such questions openly as the 1990s are upon us, more than a century since the Interstate Commerce Act and the Sherman Antitrust Act launched us on our career of federal nonmarket control.

The power of nonmarket control has become so extensive in the United States that one is reminded of the complaint in the reign of Charles I against the royal monopolies: They, like "the frogs of Egypt have gotten possession of our dwellings and we have scarcely a room free from them; they sip in our cup; they dip in our dish; they sit by our fire; we find them in the dye vat, the washing bowl and the powdering tub; they share with the butler in his bar; they have marked us and sealed us from head to foot."[17] What major line of economic activity in the United States is completely free today of federal regulation? Is the answer none?[18]

Summing up: The view developed in this book is that our federal nonmarket control structure is *partly* the product of a century of specific crises. But the ease of the governmental habit as a chosen solution to perceived market failures is also due to our tradition, the methods we find congenial. There was in the historical background and law a sufficient set of models and traditions of control which could be adapted to fit new conditions. The apparatus of control, established piece by piece, became a permanent fixture. The private economy must respond to the control as well as to its own internal information system; but the private economy must necessarily become what the control wants it to be, if the rules are followed. The nonmarket controls came into existence because, put bluntly, Americans distrust capitalism in its pure form. There is no other explanation. It was so in the 1880s, in the 1930s, in the 1960s, and as shown in the previous chapter, it is so now.

By the 1990s our long and deep-seated development of nonmarket controls had produced an economy of rule making and constraint. The Reagan administration created its full share, and more, of additional kinds of government intervention into private affairs, despite its avowed conservatism. The modern crises of drugs, AIDS, and family breakdown among the ghetto poor promise more regulation to come. Bureaucracy presides over a metastasizing social crisis, and the prospect of decisive change from the government quarter seems to be nil. The private sector has no way to free itself from the tentacles of nonmarket control except by a major reform movement at the national level, hardly a promising prospect. If Ronald Reagan and the neoconservatives would not push large-scale decontrol, who will? The dominant force for political and social reform in this country, dating all the way back to the Populists was, and is, firmly committed to the side of federal control. The Reagan-era technique of tossing the problems back to the states while keeping the funding in Washington, has produced deep cynicism about the options. The federal need for ever more funds even led to the view that the end of the Cold War would produce no peace dividend.

The original conception of the controls was always government action that was complementary to private economic decisions. What our bureaucracy has not been able to do is substitute itself and its decisions for the private economy. But it now forms a barrier of enormous proportions between individual decision makers and the objects of their decisions, all the way from the individual taxpayer to the giant conglomerate. The sudden collapse of the communist system in eastern Europe in 1989 left those economies in chaos; not a good recommendation for government control of productive resources.

Piece by piece our controls were supposed to be solutions to specific problems; in aggregate they are simply a bureaucratic congeries—a heap. Our nonmarket control tradition has a basic weakness that derives from its history, and that is the belief in the efficacy of piecemeal supervision, the origin of separateness of each agency of control from the others. Our methods amount to an ad hoc structure, and function accordingly. Bear in mind the origins, the original models. Determination of the public interest is the fundamental issue, and in medieval England and colonial American, even perhaps at the local or state level, that interest might conceivably have been determined by persons charged with the control power.

At the beginning the only public interest that mattered was primarily the source of the control itself—local landowners and a small oligarchy of officials. The wages of laborers and artisans in any district of medieval England might be set by the manor court, by local magistrates, sheriffs, or other such petty officials as are so charged in the Elizabethan *Statute of Artificers*. The interests of local society might be served with some intelligence and purpose in those circumstances. The same could be said of local colonial communities. The township selectmen charged with such responsibilities (even today in rural New England) might at least know by direct information input the local consensus on such issues. The same might reasonably be true of prices in controlled trades, or, for that matter, of entry conditions, amount, or the quality of work done.

Such problems gain complexity, however, depending on the size of the community whose welfare is supposed to be served by such basically intuitive methods. The public interest of the county or state will be more difficult for officials to determine because information becomes more diffuse and conflicting interests multiply. When these practices were elevated to control nationwide economic activity, intuitive understanding of the public interest simply became unattainable. Hence the unhappy record of the federal control structure and hence also the tendency for the public interest to become transmuted into the interest of those firms and persons subject to control. They, at least, know where their interests lie and can press the nonmarket control agencies accordingly. Having nothing but intuition, perhaps some vague theoretical guidelines, or even merely the personalities of the control officials to shape policy, the control agencies not surprisingly become the protectors and instruments of those they regulate. How could it be otherwise? Who knows in a huge community what the public interest might be? Is it lower fares on airplanes? Lower or higher earnings for airlines? Ten trunk airlines? Five? Fifty? The problem will not be solved by our methods. Neither free-market nor command-economy techniques are in use, but rather, the usual dysfunctional mixture.[19]

The control options are, of course, directives, either in laws or in the quantitative targets of some planning agency of the future. The noncontrol solution is always open. But the prospect of a massive return to the free-market decision seems to frighten politicians and private citizens alike. And nothing is more suspicious than enthusiasm from within regulated industry itself for decontrol, as was the case of our financial sector in the 1980s.

What is certain and understandable—given our history—is that intuitive control by appointed officials is not likely to work better than it has, apart from rooting out obvious corruption and incompetence. The railways, or air waves, or energy or manufacturing sectors, or financial institutions, are not deploying the technology of the seventeenth century on the scale of a New England township, or an English parish. Yet the system we use was invented for those technologies and scales of activity. We find it socially and politically congenial, but not economically efficient. It is a dilemma.

In the *Three Penny Opera*, Berthold Brecht's formula for success is happy endings. Alas, I cannot contrive such a creation out of the materials at hand. No victorious messenger is on the horizon bearing glad tidings. Decontrol seems to have come, and gone. Economics has long been known as the dismal science. The economist of 1990 is hard-pressed to earn some kindlier appellation. Has our luck really run out at last? If not, one can only hope that solutions lie hidden in the genius of the American people. But the source of our economic achievements always was there in any case. We have no evidence in the performance of government since 1960 that it can, or will, be the main avenue of escape from inflationary slow growth. Underemployment is a result of economic growth too slow to employ the existing labor force, and is not an area in which government controls are likely to help. Government seems to be more a part of the problem than of the solution.[20] The relentless increase in federal expenditures and deficits gives us money supply increases every year in excess of productivity increases. But if there are to be increased supplies of goods and services at stable or falling prices and higher levels of employment, real economic activity must increase more rapidly than does the supply of money. Since for decades now government has relied upon money-creating spending programs in the private sector to achieve its expansionary policy goals, it has no significant real resources under its own authority that could yield expanded supplies of goods and services. Our federal government is mainly an employer of bureaucrats and military people, and no extra efforts by them, no matter how heroic, can raise the supplies of real goods and services in this country. Memos are not output of capital equipment, goods, or services.

If the major long-term outcome of the controls and regulations is to protect the rents of vested interests, as most interested scholars believe, the cumulative results can be devastating in time, as industry after industry falls behind the international standard of best practice.

The current state of American manufacturing suggests that has been happening to us: in steel, in autos, in textiles, in electronics, we have seen other nations pass us by. As Joel Mokyr points out in *Lever of Riches*,[21] it has happened before to other nations who once led in phases of technological advances, but who stiffened up via rent-protecting control and regulation and were bypassed by more aggressive and adaptive competitive economies. There is a danger that our little games of nonmarket control, undertaken for whatever reasons, one at a time, are in fact subtly doing us in. Like Britain in 1914 we will look around at the host of economies that have left us in the dust and wonder how it happened.

The private sector, for the most part, is the productive sector. Any kind of policy for increased economic growth must therefore encourage new activity in the private sector. It is hard to see how the proliferation of new controls contributes to this end. Probably the most important single factor in the choices before us is simply politics. Politicians tend to do what is good for *them*; salary increases for themselves, contracts for their supporters, favors for Political Action Committees. In the late 1980s a more terrifying prospect raised its head, corruption of the regulatory system itself: the HUD scandals, and the bribery of minor officials in the IRS and in the FDA. This is a direct route to Third-World existence and must be blocked. Extensive corruption of our federal control system, huge as it now is, would undo the American economy completely.

Success in American economic development lay always in a balance between uncompromised individual freedom and the limitations society demanded to maintain order and a sense of justice beyond the market decision. But thus far we have not found the right balance between the requirements for continued economic growth and the desire, for whatever reasons, to impose controls on economic processes. At one point the idea of local enterprise zones was considered to be a way to produce economic growth in selected areas. In these areas the idea was to suspend all except the most essential controls protecting health and safety. Perhaps it would be a good idea to make the entire U.S. economy an enterprise zone. But that would take more political commitment and nerve than we have seen in government for a very long time.

Our accumulation of regulatory devices is, as I have said, no system. No one thought it out over all. It was made in separate pieces over a long period of time, and functions crazily as a part of the government. It is like a large farm where all possible crops have been planted at random, and then called agriculture. You most likely would starve from such a farm. Clearly Americans prefer a regulated economy to an uncontrolled one. But what should be the overall logic of government economic control? To what end? If tomorrow all government regulation of economic life vanished, and we were free to do it all over again, does anyone suppose we would rebuild what now exists?

As it stands we have on the ground almost every kind of regulation that could be conceived of over time, and it was made mainly by those for whom the regulation pays, for whom money can be made by regulation that the free market would never provide. If the result were merely a leveling of incomes and wealth, the process might be justified ideologically on Jeffersonian grounds. But leveling is not the result: instead it is mostly a seemingly biblical outcome: "To him who hath shall be given." Worse, though, is the fact that the economy as a whole is damaged by the random mass of regulation and restraint. If we are going to do this to ourselves, we should question the objectives of such actions. Perhaps there should be an *independent* National Commission on Economic Regulation, like the National Monetary Commission of 1908–12. Such a commission might determine and recommend which economic activities should be left free in this country, and which ones controlled and why. At least there could be a public airing and discussion of the issues involved. The way we have gone is no way to run a railroad—or a government. The stakes are enormous and should not be left to the vagaries of politics and the ambitions of special interests—and the passage of time. The way it is we have in the regulatory sphere *government by legislative accumulation*. This is no radical proposal. The National Food Security Act of 1985 (that year's farm bill) cost many billions of dollars. What was it for? Another one was hatched in 1990. Why have we done it again? Must we grow peanuts forever by grandfathered federal permits? Is it really true that farming cannot exist in this country without these giant treasury raids?

As I have emphasized repeatedly, our institutions are path-dependent. History matters. Because of regulation, we are different now than we otherwise would have been, and we ought to learn what we are doing and why, and perhaps why we ought not to continue doing this to ourselves. In regulation we are making our economic future just as surely as we do it with physical investment. But physical capital becomes obsolescent, wears out, and is replaced. Regulation tends to live on even though in many cases few know or remember anymore what it is, or was, for.

So the controls have prevailed in our era, as they did even during the great free-market expansion of the nineteenth century. We create controls (a nonelected form of government) today with the same alacrity as did our great grandfathers a century ago. It is not a question of whether the nonmarket controls have achieved their objectives, unless those objectives include perpetual bureaucratic life for the agencies of control. The problems for which the controls were invented are to be managed in perpetuity, not solved. The ruling paradigm was established by the first federal nonmarket control agency, the ICC. We may well now have the controls *because* they reduce economic efficiency; the controls are seen to save us from the uncertainties of the free market just as civil government is seen to save us from the uncertainties of anarchy. Professors of economics may not like the parallel, but they do not make laws.

NOTES

CHAPTER 1

1. Hugh Rockoff, in his recent research has isolated and identified 333 independent nodes of regulatory power in the federal government.

2. In its crudest applications, say in Cook County, Illinois, county deputy sheriffs place the furniture and personal effects of the property owner, along with the owner, in the street and seal up the house. The real estate is sold for the amount of the taxes owed at a subsequent tax sale. The owner may not regain his property without paying the tax buyer the amount owed plus interest. The right to the property tax by the state is due to the ancient right of *reserved ground rent*, an incident of the tenure of free and common socage, now called in this country fee simple, which was planted in all of the colonies by the British. The reserved rent was the right of the donor, originally the king or his tenant, and now, by marvelous legerdemain, the state of Illinois. The law is essentially the same throughout the United States. Thus the voice of the Middle Ages may still be heard in the United States.

3. "When Congress established new western territories, provision was made for a legislature that was empowered and expected to adopt civil and criminal legal codes appropriate for a new frontier commonwealth. Provision sometimes was made, as for Washington, to retain codes already in use in whatever territory each new jurisdiction came from. In some cases—including Montana, which originally had been part of Idaho—informal arrangements were adopted to retain previous codes governing land incorporated into a new territory after Congress neglected to continue a system of civil and criminal law. Idaho, however, had a more complex situation. Formed from parts of Dakota, Nebraska, Utah, and Washington territories, Idaho had no single antecedent territory with legal codes that could cover the area larger than Texas which had become a new territory with no laws identified as applicable. *Until Idaho's legislature adopted English common law, January 4, 1864*, pending enactment of a code based on Nevada's statutes, none of those four codes continued in effect. By 1866, when that oversight finally attracted judicial attention, one accused criminal managed to escape trial and two convicts were released from prison because their crimes violated no law. No one else remained in any of Idaho's jails because of offenses committed between March 4, 1863 and January 4, 1864, when Idaho lacked any criminal laws to be violated." [Merle Wells] *Idaho Yesterdays: The Quarterly Journal of the Idaho Historical Society* 25(1981): 13. Italics added.

4. Garcia v. San Antonio Metropolitan Transit Authority, 469 U.S. 528 (1985).

5. Robert Higgs, *Crisis and Leviathan: Critical Episodes in the Growth of the American Government* (New York: Oxford University Press, 1986).

6. This same conclusion also was found in the first edition of this work,

but was conjoined with the *long-term* historical propensity to use government at all levels to change market outcomes.

7. James Bryce, *The American Commonwealth*, rev. ed. (New York: Macmillan Co., 1941), p. 98.

8. James Buchanan, in 1987; Buchanan was one of the founders of the public choice school of economics. For an early approach to his views, see James Buchanan and Gordon Tulloch, *The Calculus of Consent* (Ann Arbor, University of Michigan Press, 1962). By 1975 his ideas on the problems of big government were concentrated in his powerful book *The Limits of Liberty: Between Anarchy and Leviathan* (Chicago: University of Chicago Press, 1975).

9. For a useful collection of seminal papers on growth of government, see George Stigler, ed., *Chicago Studies in Political Economy* (Chicago: University of Chicago Press, 1988). For a critique of all the major explanations of growth of government, see Robert Higgs, "Eighteen Problematic Propositions in the Analysis of the Growth of Government," forthcoming in the *Review of Austrian Economics*, 1991.

10. Joseph Schumpeter, *Imperialism and Social Classes* (New York: Meridian Books, 1955), p. 6.

11. For the view that it was mostly hubris, though, see James M. Buchanan and Richard E. Wagner, *Democracy in Deficit: the Political Legacy of Lord Keynes* (New York: Academic Press, 1977).

12. In 1971 three contributions appeared that would prove to be heavily freighted with ideas about government: Mancur Olson's book on the economics of group action, *The Logic of Collective Action: Public Goods and the Theory of Groups* (New York: Schocken Books, 1971); George Stigler's essay on regulatory agencies and their tendency to "capture" by the regulatees: "The Theory of Economic Regulation," originally in *Bell Journal of Economics and Management Science* 2 (1971), and reprinted in Stigler, *Chicago Studies*; and William Niskanen's model of government bureaus as expenditure-maximizing "firms" within congressional budget constraints, *Bureaucracy and Representative Government* (Chicago: Aldine, 1971).

13. All calculations from data in *Historical Statistics of the United States* (Washington: Government Printing Office, 1960), and *Statistical Abstract of the United States*, in relevant years.

14. Martin Feldstein, ed., *The American Economy in Transition* (Chicago: The University of Chicago Press, 1980), p. 174.

15. Usually we speak of the deficits and debt in nominal (current prices) figures. My own objection to endless deficits, thus measured, is that fiscal policy is reduced to maximum expenditures every year constrained by the debt limit, combined with Gramm-Rudman strictures and aided by various accounting sleights of hand. This condition simply eliminates discretionary fiscal policy, one reason some economists *applaud* the situation. Robert Eisner, in *How Real is the Federal Deficit* (New York: The Free Press, 1986) poses deeper problems relating to the consequences of inflation, which makes the debt seem far larger than it is in real terms; to fiscal drag, which makes the budget appear to be in deficit when in fact it is a surplus at full employment

levels; and to the failure to weigh the budgetary shortfalls against real assets, as any business firm would do in calculating its net worth. I shall not enter into these matters. But imagine the Presidio, under the Golden Gate bridge, auctioned off, all 1,400 acres, for private use, the proceeds applied to debt retirement; then one can begin to appreciate Eisner's point regarding the value of uncounted federal assets.

16. Mira Wilkins, *The History of Foreign Investment in the United States to 1914* (Cambridge: Harvard University Press, 1989), pt. 2.

17. Buchanan, *Limits of Liberty*, pp. 36–38.

18. Terry Anderson and P. J. Hill, *The Birth of a Transfer Society* (Stanford: The Hoover Institution Press, 1980).

19. Gary Becker, "Public Policies, Pressure Groups and Dead Weight Costs," *Journal of Public Economics* 28 (1985). Reprinted in Stigler, *Chicago Studies*; see esp. p. 101 on the "compensation principle."

20. George Stigler, "Director's Law of Income Distribution," *The Journal of Law and Economics* 13, reprinted in Stigler, *Chicago Studies*. "Any portion of the society which can secure control of the state's machinery will employ the machinery to improve its own position" (p. 106).

21. Sam Peltzman, "The Growth of Government," *The Journal of Law and Economics* 23 (1980), reprinted in Stigler, *Chicago Studies*; see esp. pp. 55, 74. This discussion excludes the former Soviet-bloc countries and the USSR and China, countries where until recently the deadweight of government was uniquely heavy, despite their poverty.

22. This is a generalization of Stigler's finding that small firms have more influence in a regulated industry than in the open market. In a regulated industry, a small firm has one vote, as does a large one. Stigler, "The Theory of Economic Regulation," p. 213.

23. Niskanen, in *Bureaucracy and Representative Government*, portrays government bureaus contending for budget shares much as business firms contend for market shares. Niskanen's analysis could be taken as a formal statement of Anthony Downs's argument that growing bureaucracies provide expanded opportunity for maximizing behavior by bureaucrats. To make room for promotions, they would naturally push for bureau growth. (Anthony Downs, *Inside Bureaucracy* [Boston: Little, Brown & Co., 1967].) In Niskanen, a budget increase shifts the entire expenditure function upward. In both cases growth without inside promotions in rank would do little for the individual bureaucrat, since federal salaries are tied to a fairly rigid scale of ranks. Ronald N. Johnson and Gary D. Libecap, "Agency Growth, Salaries and the Protected Bureaucrat," *Economic Enquiry* 27 (1989).

24. For a study of comparative control methods between the United States, Germany, France, and Britain targeted to solve the same range of problems, see Allen V. Kneese and Blair T. Bower, "Institutional and Organizational Approaches to Regional Water Quality Management," in *Managing Water Quality: Economics, Technology, Institutions* (Baltimore: The Johns Hopkins University Press, 1968). The Americans are singular for the politicization of their control agencies and consequent weakening of technical expertise.

25. Munn v. Illinois. 94 U.S. 113; Chicago, Burlington and Quincy Railroad v. Iowa, 94 U.S. 155; Peik v. Chicago and Northwestern Railroad, 94 U.S. 164; Chicago, Milwaukee and St. Paul Railroad v. Ackley, 94 U.S. 179; Winona and St. Peter Railroad v. Blake, 94 U.S. 180.

26. Munn v. Illinois, pp. 125–26.

27. Wabash, St. Louis and Pacific Railroad v. Illinois, 118 U.S. 557 (1886).

28. For example, Richard A. Posner, "Theories of Economic Regulation," *The Bell Journal of Economics and Management Science* 5 (1974).

29. Stanley Reiter and Jonathan Hughes, "A Preface on Modelling the Regulated United States Economy," *Hofstra Law Review* 9 (1981), esp. pp. 1404–1406, where it is shown how it will pay regulated firms to misinform regulators, who then pursue regulatory targets with incomplete information. The system goes off track and continues to drive the economy away from targeted performance. There is nothing in the system leading to self-correction.

30. J.R.T. Hughes, *Social Control in the Colonial Economy* (Charlottesville: University Press of Virginia, 1976), pp. 4–6; also Milton Handler, "Antitrust—Myth and Reality in an Inflationary Era," *New York University Law Review* 50 (1975); and "The Attack on Parker v Brown," *Columbia Law Review* 76 (1976), for a similar organization of control structure.

31. Controlling the number of participating agents stemmed from the Crown's ancient right to grant monopolies, and then the delegated powers of the early towns to restrict business activities to the gild merchants. The conditions of entry are controlled by licensing practices and are part of the traditional police powers of municipal governments, as they developed; for example, only persons of good reputation would be licensed to sell spirits. The power to control prices always existed in England; it is in the Magna Carta (the assize of bread). Quality controls are very old, beginning in English in the late thirteenth century with the rules of assumpsit. I will discuss these matters in the next chapter.

32. See Hugh Rockoff, *Drastic Measures: A History of Wage and Price Controls in the United States* (New York: Cambridge University Press, 1984), for a survey of the varied uses of one of the four control methods as far back as colonial times.

33. Alfred D. Chandler, the leading modern student of big business, attributes to displaced merchants and small businessmen the vital antagonism to the new giant firms. *Scale and Scope: Dynamics of Industrial Capitalism* (Cambridge: Harvard University Press, 1990), p. 79. I argue later, in chapter 4, for a broader source of the pressures that produced the Sherman Act.

CHAPTER 2

1. *Seeds of Liberty: The Genesis of the American Mind* (New York: Alfred A. Knopf, 1948).

2. Malcolm Rohrbough, *The Land Office Business: The Settlement and Administration of American Public Lands* (New York: Oxford University Press, 1971), p. 301.

3. "Declarations and Resolves of the First Continental Congress," October 14, 1774, in *Documents Illustrative of the Formation of the Union* (Washington, D.C.: Government Printing Office, 1927), pp. 1–5.

4. Rene David and John E. C. Brierley, *Major Legal Systems of the World Today* (London: Stevens and Sons, 1968), pp. 336–380.

5. James Kent, *Commentaries on American Law*, 12th ed., ed. Oliver W. Holmes (Boston, 1873), 3:197, 199–203, 249–50.

6. William Blackstone, *Commentaries on the Laws of England* (New York: W. E. Dean, 1840), p. 82.

7. Sir Frederick Pollock and Frederic William Maitland, *The History of English Laws Before the Time of Edward I*, 2d ed. (Cambridge: Cambridge University Press, 1968), 1: chaps. 1, 3; 2: chaps. 4, 6.

8. F. W. Maitland, *The Constitutional History of England* (Cambridge: Cambridge University Press, 1961), p. 32.

9. Marshall Harris, *The Origin of the Land Tenure System in the United States* (Westport, Conn.: Greenwood Press, 1970), chap. 2; Pollack and Maitland, *History of English Laws*, 1:291–296.

10. Francis Newton Thorpe, ed., *The Federal and State Constitutions, Colonial Charters, and Other Organic Laws of the States, Territories, and Colonies Now or Heretofore Forming the United States of America* (Washington, D.C.; Government Printing Office, 1909), p. 3789.

11. William MacDonald, ed., *Select Charters and Other Documents Illustrative of American History, 1606–1775* (New York, 1899), p. 242.

12. Harris, *Origin of Land Tenure*, pp. 91–97; Henry Christman, *Tin Horns and Calico* (New York; H. Holt and Co., 1945).

13. Thorpe, *Federal and State Constitutions*, pp. 2653–2655.

14. Kent, *Commentaries*, 3:647–648.

15. Harris, *Origin of Land Tenure*, p. 107; see Richard B. Morris, "Primogeniture and Entailed Estates in America," *Columbia Law Review* 27 (1927).

16. Morris, "Primogeniture," p. 39.

17. Ibid., pp. 25–29.

18. For a more detailed description see Jonathan Hughes, "The Great Land Ordinances: Colonial America's Thumbprint on History," in David Klingaman and Richard K. Vedder, eds., *Essays on the Economy of the Old Northwest* (Athens, Ohio: Ohio University Press, 1987).

19. Thomas Hutchinson, *The Hutchinson Papers* (Albany, N.Y.: The Prince Society, 1865), 1:33–34.

20. Theodore Roosevelt, *The Winning of the West* (New York: G. P. Putnam's Sons, 1889), 1:331.

21. William Cranch, *Reports of Cases Argued and Adjudged in the Supreme Court of the United States, 1801–1815*, vol. 6 (Washington, D.C., 1804–17), pp. 142–143.

22. Kent, *Commentaries*, 3:516.

23. David Galenson, *White Servitude in Colonial America: An Economic Analysis* (New York: Cambridge University Press, 1981); Robert Heavener, "Indentured Servitude: The Philadelphia Market, 1771–1773," *Journal of Economic*

History 38 (1978); Farley Grubb, "The Auction of Redemptioner Servants, Philadelphia, 1771–1804," *Explorations in Economic History* 48 (1988).

24. United States Constitution, article 1, section 2.

25. Abbot Emerson Smith, *Colonists in Bondage: White Servitude and Convict Labor in America 1607–1776* (Chapel Hill: University of North Carolina Press, 1947), p. 336. Estimates vary widely. Jack P. Greene holds that from 80 to 90 percent of white immigrants in the Chesapeake before 1700 were indentured servants. Some estimates for the colonial period have put the overall proportion of indentured servants in the white immigration as high as 75 percent. On the other hand, Farley Grubb, in a recent unpublished work holds that most estimates are far too high, and that the most reasonable figure lies between 29 and 45 percent. Since no one was counting, it is unlikely that we shall ever have an incontestable figure.

26. 5 Eliz. I, c. 4.

27. 39 Eliz. I, c. 4.

28. William Whitmore, ed., *The Colonial Laws of Massachusets* (Boston: City Printers, 1889), p. 53.

29. Phillip Alexander Bruce, *Economic History of Virginia in the Seventeenth Century* (New York: Macmillan, 1896), 1:593–594.

30. Hutchinson, *Hutchinson Papers*, 1:264.

31. Smith, *Colonists in Bondage*, pp. 90–137.

32. Ibid., pp. 142–143.

33. A Massachusetts law of 1642 reads: "that all parents & masters do breed and bring up their children & apprentices in some honest Lawfull calling, labour, or imployment, either in husbandry or some other trade, profitable for themselves or the Common-wealth, if they will not, or cannot train them up in learning to fitt them for higher imployments, the sayd Select men with the help of two Magistrates or the next County Court in the Shire shall take such children or apprentices from them, and place them with some masters for yeares." For boys that meant until they were 21, and for girls, until they were 18 years of age. Whitmore, *Colonial Laws of Massachusetts*, p. 136. Did the Massachusetts saints do such things? They did. Carl Bridenbaugh provides several examples. In Boston in 1656 (or 1657) Goodwife Sammon was told that her son was "living without a calling, that if she dispose him not of him in some way of employ [the selectmen] . . . will dispose of him to some service according to the law." In 1672 the parents of twelve children were told to bind them out "to serue Indentures" or the town would do it for them. Carl Bridenbaugh, *Cities in the Wilderness: The First Century of Urban Life in America, 1625–1742* (London, Oxford University Press, 1966), pp. 46–47.

34. Thomas Jefferson, *Notes on the State of Virginia* (London: John Stockdale, 1788), p. 220.

35. Edmond S. Morgan, *The Puritan Family* (New York: Harper/Torch, 1966), p. 109.

36. Farley Grubb, "The Auction of Redemptioner Servants; Philadelphia, 1771–1804," *Journal of Economic History* 48 (1988).

37. Whitmore, *Colonial Laws of Massachusetts*, p. 123.

38. Robert Fogel and Stanley Engerman, *Time on the Cross* (Boston: Little, Brown, 1974), 1:13–29. Also, Robert William Fogel, *Without Consent or Contract: The Rise and Fall of American Slavery* (New York: Norton,1989), pp. 29–34.

39. Edmund Morgan, *American Slavery, American Freedom* (New York: Norton 1975); Bruce, *Economic History of Virginia*, 2:108–22; Stanley Elkins, *Slavery* (New York: Universal Library, 1963), pp. 37–52.

40. Edward McCrady, *The History of South Carolina Under the Royal Government* (New York: Macmillan, 1899), pp. 381–385; Kent, *Commentaries*, 2: pt. 1, lecture 32.

41. Smith, *Colonists in Bondage*, p. 226.

42. Edward A. Adler, "Business Jurisprudence," *Harvard Law Review* 28 (1914-15):139.

43. Whitmore, *Colonial Laws of Massachusetts*, p. 39.

44. Charles C. Jones, *The History of Georgia* (Boston: Houghton Mifflin, 1883), 1:479.

45. Blackstone, *Commentaries*, 2:362–365.

46. Halfway through the eighteenth century *markets overt* were still being established. Governor Benning Wentworth's charters to Halifax and Marlboro townships in Vermont in 1750, and 1751 both contained provision for market days and occasional fairs. Hughes, "The Great Land Ordinances."

47. Carl Bridenbaugh, *Cities in the Wilderness* (New York: Oxford University Press, 1971), pp. 341–345.

48. Whitmore, *Colonial Laws of Massachusetts,* p. 126.

49. Ibid., p. 185.

50. James Willard Hurst, *The Legitimacy of the Business Corporation in the United States, 1780–1790* (Charlottesville: University Press of Virginia, 1970), pp. 38–39.

51. Whitmore, *Colonial Laws of Massachusetts*, pp. 192, 220.

52. Kent, *Commentaries*, 3:198–199.

53. Charles G. Haines, *The American Doctrine of Judicial Supremacy* (Berkeley: University of California Press, 1932), chap. 1, n. 1, p.

54. 27 Henry VIII, c. 25.

55. David Ricardo, *Principles of Political Economy and Taxation* (Homewood, Ill.: Richard Irwin, 1963), p. 54.

56. Whitmore, *Colonial Laws of Massachusetts*, p. 125.

57. Ibid., p. 174.

58. Ibid., p. 183.

59. 14 George 2, c. 37.

60. Benjamin Franklin, *A Modest Inquiry into the Nature and Necessity of a Paper Currency.* The American colonists appear to have independently invented paper money in the west. Previously, the Chinese had recourse to paper money off and on over several centuries, generally finding it inflationary. Mark Elvin, *The Pattern of the Chinese Past* (Stanford: Stanford University Press, 1973), pp. 150–161, 193–194, 221–222.

61. Lance E. Davis and Douglass C. North, *Institutional Change and American Economic Growth* (New York: Cambridge University Press, 1971), pp. 28–29.

62. Oliver E. Williamson, *The Economic Institutions of Capitalism* (New York: The Free Press, 1985), p. 31.

CHAPTER 3

1. Harris, *Origin of Land Tenure*, pp. 388–389.

2. Rohrbough, *The Land Office Business*, chap. 1.

3. Harris, *Origin of Land Tenure*, p. 389.

4. Albert Bushnell Hart, ed., *American History Told by Contemporaries* (New York: Macmillan, 1901), 3:155.

5. Frederick Jackson Turner, *The Frontier in American History* (New York: Henry Holt & Co., 1921), p. 47.

6. Thomas Perkins Abernathy, *Western Lands and the American Revolution* (New York: Appleton-Century, 1937), pp. 7–8, 145–146.

7. Ibid., p. 147.

8. Ibid., p. 218.

9. Harris, *Origin of Land Tenure*, pp. 385–386.

10. Abernathy, *Western Lands*, p. 368.

11. Harriet Martineau, *Society in America* (Garden City, N.Y.: Doubleday, 1962), p. 181.

12. Rohrbough, *Land Office Business*, chaps. 2–6.

13. Albert Fishlow et al., *American Economic Growth* (New York: Harper & Row, 1972), chap. 4; Howard Ottson, ed., *Land Use and Problems in the United States* (Lincoln: University of Nebraska Press, 1963); Gary Libecap, *Locking up the Range* (San Francisco, Pacific Institute, 1982).

14. Bureau of Land Management, *Homesteads* (Washington, D.C.: Government Printing Office, 1961), table 1.

15. But the lands acquired after independence remained a crucial area of fundamental dispute between the free and the slave states. The new lands, viewed by southerners as the common property of the original signatories of the federal constitution, was being distributed by the federal government to individuals and organized into new states with equal sovereignty under the land ordinances of 1785, 1787 and 1790. The situation was inherently unstable and the claims incompatible, and the issue was finally settled by the Civil War. See the forthcoming book by Professor Jennifer Roback on this topic to be published by Princeton University Press.

16. *Historical Statistics of the United States* (Washington, D.C.: Government Printing Office, 1957), tables U.10–18, and notes for the numbers. On losses, see Vernon Carstensen, ed., *The Public Lands: Studies in the History of the Public Domain* (Madison: University of Wisconsin Press, 1968), p. xviii.

17. Paul Uselding and Larry Neal, "Immigration, A Neglected Source of U.S. Economic Growth, 1790–1912," *Oxford Economic Papers* (March 1972).

18. Philip Taylor, *The Distant Magnet: European Emigration to the USA* (London: Eyre and Spottiswood, 1971), chap. 11.

19. Jefferson, *Notes on Virginia*, p. 229.

20. Taylor, *Distant Magnet*, p. 245.

21. Brinley Thomas, *Migration and Economic Growth* (Cambridge: Cambridge University Press, 1953), chap. 7, pp.

22. Joel Mokyr, *Why Ireland Starved: A Quantitative and Analytical History of the Irish Economy, 1800–1850*,(London: Allen & Unwin, 1983), pp. 265, 278–294.

23. Ibid., table 117.

24. Quoted in Carter Goodrich, *Government Promotion of American Canals and Railroads 1800–1890* (New York: Columbia University Press, 1960), p. 42.

25. Fishlow, *American Economic Growth*, pp. 468–472.

26. Goodrich, *Government Promotion*, pp. 28–41.

27. *Statesman's Manual: Presidents' Messages 1789 to 1846* (New York: Edward Walker, 1848), pp. 291, 232, 529, 534; Goodrich, *Government Promotion*, chap. 8.

28. Hurst, *Business Corporation*, pp. 22–25, 35–36.

29. Goodrich, *Government Promotion*, p. 270.

30. Fishlow, *American Economic Growth*, pp. 491–500.

31. Paul W. Gates, *The Illinois Central Railroad and Its Colonization Work* (Cambridge, Mass.: Harvard University Press, 1934); Goodrich, *Government Promotion*, p. 271.

32. Robert Higgs, "Railroad Rates and the Populist Uprising," *Agricultural History* 44 (July 1970).

33. Leland Hamilton Jenks, "Railroads as an Economic Force in American Development," *The Journal of Economic History* 4 (1944).

34. Robert William Fogel, *Railroads and American Economic Growth* (Baltimore, Md.: The Johns Hopkins University Press, 1964), chap. 6.

35. Carter Goodrich and Harvey H. Segal, "Baltimore's Aid to Railroads: a Study in the Municipal Planning of Internal Improvements," *Journal of Economic History*, 13 (1953).

36. Gates, *Illinois Central Railroad*, chap. 2.

37. Goodrich, *Government Promotion*, chaps. 5–7.

38. Carl Bridenbaugh, *Cities in the Wilderness*, pp. 341–345.

39. Richard C. Wade, "Urban Life in Western America, 1790–1830," *American Historical Review*, 64 (1958).

40. David and Brierley, *Major Legal Systems*, pp. 339–341.

41. James Kent, *Commentaries*, 2:853.

42. Ibid.

43. Ibid., pp. 857.

44. Ibid., pp. 872–75.

45. Louis Hartz, *Economic Policy and Democratic Thought: Pennsylvania, 1776–1860* (Cambridge, Mass.: Harvard University Press, 1948), p. 204.

46. Oscar Handlin and Mary Flug Handlin, *Commonwealth: A Study of the Role of Government in the American Economy, Massachusetts, 1774–1861* (New York: New York University Press, 1947), pp. 67–81.

47. Kent, *Commentaries*, 2:914.

48. Handlin and Handlin, *Commonwealth*, pp. 255–256.

49. Ibid., p. 260.

50. Hartz, *Economic Policy*, p. 204.

51. Hurst, *Business Corporation*, chap. 1.

52. Ibid., p. 1.

53. 99 U.S. 700 (1879), 726.

54. Hence the country's first multibank holding company, Utah's First Security Corporation, was chartered in Delaware by its presiding genius, Marriner Eccles, of New Deal fame. Jonathan Hughes, *The Vital Few: The Entrepreneur and American Economic Progress* (New York: Oxford University Press, expanded edition, 1986), p. 515.

55. Hurst, *Business Corporation*, pp. 146–154.

56. Karl Brent Swisher, *American Constitutional Development* (Boston: Houghton Mifflin, 1954), p. 410. These early efforts by Congress to control the railroads are evidence contrary to the notion that the Interstate Commerce Commission was the product of a conspiracy by the railroads to use the government as a publicly-financed cartel manager.

57. Herbert Hovenkamp, "Labor Conspiracies in American Law, 1880–1930," *Texas Law Review* 66 (1988):959.

58. John R. Commons et al., *History of Labor in the United States* (New York: Macmillan, 1918), 1:25–26.

59. Ibid., p. 19.

60. Supreme Court of Massachusetts, quoted in Stephen J. Mueller, *Labor Law and Legislation* (Cincinnati: Southwestern Publishing Co., 1949), p. 42.

61. Harry A. Millis and Royal E. Montgomery, *Organized Labor* (New York: McGraw-Hill, 1952), chap. 3.

62. Paul Studenski and Herman E. Krooss, *Financial History of the United States* (New York: McGraw-Hill, 1952), pp. 29–30.

63. Hamilton, who understood the imperfections of human institutions, believed sinking funds, by subordinating new debt creation to payment of old debt would enforce a measure of fiscal responsibility upon the new government. Charles Calomiris, "The Motives of U.S. Debt-Management Policy, 1790–1880: Efficient Discrimination and Time Consistency" (Unpublished paper, 1990, cited here with the author's permission), p. 46.

64. Richard Sylla, John B. Legler, and John J. Wallis, "American Banking and Growth in the Nineteenth Century: A Partial View of the Terrain," *Explorations in Economic History* 9 (1971–1972).

65. Lance E. Davis, J. R. T. Hughes, and Duncan McDougall, *American Economic History*, 3d ed. (Homewood, Ill.: Richard Irwin, 1969), pp. 185–186.

66. Ibid., pp. 194–196.

67. Bray Hammond, *Banks and Politics in America, from the Revolution to the Civil War* (Princeton, N.J.: Princeton University Press, 1957); Peter Temin, *The Jacksonian Economy* (New York: W. W. Norton, 1969), pp. 120–21.

68. Studenski and Krooss, *Financial History*, p. 7; chaps. 4–12.

69. "The notion that the federal government had the power to circulate paper money on a permanent basis during peacetime and declare it a legal

tender was a novelty of Civil War finance without constitutional authority or precedent." Calomiris, *"U.S. Debt-Management Policy"* p. 20.

CHAPTER 4

1. Davis and North, *Institutional Change*, chap. 1,
2. Karl Polanyi, *The Great Transformation* (Boston: Beacon Books, 1957), p. 3.
3. Stephen J. Mueller, *Labor Law and Legislation* (Cincinnati: Southwestern Publishing Co., 1949), p. 1.
4. Davis and North, *Institutional Change*, pp. 12–19.
5. Simon Kuznets, "Long-term Changes in the National Income of the United States of America Since 1970," *Income and Wealth*, 2d ser. (Baltimore, Md.: The Johns Hopkins University Press, 1952), tables 3, 4.
6. Milton Friedman, *Capitalism and Freedom* (Chicago: University of Chicago Press, 1962).
7. Quoted in Swisher, *American Constitutional Development*, p. 415.
8. Douglass C. North, *Growth and Welfare in the American Past* (Englewood Cliffs, N.J.: Prentice Hall, 1966), p. 176.
9. Friedman, *Capitalism and Freedom*, p. 28.
10. Robert Higgs, *The Transformation of the American Economy 1865–1914: An Essay in Interpretation* (New York: Wiley, 1971).
11. Irwin Unger, *The Greenback Era* (Princeton, N.J.: Princeton University Press, 1964).
12. John D. Hicks, *The Populist Revolt* (Lincoln: University of Nebraska Press, 1961), chap. 15.
13. Ibid., chap. 8.
14. Ibid., p. 443.
15. Ibid., p. 444.
16. Ibid., p. 440.
17. Turner, *The Frontier in American History*, p. 148.
18. Handlin and Handlin, *Commonwealth*, p. 255; Swisher, *American Constitutional Development*, pp. 402–408.
19. See chap. 1, n. 25. They were reported in spring of 1877.
20. Maurice Finkelstein, "From *Munn* v. *Illinois* to *Tyson* v. *Banton*: A Study in the Judicial Process," *Columbia Law Review* 28 (1927); Breck P. McAllister, "Lord Hale and Business Affected With a Public Interest," *Harvard Law Review* 43 (1930).
21. Cited in chap. 1, n. 27.
22. Tyson and Brother v. Banton, 273 U.S. 418 (1927), 438.
23. 94 U.S. 113 (1877).
24. Ibid., pp. 125–126.
25. Quoted in McAllister, "Lord Hale," p. 761.
26. Munn v. Illinois, p. 126.
27. McAllister, "Lord Hale," p. 769.
28. Ibid., p. 768.
29. Ibid.

30. Herbert Hovenkamp, "The Political Economy of Substantive Due Process," *Stanford Law Review* 40 (1988). Hovenkamp argues that the justices were inspired in their ideas about substantive due process directly by Adam Smith and the Scottish "realist" philosophers.

31. Wolff Packing Co. v. Court of Industrial Relations, 262 U.S. 522 (1921), 539.

32. Tyson v. Banton, p. 446.

33. 291 U.S. 502 (1934), 536.

34. William C. Coleman, "The Evolution of Federal Regulation of Interstate Rates: The Shreveport Rate Cases," *Harvard Law Review* 28 (1914–15).

35. Swisher, *American Constitutional Development*, pp. 392–393.

36. Coleman, "Evolution of Federal Regulation," pp. 36–37.

37. D. Philip Locklin, *Economics of Transportation* (Chicago: Richard Irwin, 1947), chaps. 9, 10.

38. Gabriel Kolko, in *Railroads and Regulation, 1877–1916* (Princeton: Princeton University Press, 1965), put forward an early version of the "capture thesis," arguing that the railroads exploited the federal government, using the ICC as a cartel manager. The thesis was countered by Albro Martin in *Enterprise Denied: Origins of the Decline of American Railroads, 1897–1917* (New York: Columbia University Press, 1971). Martin argued that the real capture of the ICC was by the shippers, who managed to get rates from the ICC after 1906 so low that the railroads were unable to maintain their capital equipment.

39. Charles K. Burdick, "The Origin of the Peculiar Duties of Public Service Companies, " *Columbia Law Review* 11 (1911).

40. Harry Scheiber, "The Road to Munn: Eminent Domain and the Concept of Public Purpose in the State Courts," *Perspectives in American History* (1971).

41. 169 U.S. 466 (1898).

42. Locklin, *Economics of Transportation*, chaps. 27–33.

43. I. L. Sharfman, *The Interstate Commerce Commission* (New York: The Commonwealth Fund, 1936).

44. Mark J. Green, ed., *The Monopoly Makers* (New York: Grossman, 1973), p. 20.

45. The sensational exception became AT&T, a company that really did look like a monopoly, but had quietly existed despite the Sherman Antitrust Act. After decades of happy relations with the Antitrust Division AT&T suddenly found itself out in the cold in the 1970s with a number of attacks against it via the Federal Trade Commission and a Sherman Act suit brought by the Justice Department itself. In 1982 AT&T agreed to a dissolution and restructuring.

46. For possible consequences of such a condition, see Reiter and Hughes, "Modelling the Regulated United States Economy."

47. Milton Handler, *A Study of the Construction and Enforcement of the Federal Antitrust Laws*, Temporary National Economic Committee monograph 38 (Washington, D.C.: Government Printing Office, 1941); A. D. Neale, *The Antitrust Laws of the USA* (Cambridge: Cambridge University Press, 1970).

48. Neale, *Antitrust Laws*, p. 5, n. 2.

49. Alfred Marshall, *Principles of Economics* (London; Macmillan. 1949), 4:chap. 7.

50. Swisher, *American Constitutional Development*, p. 422.

51. William Letwin, *Law and Economic Policy in America: The Evolution of the Sherman Antitrust Act* (New York: Random House, 1965), chap. 2; Hans B. Thorelli, *The Federal Antitrust Policy, Origination of an America, Tradition* (Stockholm: Akademisk Avhandling, 1954); Milton Handler, *Trade Regulation* (Brooklyn, N.Y.: The Foundation Press. 1960), chap. 2.

52. McAllister, "Lord Hale," pp. 779–781.

53. Herbert Hoover, *The Memoirs of Herbert Hoover: The Great Depression, 1929–1941* (New York, Macmillan, 1952), p. 420.

54. Northern Securities Co. v. United States, 193 U.S. 197 (1904), 403.

55. Herbert Hovenkamp, "The Sherman Act and the Classical Theory of Competition", *Iowa Law Review* 74 (1989).

56. Gary D. Libecap, "The First Federal Consumer Quality Guarantees and Antitrust," forthcoming, 1990. Cited here with the author's permission.

57. William B. Hornblower, "Anti-Trust Laws and the Federal Trade Commission, 1914–1927," *Columbia Law Review* 11 (1911):702.

58. Gilbert H. Montague, "Anti-Trust Laws and the Federal Trade Commission, 1914–1927," Columbia Law Review 27 (1927):661.

59. Alfred Chandler, *Scale and Scope: Dynamics of Industrial Capitalism* (Cambridge: Harvard University Press,1990), pp. 78–79, considers small business owners, displaced by the growth of large corporate firms, the most politically potent proponents of antitrust regulation.

60. James Bryce, *The American Commonwealth* (New York: Macmillan, 1941), 2: "Laissez Faire."

61. Ibid., p. 587.

62. Ibid., p. 588.

63. Ibid., pp. 588–589

64. Ibid., pp. 589–590.

65. Ibid., pp. 591–592.

66. Ibid., p. 592.

67. Ibid., p. 593.

68. Ibid., p. 596.

69. For a survey of this strange period in British economic history, see William P. Kennedy, *Industrial Structure, Capital Markets and the Origins of British Economic Decline* (Cambridge, Cambridge University Press, 1987). For a monetary explanation of it, see J.R.T. Hughes, "Wicksell on the Facts: Prices and Interest Rates 1844–1914," *Value,Capital, and Growth: Papers in Honour of Sir John Hicks* ed. J. N. Wolfe, (Edinburgh, Edinburgh University Press, 1968).

70. Paul Studenski and Herman E. Krooss, *Financial History of the United States* (New York: McGraw-Hill, 1952), chaps. 19–20.

71. H. Parker Willis, *The Federal Reserve System: Legislation, Organization and Operation* (New York: Ronald Press, 1923).

72. J.R.T. Hughes, *Fluctuations in Trade, Industry and Finance* (Oxford: Clarendon Press, 1960), chap. 10; also Hughes, "Wicksell on the Facts."

73. *Report of the National Monetary Commission* (Washington, D.C.: Government Printing Office, 1912), p. 41.

74. It has long been my opinion, based upon internal evidence in the Aldrich Report and the record of Pierpoint Morgan's activities in 1907–1911, that Morgan was the real author of the document with Senator Aldrich's name on the cover. Morgan was a man of vast secrecy who covered his tracks, and to the present day I know of no evidence directly linking Morgan to the document and thus to the Federal Reserve System. The time spent by Morgan with Aldrich discussing banking reform is given in Morgan's son-in-law's biography, Herbert J. Satterlee, *J. Pierpont Morgan* (New York: Macmillan, 1939). A two-way discussion of banking reform between Morgan and the playboy Aldrich is not creditable.

75. Elmus R. Wicker, *Federal Reserve Policy 1917–1933* (New York: Random House, 1966), p. 7.

76. Robert Craig West, *Banking Reform and the Federal Reserve, 1863–1923* (Ithaca: Cornell University Press, 1977).

77. Hughes, *The Vital Few*, pp. 533–539.

78. National Monetary Commission, p. 6.

79. Robert Craig West, "Theoretical and Structural Aspects of Banking Reform, 1863–1923: Real Bills and the Question of Organization" (Ph.D. diss., Northwestern University, 1974).

80. Such was the case not only in specific interventions like the National Industrial Recovery Act, but also in the experience of the then giant deficits of the World War I command economy. Marriner Eccles was inspired in his pre-Keynesian macroeconomic theorizing in part by the World War I experience. Sidney Hyman, *Marriner Eccles: Private Entrepreneur and Public Servant* (Stanford, Stanford University Graduate School of Business, 1976), pp. 96–98.

81. Murray N. Rothbard, "War Collectivism in World War I," in *A New History of the Leviathan: Essays on the Rise of the American Corporate State*, ed. Ronald Radosh and Murray N. Rothbard, (New York: Dutton, 1972); Rockoff, *Drastic Measures*, chap. 3; Higgs, *Crisis and Leviathan*, chap. 3.

82. Joseph Schumpeter, *Business Cycles* (New York: McGraw-Hill, 1939), chap. 4.

83. The cumulative figures for 1946–1986 are: total foreign aid $315.2 billion; economic aid, $196.6 billion; military aid, $118.6 billion. *Statistical Abstract of the United States: 1987*, table 1339, p. 766.

84. Studenski and Krooss, *Financial History*, pp. 280–281.

85. Arthur S. Link, *Woodrow Wilson and the Progressive Era* (New York: Harper & Row, 1954), pp. 235–240.

86. Swisher, *American Constitutional Development*, pp. 629, 684–686.

87. Ibid., p. 659.

88. Rothbard, "War Collectivism," pp. 72–75.

89. Swisher, *Constitutional Development*, p. 650.

90. Ibid., p. 681.

91. For a more detailed account of the long-term effects of the World War I command economy, see Rothbard, "War Collectivism" pp. 92–110.

CHAPTER 5

1. To many historians, the New Deal was a complete failure, even by its own measures. Ronald Radosh, "The Myth of the New Deal," in Radosh and Rothbard, *New History of the Leviathan*.

2. William E. Leuchtenburg, *Franklin D. Roosevelt and the New Deal 1932–1940* (New York: Harper/Torch, 1963), p. 337.

3. Hughes, *The Vital Few*, pp. 505–507, 524–526.

4. Herbert Hoover actually proposed "coordinated federal-state expansion of public works to remedy depressions" as early as 1921, and proposed it again, as the Hoover Plan in 1928 to the Conference of Governors. Murray N. Rothbard, "Herbert Hoover and the Myth of Laissez-Faire," Radosh and Rothbard, pp. 113–116.

5. Selig Perlman, *A Theory of the Labor Movement* (New York: Augustus Kelley, 1949), chap. 5.

6. Edward Berkowitz and Kim McQuaid, *Creating the Welfare State: The Political Economy of Twentieth Century Reform*, 2d ed. (New York: Praeger, 1988), pp. 60–66, 92–95. The Swope Plan of 1931, called "fascist" by Herbert Hoover, contained much of the New Deal to come, including unemployment insurance, coordinated planning by firms in the same industries, standardized accounting procedures in *mandatory* cooperation with the Internal Revenue Department, life and disability insurance, pensions, industrywide labor unions with collective bargaining rights, and much more, all regulated by federal agencies. J. George Federick, ed., *The Swope Plan: Details, Criticisms, Analysis* (New York, The Business Bourse, 1931).

7. Hoover, *The Memoirs of Herbert Hoover*, p. 460.

8. Ibid., pp. 461–462.

9. All data from *Historical Statistics of the United States*.

10. A stance is a posture, and not necessarily indicative of belief. Anyone who has read Herbert Hoover's autobiography is aware that his historical reputation as a do-nothing advocate of laissez-faire is more the result of his hopeless impotence in 1929–32 than of his desires. He in fact favored an activist interventionist government, especially in technical matters such as standardization of industrial measurements and the like. The interested reader may be referred to Murray Rothbard's essay on Hoover the interventionist, in Radosh and Rothbard, *New History of the Leviathan*.

11. Herman E. Krooss, *Executive Opinion: What Business Leaders Said and Thought on Economic Issues, 1920's–1960's* (Garden City, N.Y.; Doubleday, 1970), pp. 121–124.

12. Joseph P. Kennedy, *I'm for Roosevelt* (New York: Reynal and Hitchcock, 1936), p. 6.

13. John Kenneth Galbraith, *The Great Crash* (Boston: Houghton Mifflin, 1955).

14. R. G. Tugwell, *The Brains Trust* (New York: Viking, 1968), p. 113.

15. Sir John Hicks, *A Theory of Economic History* (New York: Oxford University Press, 1969), pp. 162–163.

16. Hughes, *The Vital Few*, pp. 525–526.

17. Krooss, *Executive Opinion*, p. 115.

18. Data from *Historical Statistics of the United States*.

19. Quoted in Hughes, *The Vital Few*, p. 504.

20. E. Cary Brown, "Fiscal Policy in the Thirties," *American Economic Review* 46 (1956). Also, L. C. Peppers, "Full Employment Surplus Analysis and Structural Changes: The 1930s," *Explorations in Economic History* 10 (1973).

21. Tugwell, *Brains Trust*, p. 406.

22. Studenski and Krooss, *Financial History*, pp. 398–399.

23. Phillip Alexander Bruce, *Economic History of Virginia in the Seventeenth Century*), 1:323–324.

24. Distrust of bankers was not particularly radical. Herbert Hoover wrote: "Banking, finance, public markets . . . must be regulated to prevent abuse and misuse of trust." Hoover, *Memoirs*, p. 3. So he, along with Marriner Eccles would have been astounded by the financial deregulation of the 1990s, and not surprised by the consequences.

25. Leuchtenberg, *Franklin D. Roosevelt*, pp. 39–40; Studenski and Krooss, *Financial History*, pp. 379–380. Data from *Historical Statistics of the United States*.

26. Ben Bernanke argues that the banking crisis these measures were meant to ameliorate had been so severe that the banking system, even bandaged and splinted, could not function satisfactorily again in the 1930s. Ben Bernanke, "Nonmonetary Effects of the Financial Crisis in the Propagation of the Great Depression," *American Economic Review* 73 (1983).

27. Raymond Moley, *After Seven Years* (New York: Harper, 1939), p. 160.

28. S.V.O. Clarke, *Central Bank Cooperation 1924–31* (New York: Federal Reserve Bank of New York, 1968); Charles Kindleberger, *The World in Depression, 1929–1939* (Berkeley: University of California Press, 1973), chap. 9.

29. J. K. Galbraith, *Money* (Boston: Houghton Mifflin, 1975), pp. 210–211.

30. James Madison's Record of the Constitutional Convention, May-Sept. 1787, *Documents Illustrative of the Union of the American States* (Washington, D.C.: Government Printing Office, 1927), p. 425.

31. See Hughes, *The Vital Few*, pp. 533–539 for a summary of the 1935 Bank Act, the "Eccles Bill," as it was called by its enemies.

32. Swisher, *American Constitutional Development*, pp. 866–867.

33. Robert L. Stern, "The Commerce Clause and the National Economy, 1933–1946", *Harvard Law Review* 59 (1946): .

34. L. Ward Bannister, "The Question of Federal Disposition of State Waters in Priority States," *Harvard Law Review* 28 (1914–15); Samuel C. Weil "Waters: American Law and French Authority," *Harvard Law Review* 33 (1919–20).

35. Oklahoma v. Atkinson and Co., 313 U.S. 508 (1941), 525.

36. Stephen J. Mueller, *Labor Law and Legislation* (Cincinnati; Southwestern Publishing Co., 1949), chap. 2, sec. 1.

37. Ibid., NLRA, as amended, 1947, sec. 1.

38. NLRB v. Jones and Laughlin Steel Corp., 301 U.S. 1 (1937), 41–42.

39. Bailey v. Drexel Furniture Company, 259 U.S. 20 (1922).

40. Adkins v. Children's Hospital of the District of Columbia, 261 U.S. 525 (1923), quoted in Mueller, *Labor Law*, p. 815.

41. Ibid., p. 819.

42. Lochner v. New York, 198 U.S. 45 (1905), 75. Herbert Hovenkamp has argued that this famous quip of Holmes's was totally misplaced. It was not utilitarianism that guided the Court's thinking, but rather that of the classical economics of Adam Smith and the Scottish realists: "American substantive due process was built on the political economy of an unreconstructed Adam Smith." Herbert Hovenkamp, "The Political Economy of Substantive Due Process," *Stanford Law Review* 40 (1988): 404.

43. Tugwell, *Brains Trust*, chap. 10.

44. Without the services of the ten-year-old singing and dancing moppet thousands would have faced unemployment at Twentieth Century Fox, its creditors, and in motion picture houses around the country. Little Miss Temple, and those who depended upon her earnings were saved by the "Shirley Temple Amendment" to the Fair Labor Standards Act. Shirley Temple Black, *Child Star: An Autobiography* (New York: Warner Books, 1988), pp. 234–235. The amendment actually boils down to a few crucial words: "The provisions of section 12 relating to child labor shall not apply . . . to any child employed as an actor in motion pictures." *Fair Labor Standards Act*, 1938, sec. 14 c, titled "Exemptions."

45. United States v. Darby, 312 U.S. 100 (1941), 122.

46. Russell Black, *Criteria and Planning for Public Works* (Washington, D.C., The National Planning Board, 1934). It was reproduced and distributed in typescript by the Federal Emergency Administraion of Public Works.

47. Tugwell, *Brains Trust*, introduction; Robert E. Sherwood, *Roosevelt and Hopkins* (New York: Bantam, 1950), 1: chap. 3.

48. There is a school of economic thought, the Austrian, which holds that the depression was deepened and lengthened *because* of misguided efforts by the government to intervene and raise wages and prices above equilibrium levels. The major modern study of the 1930s from this viewpoint is Murray N. Rothbard, *America's Great Depression* (Kansas City: Sheed and Ward, 1975).

49. *Historical Statistics of the United States*.

50. Joseph Schumpeter, "The Present World Depression, A Tentative Diagnosis," *American Economic Review* 21 (1931), supplement. Schumpter was an Austrian.

51. I am indebted to Professor John Wallis for these numerical improvements over the data given in the first edition. For a summary of Wallis's data, see Jonathan Hughes, *American Economic History* 3d ed. (Glenview, Ill., Scott, Foresman & Co., 1990) p. 475.

52. For a more complete survey: J. K. Galbraith, assisted by G. G. Johnson Jr., *The Economic Effects of the Federal Public Works Expenditures, 1933–1938*

(Washington, D.C., Government Printing Office 1940), National Resources Planning Board.

53. Sherwood, *Roosevelt and Hopkins*, p. 63.

54. Ibid., p. 69.

55. Arthur M. Schlesinger Jr., *The Age of Roosevelt*, vol. 1, *The Crisis of the Old Order 1919–1933* (Boston: Houghton Miffin, 1957), chap. 32.

56. Leuchtenburg, *Franklin D. Roosevelt*, p. 129.

57. H. H. Liebhafsky, *American Government and Business* (New York; Wiley, 1971), pp. 556–559.

58. Krooss, *Executive Opinion*, p. 149–150.

59. Tugwell, *Brains Trust*, p. 37.

60. Adam Smith, *The Wealth of Nations* (New York: Modern Library, 1937), p. 128.

61. Clair Wilcox, *Competition and Monopoly in American Industry*, Temporary National Economic Committee monograph 21 (Washington, D.C.: Government Printing Office, 1941); trade association figures from *Trade Association Survey*, Temporary National Economic Committee monograph 18, prepared by Charles Albert Pearce (Washington, D.C.: Government Printing Office, 1941), p. 13. Today's Business Roundtable, with its offices Washington, D.C, carries on the tradition.

62. Wilcox, *Competition and Monoply*, pp. 260–61.

63. Hughes, *The Vital Few*, p. 342.

64. Nebbia v. New York, 291 U.S. 502 (1934), 536.

65. Ibid.

66. Schesinger *The Age of Roosevelt*, 3: 280.

67. Tugwell, *Brains Trust*, p. 206.

68. Wickard v. Filburn, 317 U.S. 111 (1942), 128–129.

69. Leuchtenburg, *Franklin D. Roosevelt*, p. 256.

70. See under "The Colonial Safety Net," chap. 2.

71. Domenico Gagliardo, *American Social Insurance* (New York: Harper, 1949), chap. 16.

72. The Tudor ideal lives on today in states where Medicaid payments to nursing homes can only become available after the sufferers have been pauperized and have no further earthly means of support.

73. Mark J. Green, ed., *The Monopoly Makers* (New York: Grossman, 1973), chap. 6.

74. Liebhafsky, *American Government*, pp. 174–175.

75. D. Philip Locklin, *Economics of Transportation* (Chicago: Richard Irwin, 1947), chap. 27.

76. Sherwood, *Roosevelt and Hopkins*, 1:258.

CHAPTER 6

1. *New York Times*, June 18, 1978.

2. *Two Cheers for Capitalism* (New York: Basic Books, 1978), pp. 27–28.

3. "We Have Socialism, Q.E.D.," *New York Times*, December 31, 1989.

4. Murray L. Weidenbaum, *Business, Government and the Public*, 4th ed. (Englewood Cliffs, N.J.: Prentice Hall, 1990), p. 188.

5. See Higgs, *Crisis and Leviathan*, chap. 9, for an excellent survey of the World War II control apparatus.

6. *Statistical Abstract of the United States*, various years.

7. *New York Times*, October 13, 1974.

8. Liebhafsky, *American Government and Business*, p. 559.

9. Ibid., p. 558.

10. *Historical Statistics of the United States* and *Statistical Abstract of the United States*.

11. Sir John Hicks, *A Theory of Economic History* (London: Oxford University Press, 1969), pp. 97–99.

12. I am indebted to my colleague, Robert Coen, for these money supply figures, adjusted for changing definitions over time.

13. GNP was nominally $105.4 billion in 1940 and $5,233 billion (est.) in 1990. Federal expenditures were $9.1 billion in 1940 and $1,197 billion (est.) in 1990. The 1990 GNP figure is a factor of 49.8 higher than 1940. The 1990 expenditures figure is a factor of 132 higher than 1940.

14. Thom Shanker and David Evans, "Converting Machines and Minds" As Defense Firms Scale Back, U.S. Economy Faces Dangers," *Chicago Tribune*, Feb. 25, 1990.

15. Hicks, *A Theory of Economic History*, pp. 99, 162, 166.

16. Economists from a surprisingly wide segment of the political spectrum agree that the Vietnam War controls were failures. Rockoff, *Drastic Measures*, p. 231.

17. Joseph Schumpeter, *Capitalism, Socialism and Democracy* (London: Allen and Unwin, 1943).

18. Ibid., p. 134.

19. Ibid., p. 142.

20. Ibid., p. 146.

21. *Statistical Abstract of the United States*.

22. J. K. Galbraith, *The Affluent Society* (Boston: Houghton Mifflin, 1958); Galbraith, *The New Industrial State* (Boston: Houghton Mifflin, 1967); Seymour Melman, *Pentagon Capitalism* (New York: McGraw-Hill, 1970).

23. *Chicago Tribune*, sec. 1a, p.21, April 11, 1990. The quotes come from comments by Richard Ayres, head of the National Clean Air Coalition. He went on to say: "It was not a pretty sight watching this happen to this bill." The worst polluters in the country seem to have been exempted from this bill's restrictions. So why have the bill at all? The answers, fully sought for, most likely will be found to lie among the axioms noted in chapter 1.

24. Weidenbaum, *Business Government and the Public*, p. 37.

25. Ibid., p. 38.

26. Hughes, *Social Control in the Colonial Economy*, p. 136.

27. Dan Bertozzie Jr., and Lee B. Burgunder, *Business, Government and Public Policy*, chap. 3.

28. 343 U.S. 579 (1951), 588.

29. Ronald R. Braeutigam and R. Glenn Hubbard, "Natural Gas: The Regulatory Transition," in Leonard W. Weiss and Michael W. Klass, eds., *Regulatory Reform: What Actually Happened* (Boston: Little Brown, 1986).

30. Raymond F. Mikesell, "Trade Agreements," in *International Encyclopedia of the Social Sciences* (New York: Macmillan, 1968), 8:129–136.

31. *The New Congressional Budget Process and the Economy* (New York: Committee for Economic Development, December 1975).

32. Thomas Gale Moore, "Rail and Trucking Deregulation," in Weiss and Klass, *Regulatory Reform*.

33. Daniel P. Kaplan, "The Changing Airline Industry," in Weiss and Klass, *Regulatory Reform*, p. 45.

34. Gerald W. Brock, "The Regulatory Change in Telecommunications: The Dissolution of AT&T," in Weiss and Klass, *Regulatory Reform*, pp. 226–227.

35. Larry N. Gerston, Cynthia Fraleigh, and Robert A. Schwab, *The Deregulated Society* (Pacific Grove, Cal.: Brooks Cole Publishing Company, 1988), p. 61.

36. *Federal Regulatory Directory*, p. 71, quoted in Bertozzi and Burgunder, *Business, Government and Public Policy*, p. 110.

37. R. Glenn Hubbard and Robert J. Weiner, "Petroleum Regulation and Public Policy," in Weiss and Klass, *Regulatory Reform*, p. 114.

38. Hughes, *The Vital Few*, pp. 544–545.

39. Carl F. Christ, "The 1972 Report of The President's Council of Economic Advisers," *American Economic Review* 63, no. 4 (1973).

40. Schlesinger *The Age of Roosevelt*, vol. 1, p. 226.

41. "The Problem of Economic Instability," *Readings in Fiscal Policy* (Homewood, Ill.: Richard Irwin, 1955), p. 419.

42. Arthur Smithies, "The American Economic Association Report on Economic Instability," *Readings in Fiscal Policy*, p. 442.

43. Reprinted in Melman, *Pentagon Capitalism*, app. B.

44. Ibid., p. 227.

45. Smith, *The Wealth of Nations*, pp. 325–326.

CHAPTER 7

1. Jonathan Hughes, "Comments on Long-Run Growth and Development," *Proceedings of the 1985 Conference on Energy and the Southwest Economy* (Dallas: Federal Reserve Bank of Dallas, 1985.

2. A major source of government growth is incrementalism, a little bit added to the budget each year by each agency. One reason for this, apart from discretionary control by the OMB, is that politicians are risk averse. They understand that the outcome of nonmarket control is unpredictable, so the safe thing to do is to increase the control power (money) gradually.

3. Percentage of all persons living below the poverty line: 1978, 11.4; 1986, 13.6. *Statistical Abstract of the United States*, 1988, table 713, p. 433.

4. Franklin R. Edwards, "Studies of the 1987 Stock Market Crash: Review and Appraisal," *Journal of Financial Services Research* 1, no. 3 (1988).

5. "Bill Seeks Program Trade Curbs," *Chicago Tribune*, March 14, 1990; and in the same issue William B.Crawford Jr., "Truce Try in War of Regulators."

6. Past the eleventh hour in this dispute, *The Chicago Tribune*, on March 29, 1990 noted this fact, but not in the interests of free markets per se, but because the control proposals threatened to take business away from Chicago.

7. Roscoe Pound, *Social Control Through Law* (New Haven, Conn.: Yale University Press, 1942), p. 122.

8. Ibid.

9. Ibid., pp. 132–133

10. The pigtail once worn by Chinese men, it is said, was ordered by their Manchu rulers, the more easily to seize the Chinese without dismounting from their horses.

11. Max Weber, *The Theory of Social and Economic Organization*, ed. Talcott Parsons (New York: The Free Press, 1964), p. 335.

12. The Supreme Court has managed to justify the power of federal non-market control agencies as legal delegations of power by Congress, but this fact continues to evoke a certain amount of astonishment among students of constitutional law. Bertozzie and Burgunder, *Business, Government and Public Policy*, pp. 74–77.

13. Milton Freudenheim, "Exposing the F.D.A.: Tiny Mylan Labs Hired a Private Eye and Shook Up the Generic Drug Industry," *New York Times*, September 10, 1989.

14. Louis Uchitelle, "Moves on in Congress to Lift Secrecy at the Federal Reserve," *New York Times*, August 24, 1989.

15. "Nixon's Imprint is Deep on the Regulatory Agencies," *New York Times*, May 6, 1973; Gabriel Kolko, *Railroads and Regulation, 1877–1916* (Princeton, N.J.: Princeton University Press, 1965).

16. That is one of the general underlying arguments in the new theoretical literature on growth of government discussed in chapter 1.

17. Maurice Dobb, *Studies in the Development of Capitalism* (New York: International Publishers, 1947), p. 168.

18. In the spring of 1990 I asked a large economics class to list areas of private economic life that ought to be left free of government control. The students, upper classmen, highly intelligent, well-educated, could think of *none*.

19. Carl H. Lavin, "Battling It Out for Airport Control," *New York Times*, August 20, 1989. Decontrol of routes and fares has given trunk lines, through their long leases of airport gates from the government owned major airports, nearly monopoly control at various airports: 85 percent of passengers at Pittsburgh fly U.S. Air; 82 percent at St Louis fly TWA; and even at Chicago's giant O'Hare, fully half fly United. This was an unexpected outcome of deregulation. Airplanes have to take off and land, so available airport space has largely determined the number of trunk lines. Government planning, not market forces, determined the amount of available airport space. At least the fares have come down for some kinds of service since the CAB left the scene.

20. Andrew Pollack, "Innovators and Investors Hindered in the Business of Pollution Controls," *New York Times*, August 29, 1989. Controls that set standards may become a barrier to progress if technology outruns the control agencies themselves. "Almost everyone agrees that the biggest obstacle for the new industry [pollution control] is the way the government sets the environmental standards in the first place. . . . Many Federal pollution control laws require polluters to treat wastes using the best available technology or its equivalent. Although the EPA is supposed to upgrade the standards as new technology becomes available, such upgrades are made only sporadically and require a long review process. Once a technology is established as a standard, companies have little incentive to try anything new."

21. Joel Mokyr, *The Lever of Riches: Technological Creativity and Economic Progress* (New York: Oxford University Press, 1990), esp. chap. 11.

INDEX